Design Culture in Liverpool
1880–1914

For Sophie and Johnny, two Australians born in Liverpool

Design Culture in Liverpool 1880–1914

The Origins of the Liverpool School of Architecture

Christopher Crouch

LIVERPOOL UNIVERSITY PRESS

First published 2002 by

Liverpool University Press
4 Cambridge Street
Liverpool
L69 7ZU

British Library Cataloguing-in-Publication Data
A British Library CIP record is available

ISBN 0 85323 884 7 cased
ISBN 0 85323 894 4 paperback

Typeset by Carnegie Publishing, Lancaster
Printed in Great Britain by
Bookcraft, Bath

Contents

Acknowledgements

This book would not have been written without the encouragement of the late David Thistlewood, who got me started and kept me going. I would also like to thank Jane Pearce for her constant sound advice. Thanks also to Simon Pepper and the late Frank Horton at the Liverpool School of Architecture, and the staff at Liverpool City Libraries who diligently hauled dusty books from out of dark corners.

Illustrations

1 Reilly's legacy, the new Liverpool School of Architecture, perspective drawing of Chestnut Street and Bedford Street elevations.

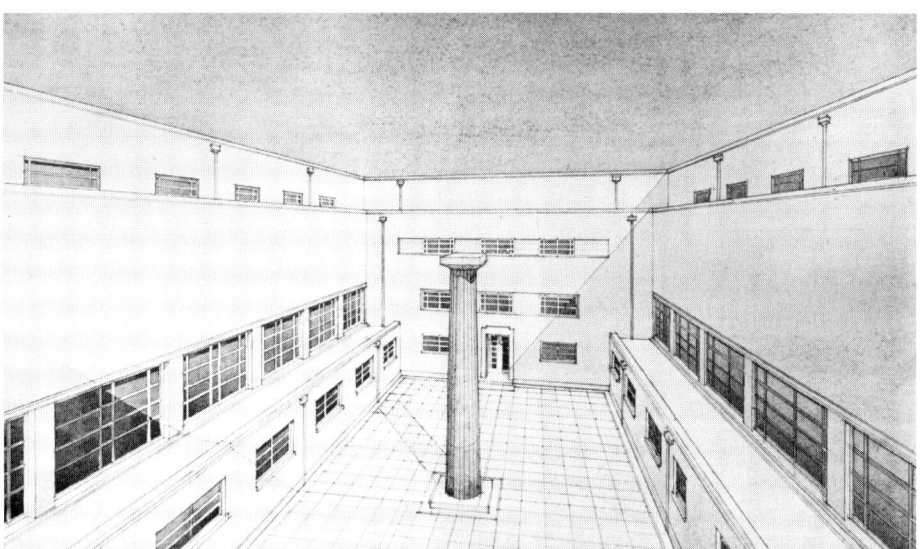

2 The classical tradition allied to modernity: Liverpool School of Architecture, perspective drawing of Central Court. (Architects C. H. Reilly, L. B. Budden and J. E. Marshall.)

Preface

Britain, culturally introverted as it was in the early 1900s, was never-theless still part of the wider processes of cosmopolitanism associated with early European Modernism. Liverpool, because of its cultural and geographical circumstances, found itself closer to American ideas of modernity: in relation to architecture, particularly American ideas about building technology and how it could relate to design. These ideas became institutionalised within the city's cultural structures and further, as they became increasingly influential nationally, and then internation-ally, were to play an important role in the spread of design practices that we now characterise as culturally progressive.

That there was a clear relationship between some ideas seen as belonging to the Arts and Crafts, and to those of the Beaux Arts as conceived in Liverpool, is indisputable. These ideas relate to the Arts and Crafts conception of the ideological purposes of design; what its methodology should be, and what it expresses, or should express, socially. The difference between the Arts and Crafts and the Beaux Arts is merely one of physical expression. The look of objects has tradi-tionally been seen as the most significant means of their analysis, because it emphasises differences immediately. If however one looks for correspondences and continuities between objects and their design methodologies the evolution and development of ideas from one style into another becomes clearer. During the period 1880–1914, the Arts and Crafts conception of a vernacular, commonplace design – representing a material-based design philosophy co-operatively instigated – developed nationally into a baroque, art nouveau, individualistic design that bore stylistic similarities to the Arts and Crafts but which negated its agenda of the collective. At the same time as this transition took place, so did a rejection of the stylistic coding of the Arts and Crafts which had come to be seen as incapable of expressing what it had before: a cooperative, universal design ideology. This book explores developments in Liver-pool, where the adoption of new industrial technologies and educational practices from the United States of America occurred alongside the adaptation of past ideas about the handcrafts. The new form in which these ideas were to express themselves was Beaux Arts derived. During this period the established Arts and Crafts union of methodology and style split into two. The Art Nouveau style continued and developed the Arts and Crafts physical appearance, while the Beaux Arts, promoted by the Liverpool School of Architecture, continued by developing its ideological position.

Previous research[1] has concentrated upon the Applied Arts and Arts and Crafts aspects of the early phase of the Liverpool School. The exclusive investigation of this aspect has been a major error in past interpretations, compounded by the examination of the work of selected individuals within the School. In this way the work of Herbert McNair, because of his associations with the Glasgow Four and the recent fashion for Art Nouveau, has assumed a significance at odds with his contemporary influence. Herbert Bloomfield Bare, who exercised such an important role in formulating the ideas for the School within the city, and publishing its achievements in the art press, has suffered in comparison. Equally, Charles Reilly's reputation has eclipsed that of Frederick Simpson's, yet examination shows that his considerable personal achievements could not have been made without the substantial cultural and administrative base created by Simpson at Liverpool. Philip Rathbone has been sidelined as a bureaucrat on the edges of artistic endeavour, when he can alternatively be characterised as part of the city's progressive intelligentsia, central to the unfolding of cultural events.

A further omission in past research has been the investigation of events within the cultural community in which they took place, and the role that institutions had in instigating and administering cultural change. Thus the role of the 1888 Congress of the National Association for the Advancement of Art and its Application to Industry in Liverpool has been seen as an irrelevance; Willet for example looks at how its significance was perceived by William Morris,[2] rather than viewing it as the trace of a debate about design education within the city. It is erroneous to assume that 'national' issues concerning cultural development are always universally applicable. A close reading of events in Liverpool in the 1890s indicates specific cultural interests related to regional circumstance. In this way regional issues can be identified which reflect upon the dominant culture, rather than vice versa. The Liverpool School of Architecture and Applied Art was an innovative institution in terms of its funding, and in its attempts to set a new educational agenda for design. The local interpretation of the possibilities inherent in the funding mechanisms of the Technical Instruction Act can be seen as having played some part in the further development of craft education in London. George Frampton's close association with the staff at the Liverpool School, his work as an Art Advisor for London County Council, and his relationship with William Lethaby are all equal parts of the process that was to lead to the establishment of the Central London School of Arts and Crafts.

Liverpool also acted as a centre for the spread of ideas about architectural education in the USA. The port's economic and cultural links with the USA, its similar, though smaller scale, concerns about architectural construction, all led to the adoption of American practices in the mid 1890s, a full decade earlier than has previously been acknowledged. Frederick Simpson's involvement with the formal structures of architectural education and his familiarity with American educational procedures must be seen as a prelude to the success that the Liverpool School was to achieve under the charismatic direction of Charles Reilly. To acknowledge this is to add another strand to the complicated evolution of modern design in the United Kingdom.

Just as there were conceptual links between the Arts and Crafts and the Beaux Arts, so too are there links between the Beaux Arts as practised at Liverpool and the nascent Modern Movement. The cultural views of the Beaux Arts practitioners were to be reinforced by the immediate post-war rationalisation in the construction of municipal housing estates,[3] where economic necessity meshed with the Liverpool School's pre-war rejection of Garden Suburb architecture in favour of a set of planning precepts based on the formal relationship of the part to the whole. The School of Architecture at Liverpool was to play an important role in the dissemination of European Modernism in the 1930s. Why was this? It can only be the case that the rationalising, technologically-based view of architecture that Reilly inculcated at Liverpool was immediately receptive to the underlying ideology of European Modernism.

A final comment can be made about the role of individuals within the book's narrative. I have concentrated upon a few players whose personal skills and successes are already well known. I have previously argued that concentration upon individual achievements can distort the wider perception of events. This is not to deny the extremely important role that some individuals, notably Charles Reilly and W. H. Lever, played. However, even such charismatic figures as these were not able to transcend the cultural environment in which they found themselves. They were simply part of a complex interlocking of personalities and events that is given coherence only in retrospect, and as such, many years and 12,000 miles away, can only ever claim to be an interpretation of events, rather than its replication.

Perth, Western Australia

Notes

Place of publication is London unless given otherwise.

1 M. Bennet, *The Art Sheds*, Liverpool: Walker Art Gallery, 1981. Q. Hughes, 'Before the Bauhaus', *Architectural History*, Vol. 25, 1982. J. Willet, *Art in a City*, Methuen, 1967, pp. 51–61.
2 J. Willet, *Art in a City*, p. 54.
3 S. Pepper and M. Swenarton, 'Home Front. Garden Suburbs for Munition Workers', *Architectural Review*, June 1978.

3 The 'Liverpool manner' at its most unambiguous: Egyptian State Telegraphs and Telephones Building, Cairo, main entrance. (Architect M. Lyon.)

4 Georgian revivalism fed by nostalgia for American colonial architecture and Liverpool School training: house for William F. Raskob, Wilmington, Delaware. (Architect E. W. Martin.)

5 A modernist structure with its stylistic origins in the understanding of neo-classical form: Union House, Johannesburg. (Architect F. Williamson, with Stucke and Harrison.)

Introduction

There is a Lumière Brothers' film of 1896 – among the first made for the Lumière Cinematographe – of the Liverpool Overhead Railway that ran the length of the city's docks. In addition to its main subject, the film, which is of several reels' duration, shows a city of machines and people in a frenzy of activity. Liverpool at the turn of the nineteenth century was a busy cosmopolitan port where the new was both welcome and necessary. It was a city that relied on technological innovation for its continued financial success, and its success meant the influx of objects and ideas from other cultures. The Mersey was a link with the rest of the world, and at the turn of the century Liverpool was one of the most prosperous ports in the world. As a consequence of this, the city saw itself as looking out from, rather than into, the island culture in which it was situated. The city was part of the early modernist dialogue of internationalism, the city's cultural institutions expressing their cosmopolitanism largely through the adoption of American rather than European ideas.

The particular conditions that formed Liverpool as a city and cultural centre encouraged the intellectual transgression that characterised Modernism, and stimulated investigation into the the arts and sciences. The port and its town was physically and intellectually new, as isolated from the cultural history of England as it had been physically isolated from the centre of power. In 1907 Walter Dixon Scott wrote that Liverpool was

> quite frankly, an almost pure product of the nineteenth century, a place empty of memorials, a mere jungle of modern civic apparatus. Its people are people who have been precipitately gathered together from north, from south, from overseas, by a sudden impetuous call. Its houses are houses, not merely of recent birth, but pioneer houses, planted instantly upon what, so brief a while ago, was unflawed meadow-land and marsh. Both socially and architecturally it becomes, in large measure, a city without ancestors.[1]

It was the modernity of Liverpool that made it remarkable in Britain. It was not unlike the cities of the United States, and its constant physical expansion was clearly visible as its maritime and mercantile structures increased. The dominance of trade with the United States led to a cultural environment in which the influence of ideas upon the Liverpool intelligentsia by American cultural institutions were particularly fruitful. By the the end of the 1930s the Liverpool School of Architecture was probably the most famous British school of architecture in the world. Its graduates taught, and practised, all over the world, and would change the face of cities from Ottowa to Beijing, Cairo to Perth, Australia.[2] It had a reputation that in retrospect seems almost too good to be true, it was an institution that produced dependable, efficient architects, and yet which remained at the cutting edge of avant-garde practice.

By the end of the nineteenth century, Liverpool was home to vigorous cultural institutions, 'unfettered by ancient rules, prejudices, traditions and sentiments that [had] grown obsolete and meaningless'.[3] Liverpool was a wealthy city with little tradition but with a substantial building programme that was necessary to sustain its constant expansion. The successful economic environment of the city meant that its cultural life was unusually active for an English regional city. It is easy to forget in our contemporary world of collapsing cultural institutions that,

> Liverpool, when the Queen died was a singularly pleasant place in which to live ... There was nothing narrow about its life, and as there was a steady flow of visitors on their way from or to the New World it was by no means isolated from the main currents of international activity ... lectures were frequent and well attended; there were ample facilities for the study of art, music, and letters.[4]

The city was cosmopolitan, broad-minded and tolerant, with a reputation for progressive intellectual and political activity. Contemporaries thought 'the innumerable voluntary societies and associations that exist in Liverpool show how deeply the co-operative spirit has taken root among all classes of citizens'.[5] It was in this atmosphere, in 1885, that the Roscoe Professorship in Fine Art was established at University College Liverpool (University College Liverpool was founded in 1881 with University College Leeds, and University College Manchester, constituting together the Victoria University) which in turn was to ultimately lead to the founding of the Liverpool School of Architecture. It was part of the process of formalising and institutionalising the intellectual momentum established in the City during the latter part of the eighteenth century.[6]

The port, whilst dating back to the thirteenth century and founded on trade with Ireland,[7] became wealthy with the development of the cotton trade in the late eighteenth century.[8] At the end of the nineteenth century, Liverpool concerns owned one third of British shipping, and one seventh of the world's registered shipping. One in ten of the world's ships visited the port, which by 1900 had a lineal quayage of 35 miles.[9] Massive investment in warehousing was undertaken by the Dock Board from the 1840s on, firstly under the Dock Engineer Jesse Hartley and his son, and from 1861 by George Lyster. The city was almost totally dependent upon shipping and its allied services,[10] and unlike Manchester, Leeds and Birmingham had no diverse manufacturing base. Because of this, a substantial part of the working population was dependent upon casual labour. The city was also home to a large transient population of emigrants on their way to the United States and Australasia. This unstable population added to the economic dynamism of the port, because wages could be kept low. This enabled the rapid servicing of the docks and facilitated the City's building programme. It also meant that counterbalancing the wealth and prestige of the port, there was a dispossessed class whose poverty and potential for social unrest was particular to the city, and unusual in the rest of Britain. The general transport strike which convulsed the city for two months in 1911 when Liverpool was the greatest cotton market in the world, was eventually brought under control by 6000 armed troops, leaving two strikers shot dead and hundreds injured in skirmishes in its last days.[11]

This social disparity was reflected architecturally in the differing quality between the slum court houses with no sanitation, and the substantial town houses and suburban villas of the merchant class. Enormous wealth and absolute squalor existed side by side. One consequence of this was the common use of vigilante groups to contain social unrest, as Eric Midwinter describes:

> At the north end of Toxteth Park, 20,000 impoverished and depraved beings were packed into squalid courts of houses erected by the Earl of Sefton, and their 'depredations' (to use the vogue-Victorianism) were such that the inhabitants of the wealthier southern side side of Toxteth Park felt obliged to establish a private patrol to defend their property.[12]

Private patronage and municipal action went some way to relieving the social tensions. Two housing estates attached to industrial works were built in the Liverpool hinterland before Lever's substantial development at Port Sunlight. Hartley's (the jam makers) estate in Aintree, and Price's candle works estate in Bromborough were built in the

1850s, each of one hundred or so dwellings. Port Sunlight was of this scale initially in the late 1880s, but had always had a wider social agenda and was to become much larger, reaching completion in the l930s.

Municipal responsibility for housing really began in 1846 after one fifteenth of the city's population had died in cholera and typhus epidemics, caused largely as a result of insanitary and crowded housing conditions. To try and contain the problem, Liverpool created the post of Medical Health Officer. This was the first such position in the country, and was a measure forced as much through necessity as benevolence. The regular inspection of housing conditions led ultimately to the provision of municipal housing. In 1864 with powers obtained under the Liverpool Sanitary Amendment Act,[13] the Liverpool municipal authorities began the construction of a number of four storey tenement dwellings for rent. In 1885 a municipal five storey housing scheme in the city was awarded a Gold Medal at the 1887 International Health Exhibition. Large tenement developments continued from this point on, with the municipal authorities starting to build city 'cottage' housing in conjunction with tenement schemes in 1912.[14]

The planning of housing was not a new development in Liverpool. The bulk of the housing stock built in the city from the 1790s to the 1850s was Georgian in style, if not by date. This housing, in a locally manufactured brown brick and with red sandstone detailing, stretched from the Dingle in the south of the city to Everton in the north, finishing at the sandstone ridge that runs parallel to the Mersey. The majority of it was speculatively built by private builders, but John Foster Senior, the City Surveyor until 1846, laid out the infrastructure for housing developments in Abercromby and Faulkner Squares and the surrounding streets. He also recommended a uniform treatment of buildings in their height and style. Thus, merchant housing of this period in Liverpool has a consistency of appearance that is the result not only of historical circumstance, but also of planned styling. This also accounts for the late use of the Georgian style within the city, and was to influence the teaching of design at the Liverpool School of Architecture.

The development of parks in the city was primarily a municipally led development. Birkenhead Park, designed by Joseph Paxton in 1843, and modelled on the parks of Paris, was a municipal venture on the other side of the Mersey. It was built at the same time as the 44 acre Prince's Park was being developed privately in Liverpool. Liverpool's municipal parks were begun in 1868 with the development of three parks; Sefton, Newsham and Stanley, distributed in a curve around what was essentially the 'Georgian' city. As the city expanded outwards from the parks, the city's housing lost its indigenous identity, and

6 The neo-classical context of the city: Lime Street, looking towards St George's Plateau.

both the huge suburban villa and mean terrace house tended to be built of red pressed brick with a Welsh slate roof. As in any wealthy city, the style of the buildings varied according to the immediate fashion of the period.

The form of the city was also determined by the technology of transport. The smooth growth of the 'Georgian' city based around the port was curtailed by the development of rail transport as much as the economic doldrums of the 1840s. Edge Hill railway station, the world's first, was built on what was then the perimeter of the city in 1830. The travel afforded by railway fragmented the town as the wealthy moved further away, and then subsequently aided its development as suburban rail travel increased in its complexity. The building of Lime Street Station in 1836 gave the plateau, for so long a stretch of undeveloped heath, a social importance which was reinforced by the building of St George's Hall in 1842. This huge neo-classical concert hall set the agenda for the style and purpose of what was now St George's Plateau, which by the beginning of the twentieth century had arrayed around it in neo-classical form the City Technical College (1902), Museum (1860), Library (1875), Art Gallery (1877) and Law Courts (1884).[15]

As rail had determined the civic centre, ocean travel determined the

7 The neo-classical Town Hall, Castle Street, looking north.

8 The neo-classical Customs House, Castle Street, looking south.

commercial centre. The historical axis of the town was Castle Street, with the Town Hall designed by John Wood of Bath in 1749 [16] at one end and the Custom House (designed by John Foster in 1828) at the other. After 1900 this banking, office and administrative area was no longer able to cope with the increasing commercial needs of the port. Further exchange buildings and office developments were built to the north of the Town Hall, and the Pier Head site, already an important communications centre, was developed as a grandiose waterfront. Pier Head was where local and international travel met:

> It is, in fact, the finest of Liverpool's parks, furnished with its sheet of water, provided with its cafes, its bookstalls, its seats. Merchants and clerks ... slip down here at lunchtime, mothers bring their children from the recesses of the suburban plume. The actual people of Liverpool are here at last to be seen in vital conjunction with the weapon they employ.[17]

Alongside the great ocean going passenger ships that embarked and disembarked on the floating landing stage, were river ferries. Once off the ferries, commuters were immediately at the terminus of the city's electric tram system. It was the ideal setting, both socially and culturally, for the construction of the first of the three Pier Head buildings, the Mersey Docks and Harbour Board Offices in 1907. A year later work began on the Liver Building, a multi-storey structure that exploited the new reinforced concrete technologies.[18] The last of the group, the Cunard Building (1914), is the finest early example of Liverpool School styling.

   The Pier Head site was also the subject of an architectural competition 'A New Liverpool Water Front' in 1913, sponsored by Lord Lever. The cultural atmosphere of Liverpool stimulated ambitious men like Lever, and 'the lure of Liverpool, both as a source of livelihood and prospective fortune and as a centre where education and culture could be acquired, was undoubtedly great. Young men of ability began to leave the farms and fields of their ancestors and seek new careers in shipping, merchanting or shipbuilding'.[19] The talents of these new men, amongst them Americans, together with the prestige and experience of established merchant families such as the Roscoes, Gladstones and Rathbones combined to make a commercial culture capable of supporting the arts to a sophisticated level. Typical of the 'newcomers' to the city was F. R. Leyland who started off as a clerk in a shipping office, learnt several Mediterranean languages and on the basis of his linguistic skills built his own shipping line. He had a house in Prince's Gate, London, and in Liverpool he lived in Speke Hall, a large timber-frame Elizabethan manor on the outskirts of the city. Both homes were filled

9 Aerial view of Pier Head showing, left to right, the Liver Building, Cunard Building and the Mersey Docks and Harbour Board Building.

with contemporary art works, and a collection of Italian Renaissance paintings. Known as the 'Liverpool Medici', Leyland was Whistler's main patron, suggesting the use of musical terms to describe his works. On the other hand Philip Rathbone was representative of the established families in the city. From a liberal Nonconformist background, he was educated abroad and travelled the world before returning to Liverpool to work in shipping and entering Liverpudlian politics. From this power base he agitated for a civic, didactic role for art and architecture.

University College Liverpool was founded after a meeting in the city in 1878 at which interested parties, such as Rathbone, promoted the idea of a college of 'higher learning'. It was the product of an enlightened capitalist patronage in the city that had its roots in the traditions of Unitarianism and Republicanism that developed in Liverpool in the 1790s. It was really the last of many local initiatives in education, following the establishment of such societies as the Liverpool Academy of Art and the Philharmonic Orchestra, amongst a plethora of smaller but no less valuable institutions. Lobbying from the architectural community in the city for architectural education to become part of the

University's brief succeeded in turning University College's Fine Art Professorship into a Chair of Architecture in 1895, when The City of Liverpool School of Architecture and Applied Art was inaugurated under Frederick Simpson, its Director from 1894–1904. The City of Liverpool School of Architecture and Applied Art was an innovative institution, funded jointly by the University and the Municipality, and initially promoted the design ideals of the Arts and Crafts movement. In 1904 the School split into a University-funded School of Architecture (the first national institution to offer an Architectural degree), and an Applied Arts section which amalgamated with the city's increasingly successful School of Art. By 1908 under the Directorship of Charles Reilly, the second Roscoe Professor,[20] the School of Architecture had gained a national reputation as one that largely modelled itself upon the Ecole des Beaux Arts.[21] Within a year a Department of Civic Design (the first in Britain) had been added. In 1913 a student of the Liverpool School of Architecture won the first British Prix de Rome and, 'by 1914 the work of the School had profoundly influenced the course of English Architecture'.[22]

Charles Reilly was appointed head of the School of Architecture at the University of Liverpool in 1904 at the height of the port's commercial powers. Trained as an engineer at Cambridge, he was in many ways typical of the personalities that found success in the city during this period. Vivacious and hedonistic, his flair for organising the arts generally (he was largely responsible for the founding of Liverpool Playhouse, the country's first repertory theatre) was matched only by his flair for self publicity. In the days of the Mersey Privateers, the sailors who worked these ships were considered the most dashing and daring on the river, 'half-horse, half-alligator, with a streak of lightning'.[23] In a city of excess, Reilly played the role of cultural privateer. His predecessor, Simpson, was much more formal and meshed with the world of learned societies, plotting a discreet course through the choppy waters of aesthetic education. Reilly had been one of the entrants for the Liverpool Cathedral Competition in 1902, along with such luminaries of the British *fin de siècle* as Charles Rennie Macintosh and William Lethaby. In comparison to their Art Nouveau/Arts and Crafts submissions, Reilly presented a formal perspective of a domed neo-classical basilica, more in tune with what was to happen in architecture, rather than what had gone by.

When the Liverpool School of Architecture and Applied Art had opened its doors in 1895, the University's annual prospectus noted that 'a somewhat similar scheme has been in existence for several years in the principal towns of America and has been found to work most successfully'.[24] This American influence was to change more than just architectural education at the University. Ideas about the role of style, based on contemporary American architecture, became an important issue, at first in Liverpool and then nationally. It was through this initial importation of American ideas in architectural education that Liverpool was to change the face of English architecture for several decades to come; so that when Walter Gropius opened a London exhibition of work from the Liverpool School of Architecture in l936, the *Manchester Guardian* was able to say in an editorial, 'The Liverpool School of Architecture is a wonderful creation'.[25]

Rather than enumerate the history of the art and architecture of Liverpool, this book will examine those *attitudes* to design (predominantly architectural) held by patrons, practitioners and theoreticians within the city from the founding of University College to the beginning of the First World War. The war was to alter the momentum of British political and economic life and as the British Empire's great port, Liverpool was also to change, to look less to the United States for its cultural links and more to Europe. It is at this point that my narrative will close.

Past research which has looked solely at artefacts [26] and programmatic pronouncements from the school in isolation from their context [27] has provided a lopsided view of the development of the Liverpool School in which research on the Arts and Crafts legacy, important though it was, has completely subsumed the early Liverpudlian interest in American architectural education. Although architectural form is an important issue, I shall be examining cultural attitudes and processes illustrated by architecture, rather than architecture itself. Two cultural poles can be identified in the city during this period, each linked with national aesthetic concerns: the gradual institutionalisation of Arts and Crafts attitudes, and the subsequent decline of their status, followed by the replacement of that style and the development of a new design approach. This was substantially based upon the French-derived Beaux Arts practices that were used and given currency by the contemporary American schools of architecture. Both are linked in Liverpool, to an extent not readily identifiable elsewhere in the UK. In Liverpool it is possible to see that the late experiments in the Arts and Crafts, and the early experiments in the Beaux Arts style share a common ideology which valued the collective and the co-operative above that of the individual. Practitioners in both styles were aware of the importance of signifying these notions through stylistic means, and both design approaches shared a common methodology that emphasised the unity of the arts under architecture.

The two traditional focal points for Arts and Crafts activity in Liverpool, Lever's Port Sunlight Village development, and the City of

Liverpool School of Architecture and Applied Art, have been seen as complementary. Both are often seen as sharing the same set of aesthetic and cultural values. A closer examination of the motivating factors behind the two will show a difference in concerns that is obscured if physical appearance is the sole criteria for judgement, and ideological motivation is ignored.

That there was an environment in the city sympathetic to the aims of the Arts and Crafts movement and its associated aesthetic concerns is clear. It had been established in the early days of the Liverpool Academy,[28] with its championing of Pre-Raphaelite painting, and the closeness of contact that its artists had with John Ruskin (Ruskin was, by way of example, a close correspondent of the Liverpool painter William Davis, and W. G. Collingwood, the son of the Liverpool water-colourist William Collingwood, was later to become his private secretary and biographer).[29] Local patrons such as Philip Rathbone played a considerable role in creating an environment that manifested a pronounced bias towards an Arts and Crafts aesthetic. It was a flexible aesthetic, and an open and liberal approach to art and archi-tecture was created that emphasised the didactic cultural role that the arts should play. However, beyond this superficially unifying atmos-phere there were profound differences in the role that style was to play in the hands of Lever and in the Liverpool School of Architecture and Applied Art.

A 1988 examination of the architecture of Port Sunlight,[30] the village built by William Lever for the workforce at his soap factory, said of Lever that his 'interests and tastes must have received guidance and impetus from the social contact which was maintained with architects'.[31] Lever employed predominantly local architects, but that is not to say that there was any consistent or shared cultural programme between patron and architects. Later he was to become intimately involved with financing the School of Architecture. This does not indicate his entry into theoretical architectural debate, though the development at Port Sunlight does illustrate the transition of styling that I shall be examin-ing. Port Sunlight village initially reflected a self-conscious Arts and Crafts style, adopted to signify all that was progressive about Arts and Crafts attitudes and methodology. It was however a directed archi-tecture, it was not an architecture that emerged organically – created collectively and collaboratively by a self-determining work force – as demanded by Arts and Crafts theorists like William Morris. Neither was it the product of a utopian socialist experiment, but can be seen as the result of conscious styling that acted as a piece of cultural propaganda for benevolent capitalism. If this is the case, then this adoption of a significant style, in opposition to its original social and cultural context must lead to questions about received attitudes towards the village's development.[32]

At first sight it would appear that the cultural attitudes espoused by the Liverpool School of Architecture and Applied Art came close to the Arts and Crafts ideal. What was proposed at this institution was an architecture created by a skilled artisan workforce under the administration of an architect familiar with handcrafts, rather than an architect who acted as sole progenitor of the artefact. This approach to design was obviously that of the Arts and Crafts movement, and was important not only in a Liverpudlian, but also in a national context, as the School was the first of its kind in England. On closer examination of the evolution of the course it becomes clear that this initial Arts and Crafts premise was eroded and replaced by a system closer to that of the Beaux Arts far sooner than has been generally accepted.

Cultural life in Liverpool can be seen as a microcosm of the national dilemma faced by contemporary practitioners of an Arts and Crafts aesthetic. During a period of 30 years a method of working had become codified and adopted as style, whereas its essence was essentially that of 'stylelessness'. This contradiction can be seen as acting in two ways. The Arts and Crafts 'style' becomes increasingly without value the more that it was used, its ideological dilution diminishing its potency. The notion of 'stylessness', and its associated disregard for the notion of stylistic significance, also leads to a form of aesthetic anarchy. The regular codification of meaning that all artefacts are dependent upon in order to convey sense, becomes confused. It is at this juncture that the founding of the Department of Civic Design at the University of Liverpool plays an important role in reinforcing an aesthetic solution to this problem, a solution conceived by Frederick Simpson and promulgated nationally by Charles Reilly through the School of Architecture.

In Germany before the First World War, the issue of an Arts and Crafts based stylistic anarchy became a concern that was publicly debated by members of the *Deutscher Werkbund* and resolved by the promotion of an aesthetic that was based upon 'the machine'.[33] This solution led to a new style (that its contemporary practitioners saw as rational stylessness) which signified in a way that the old craft-based conception had ceased to do. It conveyed ideas of 'modernity', 'efficiency' and 'unified design' in a way that its predecessor could not. This was not because of any inherent failure of the Arts and Crafts aesthetic but simply because the issue of signification that Modernism solved was not perceived as a problem by its predecessors. In England this debate was not solved in the same way. The lack of signification of an Arts and Crafts style was equally disliked, but a unifying design system was found in a civic architecture based upon a Beaux Arts-derived style, one that was to a very large extent enriched by the contemporary City Beautiful movement in the USA. It is here that Liverpudlian cultural life acts as a national forum for the debate. The Department of Civic Design under Stanley Adshead, and its Journal, *Town Planning Review*, acted as both vanguard and focal point for the new ideas. On the staff at the School of Architecture was the City's Chief Engineer John Brodie who put into operation on a city-wide scale much of the department's theory of planning; laying out the infrastructure of modern Liverpool, meeting the challenge of the mechanised future influenced by American ideas on city planning.

It is the dialogue between architectural style and ideological motivation, the dialogue between the Arts and Crafts and the Beaux Arts as they emerged within the city's cultural life, and the importance of institutional discourse, that this book is about.

Notes

1 W. Scott Dixon, *Liverpool 1907*, A. & C. Black, 1907, p. 6.

2 Herbet Rowse in Ottowa, Maurice Lyon in Cairo, Charles Chen in Beijing and Gordon Stephenson in Perth.

3 W. T. Pike, (ed.), *Liverpool and Birkenhead in the Twentieth Century*, Brighton: Pike and Co., 1911, p. 61. Also: 'The Liverpool University was lately described as the most energetic in the Kingdom, and praise from the outside is always welcome. The article on "Northern Universities" by Mr. Talbot Baines, in the current number of the "National Review" is an eloquent appreciation of the work done here.' *The Courier*, Liverpool, 17 February 1907.

4 C. Petrie, *The Victorians*, Eyre and Spottiswood, 1960, p. 99.

5 Pike, *Liverpool and Birkenhead*, p. 45.

6 G. Chandler, *William Roscoe of Liverpool*, Batsford, 1953.

7 W. Tyndale Harries, *Landmarks in Liverpool History*, Liverpool: Philip Son and Nephew, 1946 pp. 9–26.

8 B. H. Tolly, *Liverpool and the American Cotton Trade*, Longman, 1978, pp. 27–60.

9 Petrie, *The Victorians*, p. 78–79.

10 See 'Port Investment, Administration, and Competition, 1858–1914' in F. E. Hyde, *Liverpool and the Mersey: The Development of a Port 1700–1970*, David & Charles, 1971.

11 H. Hikins, *The Liverpool General Transport Strike 1911*, Liverpool: Toulouse Press, 1980.

12 E. Midwinter, *Old Liverpool*, David & Charles, 1971, p. 57.

13 See 'The Struggle for Water and Drains' in Midwinter, *Old Liverpool*, and Q. Hughes, *Seaport*, Lund Humphries, 1964, pp. 121–36.

14 'A Review of Housing and Planning', Liverpool: Liverpool City Council, 1952.

15 For more detailed information about the architecture of Liverpool see *Buildings of Liverpool*, Liverpool: Liverpool City Planning Department and the Liverpool Heritage Bureau, 1978.

16 With additions by Foster later on. See *Buildings of Liverpool*.

17 Scott Dixon, *Liverpool 1907*, p. 39.

18 The first experiments in using cast iron technology for prefabricated buildings took

place in the city in the early years of the nineteenth century, in St Georges Church, Everton in 1812, and St Michaels in the Hamlet in 1814. Partial steel frame buildings were being built in the 1890s, for example the Royal Insurance Building in 1893, and the first completed steel frame building was started in 1906 (Tower Building on the Strand).

19 Hyde, *Liverpool and the Mersey*, p. 46.

20 The Roscoe Professorship was named after William Roscoe, 'Radical and Gentleman of Taste', who played such an important part in establishing the arts infrastructure in Liverpool at the turn of the eighteenth century. His name was invoked regularly at crisis points in the city's cultural history, as a touchstone of all that was progressive and humanistic in the arts. See Chandler, *William Roscoe of Liverpool*.

21 Editorial, *The Builder*, 12 December 1908: 'We have already pointed out that in several respects the Liverpool School of Architecture resembles in its course of study the Ecole Des Beaux Arts at Paris.'.

22 'Heil Reilly', *Architects' Journal*, 17 November 1938, p. 785.

23 J. Aspinall, *Liverpool a few years since: By an Old Stager*, Liverpool: Holden, 1869, p. 15 (a collection of reminiscences published in the 1850s in *The Albion* newspaper).

24 University College Liverpool Calendar for Session 1895–96.

25 *Manchester Guardian*, 31 March 1936.

26 Bennett, *The Art Sheds*.

27 Q. Hughes, 'Before the Bauhaus', *Architectural History*, Vol. 25, 1982, pp. 163–77.

28 See H. C. Marillier, *The Liverpool School of Painters*, John Murray, 1904.

29 Ibid.

30 E. Hubbard and M. Shippobottom, *A Guide to Port Sunlight Village*, Liverpool: Liverpool University Press, 1988.

31 Ibid. p. 4.

32 S. Bayley, *The Garden City*, Milton Keynes: Open University Press, 1975.

33 At the *Deutscher Werkbund* congress, Cologne, July 1914. Particularly the debate between Van de Veldes and Muthesius. See 'Arts and Crafts and Architecture in Germany' in, C. Benton, *Documents: A collection of source material on the Modern Movement*, Milton Keynes: Open University Press, 1975.

Chapter One

The Styling and Ideology of the Arts and Crafts in Liverpool

THE Liverpool School of Architecture and Applied Art started its life as an institution with its educational principles rooted in the ideological assumptions of the Arts and Crafts movement. It is necessary to immerse ourselves in the cultural milieu in which the institution emerged, for the relationship between the English Arts and Crafts' and American Beaux Arts' methodology is more closely intertwined than might at first be thought. Central to understanding this relationship is an awareness of the dialogue between architectural form and content, between what is signified through the adoption of a particular style and how this relates to the processes of its manufacture. The assumption is often made that all Arts and Crafts styling is a reflection of the cultural aspirations of William Morris and John Ruskin, and reflects their socially progressive position. However, there is nothing intrinsic in the adoption of a vernacular style which guarantees this. As close examination reveals, the stylistic similarity of buildings within the city does not necessarily mean a similarity of ideological intent by their designers. If we can separate out the difference between style-based architectural signifiers and the circumstances under which a building is conceived and then constructed – its methodology – then the move from Arts and Crafts to Beaux Arts styling at the Liverpool School is much easier to understand.

In interpreting the design base bequeathed by the Arts and Crafts movement in Liverpool's cultural superstructure, two architectural 'institutions' present themselves as paradigms. One is Port Sunlight,

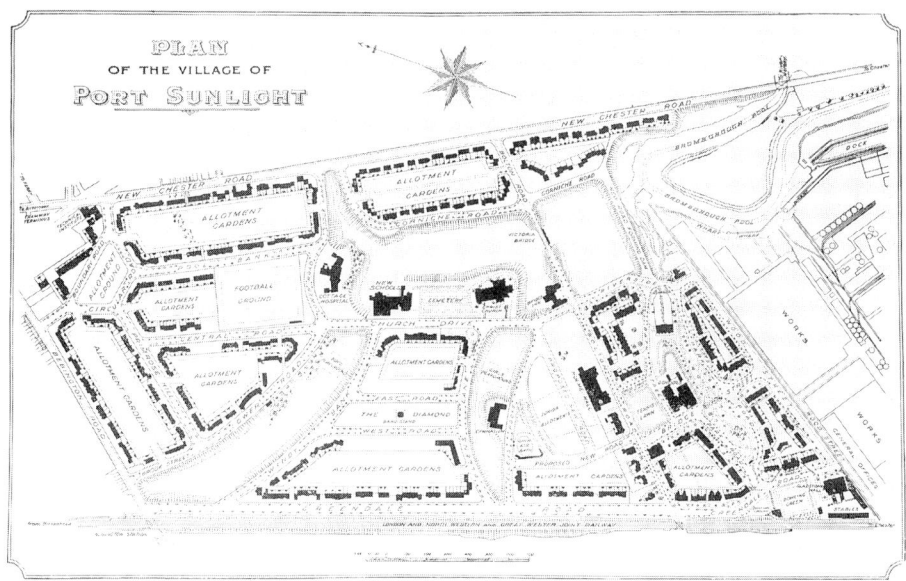

10 Plan of the village of Port Sunlight before the Beaux Arts plan.

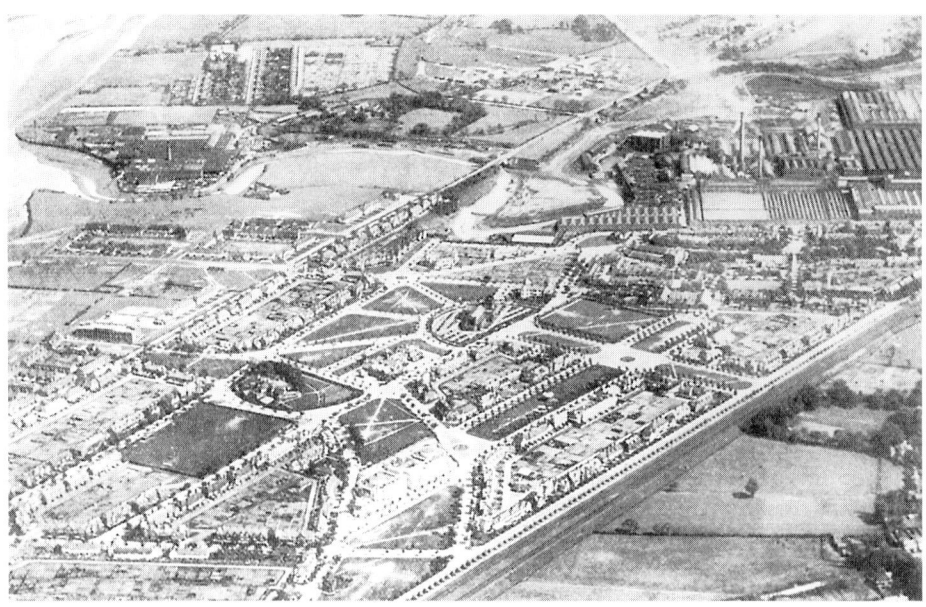

11 Aerial view of Port Sunlight.

the other the Liverpool Cathedral Competition of 1902. Port Sunlight village was, and is, an important example of social housing on Merseyside, whose construction began a decade before the founding of the Liverpool School. By looking at the received attitudes towards the village, examining the motivations for its construction and its vernacular and rustic appearance, we can begin to understand the meanings attributed to the cultural practices of the Arts and Crafts. An examination of the acrimonious debate surrounding the decision to build a new cathedral in the city in a Gothic style further elucidates the city's architectural culture, and reveals that the radical architectural voice in Liverpool was of the opinion that the Arts and Crafts no longer provided an appropriate voice for the new nineteenth century.

Port Sunlight's development can be divided into two. What started as a quasi-rural, domestic piece of planning later became formalised under the influence of the Liverpool School's American-derived planning ideas. The following brief account stresses the village's architectural style. The village was conceived as much as a public architectural statement as an efficient environment for the employees of Lever Brothers Ltd. The architectural development at Port Sunlight, in all its varying forms, was the direct result of the enthusiasm and ideas of William Hesketh Lever, later Lord Leverhulme,[1] and is often unrelated in scale and scope to the smooth functional workings of a comparable estate of its size. The village is treated with great respect, for obvious reasons, as an unparalleled success in the development of social housing. But just as Lever is often credited with a 'generous humanitarianism'[2] in relation to his provision of workers' housing which on closer examination can be seen in a more realistic light, so Port Sunlight itself can be seen to differ from the received view of its architectural context and form. The physical appearance of the architecture is impressive, and successful, because its form reflects values associated with the Arts and Crafts movement. The village's built environment can be seen as one in which aesthetic values were of great importance, and one that was actively progressive in the way that it enhanced the life of the firm's workers. Lever reinforced this aspect of the village with the commissioning of George's book, *Labour and Housing at Port Sunlight*.[3] It is undeniable that the village greatly improved the living conditions of the majority of those living in it. Whilst the stylistic form of Port Sunlight appears to reflect the ideas of the adherents of the Arts and Crafts movement, its reality is in some ways far removed from it. What the imagery of the village portrays, how it signifies architecturally, differs considerably from the ideological reality underpinning its creation. Stephen Bayley's view in his essay *The Garden City*,[4] is in many ways typical of the predominant attitude towards the development:

> Port Sunlight is an exceptional creation in that it is both
> beautiful and socially successful; it was created by a man with

money to spare, able to employ the best architects of his day
to create a faultlessly ideal community redolent everywhere
of the influence of William Morris.[5]

From an alternative viewpoint, the appearance of Port Sunlight is
largely the result of an applied style (rather than a style that emerged
through a process of specific problem solving) and is to some degree
the antithesis of what Morris and a large part of the Arts and Crafts
movement stood for. As such, it is a good indication of why it was
considered necessary by so many designers to reinvent the language
of design. If it were really the stuff of Bayley's description there would
be no intellectual justification for moving design forward, looking for
new forms of social expression. If the architectural and social ideas of
John Ruskin and William Morris (who was so profoundly influenced
by Ruskin's *The Nature of the Gothic*[6]) are examined, it is possible to
distinguish in the form of Port Sunlight an empathy with the Arts
and Crafts movement, but with an emphasis placed more upon the
movement's historicist and picturesque aspects than on any other. This
can be seen in opposition to the radical attitudes towards methodology
that were initially espoused in the Liverpool of the School of Architecture and Applied Art, and which were among the original motivations
for the establishment of the School.

It is a thankless task trying to define Arts and Crafts practice as a
coherent body of ideas. The first phase of housing development at Port
Sunlight, the Arts and Crafts phase, was completed by 1897. If the work
of the architects responsible is put into the context of the national
evolution of the Arts and Crafts movement, it is possible to see its
development placed at an important juncture where the second generation of Arts and Crafts practitioners were establishing themselves into
formal groupings.[7] This formalisation inevitably meant some form of
codification of style, outlook and identifiable approach. Alongside this
codification of style was also a development in ideas about the functioning of designed objects and how that functioning related to the
object's materials. The two issues were not necessarily paired.

This second generation of Arts and Crafts practitioners were to a
large extent removed from the ideological position of Ruskin and
Morris. Whilst liberal in cultural terms, they had not adopted the
political outlook of the mature Morris.[8] The gulf that existed between
the instigators of the Arts and Crafts stylistic approach and its younger
codifiers is well illustrated by an account of Charles Ashbee's first
meeting with William Morris. When Ashbee visited Morris it had been
only a few weeks since the debacle of 'Bloody Sunday'. During the
course of a political demonstration, amongst whose organisers was

Morris, a number of demonstrators had been killed by the police. It was becoming increasingly clear to Morris at this point that no amount of artistic activity could fragment the economic and political climate that militated against the fulfilment of his initial aesthetic aims. The purpose of Ashbee's visit in December 1887 was to gain Morris's blessing for the establishment of the Guild of Handicraft. Ashbee wrote in his journal:

> William Morris and a great deal of cold water. Spent last evening with him – by appointment – apropos of Art Schools. He says it is useless and I am about to do a thing with no basis to do it on. I anticipated all that he said to me ... I could not exchange a single argument with him until I granted his whole position as a Socialist and then said, 'Look, I am going to forge a weapon for you; and thus I too work with you in the overthrow of society', to which he replied,' The weapon is too small to be of any value.[9]

Morris can be considered as a progenitor of the Arts and Crafts movement, but not necessarily its representative voice. By the time of Port Sunlight Village's construction, and the establishment of the Liverpool School of Architecture and Applied Art in 1894, the Arts and Crafts had many voices. In focusing attention on aspects of Ruskin's work, Morris took from the Gothic revival and transcended its historicism in order to build a wider conception of a social art practice. It was this foundation, based upon the intrinsic social and cultural value of hand labour that the Arts and Crafts movement in turn developed in an ad hoc way. I think it is important to remember that the Arts and Crafts movement was a grouping of disparate personalities that argued for the necessity of hand manufacture, and who held generally concurrent views as to the necessity of collective and collaborative working, rather than a coherently motivated body of ideologues, with a formal administrative structure and cultural programme. This helps explain the many inconsistencies and contradictions that are often found within the movement.

In 1886 William Hesketh Lever found that because of the increased demand for his product, his soap works in Warrington were no longer sufficient for his needs. New premises were sought and subsequently found at Bromborough Pool in the Wirral. Its position afforded easy dock development, and was outside the control of the Mersey Docks and Harbour Board. However, the quality of the ground for a potential building site was poor, the shore being tidal and the land marshy. Thus the conception for the site lay not in building in an already ideal environment, as was the case with the guild developments, (for example

The Guild of Handicraft in Campden, Gloucestershire, and the Guild of St George in Abbeydale, Yorkshire); but in finding cheap land in order to create maximum wealth. It is important to consider this distinction between the pragmatic Lever and the utopian principles that he is sometimes credited with. By 1887 the land had been drained and the process of land management begun. The following year the building programme was formally inaugurated by Lever's wife who cut the first sod on 3 March 1888. Initially 24 acres were allotted to the factory site, and 32 to the village. The following year, 1889, saw the completion of the factory and within the next six months the first 28 dwellings, an entrance lodge and several blocks of cottages, were finished. William Owen, a Warrington architect whom Lever had used previously for factory work in Warrington, designed the factory and the first few dozen houses. More houses were designed and built by Owen in 1890, when the first phase of the village reached its conclusion.

In 1891, with Owen still as principal architect, Lever opened up the architectural development to the Liverpool firm Grayson and Ould, and the Chester architects Douglas and Fordham. Both practices had a reputation for working within a range of picturesque styles. Douglas had worked for Lord Derby at Croxteth Hall on the outskirts of Liverpool, concentrating on picturesque elements to complement the vernacular additions to the hall by Wyatt in 1874.[10] Grayson and Ould's work in Liverpool included a bank for Martin's Bank Ltd., and the churches of St Peters at Woolton, and All Hallows at Allerton with its Morris and Company stained glass.

The year 1896 saw the completion of the village as it had been originally conceived; designed by Owen, closely directed by Lever. From this year on Lever started to use architects with a national reputation rather than a local one, all of them working within a vernacular style. Buildings of cultural or symbolic importance remained in the hands of Lever's initial choice of architects: Owen was responsible for Hulme Hall and Christ Church; Grayson and Ould for the Cottage Hospital and the open air Auditorium. However the main body of the 400 dwellings finished by 1900 were the work of an assortment of architects.[11] The third phase of building at Port Sunlight was instigated in 1910, and a pronounced change in the style of the village's design, that coincided with the increasing national status of the Liverpool School's American influenced design philosophy. In this year Lever held a competition that was open to students at the School of Architecture's Department of Civic Design, whose funding he had been responsible for in 1909. The brief was to design a plan to complete the village. The winning design was a piece of Beaux Arts planning by a third year student, Ernest Prestwick. It was revised and put into work

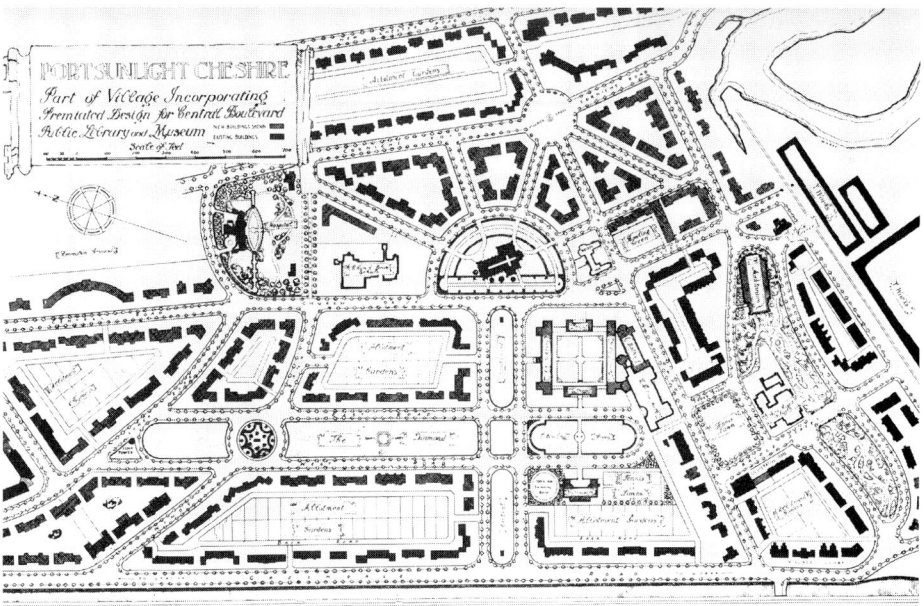

12 Plan of the village of Port Sunlight, Ernest Prestwick's scheme showing the Beaux Arts redesign.

by J. Lomax-Simpson, the then company architect, and the landscape architect T. H. Mawson, a lecturer in the Department of Civic Design. The final indication of this change in stylistic approach from a historicist, Arts and Crafts derived style to the new styling promoted by the Liverpool School, was Owen's conception in 1913, in neo-classical style and faced in Portland stone, of what was to be the Lady Lever Art Gallery.

If we return from this history to the idea of Port Sunlight as the paradigm of all that William Morris stood for, we are faced with a conundrum. Architectural styling obviously played a fundamental part in the village's development. Morris, however, had no sympathy for 'stylistic' design, and viewed the copying of the past as a pointless activity. He was a reluctant admirer of the Queen Anne 'revival', and was an admirer of Shaw's work at Bedford Park [12] but, like John Ruskin, he made a great distinction between architectural style and usage. Echoing Ruskin, Morris admired the Gothic for its pragmatism, seeing it as the exclusive base for a 'living art which is free to adapt'.[13] One means by which this 'living art' would be expressed was in the form of the cottage. His hope was 'that it will be from such necessary unpretentious buildings that the new and genuine architecture will spring, rather than from our experiments in conscious style'.[14]

Morris's conception of architectural style, like that of Ruskin, was a social one. In Morris's view a future design form would emerge from a vernacular tradition, because this tradition was the materialist base for design. If it is possible to accept this as a reasonable, if generalised, summary of Morris's position, then the question must be asked whether the development at Port Sunlight really is 'redolent everywhere of the influence of William Morris',[15] or whether the use of Morris as a representative measuring stick is erroneous. It is clear that a large part of the village's early development was in a style consistent with a rural building style that was to be found in Cheshire. But it is also worth remarking that the village's 'vernacular' building also used styles from other cultures. The village has a flavour of the Arts and Crafts, but already there is more than a suggestion that in purist terms the village might well be a stylistic husk, lacking that kernel of political and social commitment, which, were it based on the ideas of Ruskin and Morris, should be the motivating force behind its appearance. It is possible to go some way towards solving this question by looking at Ruskin's ideas and examining Lever's ideological reasons for wanting to build the village.

As an undergraduate at Oxford, Morris had been greatly influenced by John Ruskin's *Stones of Venice*,[16] in particular the chapter 'The Nature of the Gothic'. He was so impressed with it that it was among the first publications from his Kelmscott Press. Morris referred to it as 'A new gospel and a fixed creed'.[17] In his introduction to the text published in 1892 he went even further, considering the work 'as one of the few necessary and inevitable utterances of the century'.[18] What Morris identified as its importance lay in its provision of an ideological base for art production. Ruskin went beyond physical appearance in his attempt to provide an alternative co-operative design in opposition to the contemporary capitalist one.

The importance of this particular text for proposed future art practice cannot be underestimated. *The Nature of the Gothic* was first printed on its own in 1854, as an instructional text for Dr Furnivall's Working Men's College, all profits from the sale of the reprint going to the upkeep of the college.[19] *Stones of Venice* was republished in a edited form (containing *The Nature of the Gothic*) in 1879. W. G. Collingwood, Ruskin's secretary, wrote that the reissue of this text had a didactic purpose, 'to the art teaching of it [Ruskin] adhered. Of that teaching he desired to "re-affirm every syllable"'.[20] Ruskin thought that no other of his books had, 'had so much influence on contemporary art as the *Stones of Venice*'.[21]

It is possible to distinguish three distinct attitudes towards the Gothic during the latter half of the nineteenth century, and Ruskin is responsible for two of them. One view sees the Gothic as having an almost exclusively spiritual role (this is important in relation to the following discussion of the Liverpool Cathedral competition of 1902); this attitude is Pugin's and not Ruskin's.[22] Using the analogy of larks led into a trap through the use of glittering broken glass, Ruskin strongly criticised Pugin's use of the Gothic as an aesthetic bait for the sensually deprived masses.[23] This criticism was part of Ruskin's programme for the secularisation of the Gothic.[24] The second view, Ruskin's view, and the one adopted by others in the Arts and Crafts movement, was that the Gothic was an appropriate base for the creation of a vernacular architectural form, amongst other reasons because of the importance of hand labour. This meant though, that in order to maintain the significance of the style, it was also necessary that it should be contextualised or it would cease to have meaning. Ruskin talked about this when he saw, to his horror, a Gothic styled porch on the front of a public house: 'this good and true piece of brickwork was the porch of a public house, and its total motive was the provocation of thirst, and the encouragement of idleness'.[25] Ruskin's objection to this use of the Gothic is analogous to his dislike of Pugin's appropriation of it, suggesting that the Gothic style's worth was self referential. The Gothic was seen as proclaiming its value through its intrinsic processes of creation and manufacture. A final view of the Gothic style, and one which was acknowledged by Ruskin as the consequence of his writing, was directly related to the above issue – the adoption of the style by speculative builders leading to the style losing its meaning:

> I have had indirect influence on nearly every cheap villa-builder between this and Bromley; and there is scarcely a public house near the Crystal palace but sells its gin and bitters under pseudo-Venetian capitals copied from the Church of the Madonna of Health or Miracles. And one of my principal notions for leaving my present house is that it is surrounded everywhere by the accursed Frankenstein monsters of, indirectly, my own making.[26]

Ruskin's attitude differed considerably from that of the Gothic stylist in that he was not solely concerned with the itemisation of stylistic parts (as was for example Thomas Rickman).[27] Ruskin was an interpreter and saw little reason for a systematic, and by inference dogmatic, architectural system, suggesting that it was as unlikely 'to derive either pleasure or profit from an architecture whose ornaments are of one pattern, and whose pillars are of one proportion, than we should out of a universe in which the clouds were all of one shape, and the trees all of one size'.[28] He differentiated between building as an economic activity which was 'not art but manufacture',[29] and building which was expressive of 'some great truth commonly belonging to the whole race'.[30] Logically, this argument could be related to any particular style, however Ruskin justified his position by defining the Gothic as much by the way that it was made than by anything else. It was this social conception of art that led some of his contemporaries to view him as 'a radical' and as 'having communistic tendencies of no uncertain colour'.[31]

Ruskin's definition of the Gothic style was a fluid one,[32] where its qualities centred around the notion of 'perpetual novelty' and where style operated in 'profound sympathy with the fullness and wealth of the material universe'. The Gothic variety of form, Ruskin argued, was the direct result of the way that the buildings in question were made. In relating the nature of the manufacture of the object to the finished product, Ruskin created a new definition of an ideal object that was the direct result of a need, rather than a premeditated want and its associated affectations.[33] It was to be made by freely given labour. The more repetitive a task, the more degraded the worker became in Ruskin's eyes. Industrialisation had achieved in architecture what it had done in other design disciplines, and that was to remove repetitive manual tasks from any social context, and place them entirely into the context of successful economic performance.[34]

Though never presented in precisely the following terms, in effect it could be said that Ruskin was arguing for an architecture that had an ideological, rather than an economic, value. This interpretation was taken up without hesitation by his contemporary followers. In interpreting Ruskin's *Political Economy of Art* for a contemporary audience Collingwood wrote that the state should 'undertake education and be responsible for the employment of the artists and craftsmen it produced, giving them work upon public buildings', and that the re-establishment of guilds 'would be of great service, especially in substituting a spirit of cooperation for that of competition'.[35]

Ruskin himself wrote:

> I plead for the introduction of the Gothic form into our do-
> mestic architecture, not merely because it is lovely, but because
> it is the only form of faithful, strong, enduring, and honourable
> building, in such materials as come daily to our hands ... And
> I trust that there will come a time when the English people
> may see the folly of building basely and insecurely.[36]

To Ruskin the Gothic style was primarily one of aesthetic vivacity achieved through co-operative labour. A 'whole' building was made up from many personalised parts that 'indulgently raise up a stately and unaccusable whole'. The meaning that was generated from this communal architecture was 'a freedom of thought' expressed through the work of a liberated workforce which 'must be the first aim of all Europe at this day'.[37] It is not difficult to dismiss this earnest, and historically wilful, vision of the Gothic past[38] but that would be to miss the value of Ruskin's argument that 'style' does not imitate; it explains, manifesting meaning in the way that it tells or makes.[39]

A final point about Ruskin and style. One of the characteristics that the Gothic held for him was the quality of 'changefulness'.[40] In his essay 'The Deteriorative Power of Conventional Art' Ruskin addressed the lack of social realism in stylistic revivalism. He dismissed 'mysticism and symbolism' and argued that the 'patriotic' and 'romantic associations' of the Gothic were 'worse than useless, they are false. Gothic is not an art for knights and nobles; it is an art for the people; it is not an art for churches and sanctuaries; it is an art for houses and homes'.[41] It was the Gothic's flexible pragmatism that was to make it a fit stylistic base for the modern world: 'In these experimental days [it is] incumbent upon [the architect] to invent a new style worthy of civilisation in general; a style worthy of our engines and telegraphs; as expansive as steam, and as sparkling as electricity.'[42] It is hard to think of Port Sunlight in these terms. Its revivalist styling and nostalgic coding, made even more strange by its placing next to the large industrial soap works, evokes a retreat into past times, rather than a blueprint for the future.

Many of Lever's contemporaries argued that Port Sunlight village was 'more of a hobby than a serious business proposition'.[43] This is both a misinterpretation of Lever's commitment to the estate, and an underestimation of the sophistication of Lever's attitude to the estate as an integral part of his business's superstructure.

There was an established tradition of benevolent patronage by employers that took the form of model industrial communities, the economic benefits of these communities were well understood.[44] The most famous is probably Sir Titus Salt's Saltaire, a village of workers' housing built in 1853 around Salt's mill in Yorkshire. There were smaller scale developments such as Julian Hill's Bromborough Pool Village in Cheshire, built for Price's Candle Company from around 1853, that were equally productive. Other forays into a more equitable association between employer and employee had led to various experiments in profit sharing; by the time the Board of Trade had published its report on profit sharing in 1894, 101 firms employing 28,000 people were using the system.[45] That was not a large percentage of the British workforce, but amongst whose number were Lever's employees.

Profit sharing involved a process of payment in excess of standard wages when business did well, it also logically entailed a loss of wages for the workforce in months when trading was bad. Many profit sharing firms kept secret the proportion of profits given as bonuses to the workforce, and Lever, amongst others, considered that this robbed the idea 'of all merit'.[46] The system was not liked by the trade union movement who saw it as a way of eroding the role of the union as the means of interface between labour and capital. Lever devised a version of profit sharing, deeply paternalistic in its conception, that he called 'Prosperity Sharing', the physical manifestation of which was Port Sunlight village. The village was considered by Lever as neither philanthropic endeavour,[47] nor as a dividend earning concern for the tenants. It was an attempt, in his own words, 'to socialise and Christianise business relations'.[48]

Lever was well aware of the opposing nature of capital and labour. In a paper read to the Birkenhead Literary and Scientific Society,[49] Lever admitted to the moral failure of the capitalist wage system. Four years later in a paper that was read to the Port Sunlight Mutual Improvement Society and also published in the company magazine,[50] Lever agreed 'that evils exist in the great extremes of wealth and poverty in the world today'.[51] He was conscious of the debilitating social effect of industriali- sation and as such can be said to adhere to the analysis of the capitalist system by such people as Morris. However as an employer, any form of alienation of his workforce would be an impediment to the success of his business, and he saw that more cooperative working methods were of benefit to him. He wanted to return 'the office, factory and workshop to that close family brotherhood that existed in the good old days of hand labour'.[52]

Up to this point it can be seen that there is a good deal in common between Lever's views, utopian Socialism and the general antagonism to industry found in large sections of the Arts and Crafts movement. However, Lever's vision of co-operation was an idiosyncratic one, he viewed co-operation as having no general merit as an intrinsic prin- ciple. He rejected co-operative systems for having failed 'to increase the share of profits going to management and labour'.[53] Profit in co- operative schemes, according to Lever, increased the share of profits that would continue to be returned to the capital investment and did not insure its movement elsewhere. This sometimes tortuous and often confusing argument against co-operative systems found an echo in Lever's equally amorphous definition of prosperity sharing. The aim of Lever's system of prosperity sharing was to 'create increased prosperity by common effort sufficient to provide a share of that prosperity for Labour, and also to enlarge the prosperity of Capital and Management'.[54] Essentially, Lever viewed management as a central force independent of labour and capital, who in their turn were both dependent upon it. In this economic view, prosperity sharing was indistinguishable from profit sharing, where all control rests with management structure.

Lever's notion of prosperity sharing was essentially paternalistic where long-term economic stability was seen as a fundamental part of a programme of moral improvement. To him, prosperity sharing was an attempt to elevate the notion of economic richness to that of moral wealth. There are strong echoes in Lever's exposition of the concept of prosperity sharing of Ruskin's attitudes to economics and morality expressed in his essay 'Ad Valorem'. Ruskin wrote that:

> There is no wealth but life. Life, including all its powers of love, of joy, and of admiration. That country is the richest which nourishes the greatest number of noble and happy human beings; that man is richest who, having perfected the functions of his own life to the utmost, has also the widest helpful influence, both personal, and by means of his possessions, over the lives of others.[55]

Lever speaks of prosperity sharing having 'a distinctly elevating tendency on Labour so as to raise Labour both in the social and intellectual scale with increased power for enjoyment within itself and greater power for usefulness outside itself.'[56] Whilst there is a similarity in sentiment between the two views expressed, it must be borne in mind the different directions from which they originated, and the differing ways by which the ideas were put into operation by the two men.

Prosperity sharing was a form of profit sharing where the workers' share, or dividend, instead of being paid to each individual, was considered by management as having been earned collectively, and thus was the property of the community (as defined by the management). So instead of financial bonuses over standard rates, wages were looked upon as a totality and profits above an adopted limit were used to maintain the architectural fabric of the village. Expenditure was kept consistent to avoid problems during bad economic periods and surpluses were banked. The purpose of the reservoir of funds was firmly fixed, pensions from the firm were purely discretionary, and the workforce was clearly told that it was beyond its brief to demand pensions or benefits as part of a contract of employment. The actuality of prosperity sharing was such that it differed little from profit sharing, short of its reluctance to part with cash. There were benefits: rentals on the estate were lower than the local average. Whereas in Liverpool rent could be expected to absorb one third of the average worker's wage, tenants on the Port Sunlight estate were paying around one quarter to one fifth of theirs,[57] but a Port Sunlight employee was not automatically entitled to be housed by the firm. Company policy was to 'provide as

much as possible for those whose occupation at the works is permanent'. Effectively this meant a two-tiered employment policy was
operated, where those hired on a more temporary basis, or those not
allocated accommodation, received no benefits from the prosperity
sharing scheme.

The benefits of the system were seen as freeing the workforce from
cash dividends so that they would require, 'no protection against
themselves [the main critique of profit sharing]'. This idea of the
emancipation of the worker from his spending power was further
developed so that 'instead of the worker being subjected to the demor-
alising influence of irregular bonuses, he is given the opportunity of
occupying a good house at a low rate in pleasant surroundings and
of taking part in communal life.' [58] This attitude sits awkwardly with
Lever's pronouncements on the economics of the commodity market,
where he believed that 'social progress is promoted just as much by
consuming wealth as by saving wealth' and that 'the successful investment of capital in machinery is only possible in proportion to its power
to cheapen production whilst raising wages and so giving increased
consumption to Labour.' [59]

Lever firmly believed that within Port Sunlight the tenant body
enjoyed 'the fullest liberty in managing its own institutions outside the
business, whilst management is maintained in its proper place inside
the business'.[60] However communal life on the estate, so valued as part
of prosperity sharing, was controlled by the management, who defined
the needs of the tenants and then set about supplying them. Lever was
petitioned on this issue by tenants who felt dissatisfied at paying for
facilities they had not instigated.[61] Control of the environment, both
physical and moral was absolute. To teach 'sobriety, cleanliness and
respect for the law',[62] something more than a good cottage was needed.
Lever considered that whilst profit sharing schemes left begging the
questions of health, morality and education, Port Sunlight with its
educational and health facilities created an ideal social environment.
That it was an environment which meant the improved physical well-
being of its tenants is undeniable, however it is worth noting that critics
of Lever's prosperity sharing were unaware of the qualitative difference
between it and profit sharing: 'No man of an independent turn of mind
can breathe for long the atmosphere of Port Sunlight … The profit
sharing system not only enslaves and degrades the workers, it tends
to make them servile and sycophant.' [63]

The creation of Port Sunlight village by Lever was not an idle pastime,
although he gained great satisfaction in directing the physical progress
of the institution. Neither was it an act of benevolent financial patronage
comparable to Ruskin's funding of the Guild of St George. The village

was seen by Lever as an essential part of his company's economic substructure, and whilst there can be no doubt of its achievement in contemporary social and cultural terms, its creation and implementation was the result of traditional hierarchical organisation. As such it bears no relationship with the new forms of cultural and social organisation, based on the ideas of Ruskin and Morris,[64] that many Arts and Crafts practitioners were attempting to establish with varying degrees of success. This of course does not explain the form of village; in its early stages it was very closely supervised by Lever who nevertheless was ultimately dependent upon the specific skills and interests of his architects to put into practice his general schemes. (This is more clearly demonstrated in his remodelling of the village of Thornton Hough, where in essence a traditional village was reconstructed in pastiche form.) It would appear that Lever was aware of architectural fashion and the messages that it conveyed, otherwise the development of the village along utilitarian lines, on a grid pattern using standard by-law housing specification would have been perfectly feasible. His use of Edward Ould and Maurice Adams as architects elucidates this point. An examination of their personal attitudes to architecture and the Arts and Crafts movement further reveals the gulf between the stylistic adoption of the vernacular as a simple signifier of rusticity, and the ideological adoption of its methodologies.

Edward Ould joined George Grayson in partnership in Liverpool in 1886, having previously worked with John Douglas in Chester (Douglas was another of Lever's early architects at Port Sunlight). His training was in the vernacular style. As a partnership, Grayson and Ould were responsible for 25 blocks of cottages at Port Sunlight,[65] and the majority of the work at Thornton Hough. Ould's personal views on architecture can be easily established from a look at his presidential address to the Liverpool Architectural Society in 1900.[66] As one might expect from the ornate vernacular work of his partnership at Port Sunlight, Ould talked about the architecture of Rome with the partisan attitude of the Arts and Crafts aficionado, 'there is very little architecture there, pure and simple, that is worth going to see, and the picturesque and purely artistic element is altogether wanting'.[67]

Edward Ould's book *Old Cottages, Farmhouses and other Half Timbered Buildings in Shropshire, Herefordshire and Cheshire* was published in 1904. Two issues can be extracted from the text; the implicit attitude that such buildings have an intrinsic worth, and that they can be seen as an architectural paradigm to follow. Ould wrote:

> The question naturally arises, whether timber nogging is a
> suitable style for a modern house, and as one who has had

> some experience of such building, I would say that, given a
> suitable client, one who is worthy of the privilege in living in
> a timber house, who will appreciate the advantages and put
> up with the drawbacks – it is an immensely suitable style for
> a house of moderate dimensions.[68]

This doesn't really sound like the voice of a man committed to radical
social and cultural change. Ould's architectural concerns can probably
best be characterised as one concerned with the picturesque. He did
deal with the relationship between appearance and manufacture of
timber-framed houses and the material conditions formative in their
construction. In so doing Ould treated the historical housing form as
a practical design solution related to quite specific physical circumstances. The decorative form found on such housing was treated to a
similar analysis, its lack of sophistication attributed to the countryside's
inaccessibility for skilled artisans. The decoration was valued however
despite, or maybe, because of this:

> The sculpture and carving on the timber building we are
> considering … were not usually the work of trained artists,
> but the simple, traditional, but [very often], most effective
> ornament of the village carpenter. The elaboration of ornamen-
> tal forms in the timber work … is more apparent the further
> north you travel and culminates in the multitudinous forms
> and ingenious devices appearing in the framing of the Manor
> Houses of Cheshire and Lancashire.[69]

Whilst this approach to the tradition and application of handcrafts
links him to aspects of the Arts and Crafts movement his absence of
comment upon the desirable application of the use of 'simple carpenters'
in the construction and decoration of contemporary cottage architecture
separates him from a full assimilation into the radical aspects of the
movement. Although he was aware that past timber housing form
emerged from specific physical conditions, it did not constitute a convincing argument for the recreation of those conditions in order to
recreate the form. The vernacular form in the early twentieth century
was to be chosen by the architectural patron in much the same way
that a gourmet will choose a wine. The adoption of a style and not the
processes of construction was ultimately what motivated Ould.

   Ould viewed the cottage form in broad aesthetic terms, approving
of the use of natural materials because of their ability to blend effectively and unobtrusively with the dwelling's setting. His descriptions
in his book betray a predilection for this aesthetic role of architecture,
almost on occasions to the point of parody: 'The timber structure is

SHAKESPEAR COTTAGES   COTTAGES. PARK ROAD

13 The 'Arts and Crafts' nostalgia of the first stage of Port Sunlight's development: cottages, Park Road.

delightfully promiscuous and unsymmetrical, but wholly satisfactory. The timbering of the gable is quite unique in arrangement but strictly constructional. Partly flagged and partly tiled, as a piece of colour it is wonderful, especially when the autumn tints have fired the virginia creeper.'

If the setting for buildings was an important consideration for Ould, so too was the use of traditional materials. Included in this sense of 'rightness' of materials, an attitude readily identifiable with the Arts and Crafts, was the adoption of the idea that the patina of age contributed to the aesthetic qualities of a building. This suggests an architecture that is illusionistic, falsifying the present in order to create a pretence of the past, rather than an architecture using traditional forms in order to solve contemporary design problems.

> No style of building [like the timber frame house] will harmonise so quickly and so completely with its surroundings and so soon pass through the crude brand new period, and none continue to live on such terms of good fellowship with other materials, whether rosy brickwork, grey lichen-covered masonry, or pearly flag slates, which last it loves most of all.

It is obvious that Ould's love of the picturesque and his use of vernacular form could place him within the common definition of the Arts and Crafts aesthetic. However if we accept that there was also a strong element of ideological commitment to working method and process in that aesthetic, then there is no evidence of any other points of connection. He does at one point in his book refer to the contemporary application of the traditional black and white form as being 'not cheap', though he makes no further examination of the economic issue. In this he is the opposite of Maurice Adams who viewed the cottage form as having a positive economic advantage.

Maurice Adams was responsible for the building of 20 cottages in three blocks at Port Sunlight; two blocks in 1889 and one in 1907.[70] His book *Modern Cottage Architecture*[71] was published half way through his work at the village. What emerges from his text is his intelligent pragmatism with regard to the quality and styling of cottage architecture,[72] and his lack of sympathy with the general ideological aims of the Arts and Crafts and associated Garden Suburb/City movements in their more political manifestations. It is not necessary here to understand why Adams took this attitude – obviously he was a man who designed buildings for a living, unlike many of the Arts and Crafts practioners.[73] What *is* relevant however is that his work at Port Sunlight can be misread in terms of stylistic encoding, as part of a general Arts and Crafts approach to housing.

Adams showed little interest in his book in the cultural motivation behind much cottage style building of the period, despite his involvement in both Port Sunlight and Bedford Park. Small holdings, garden suburbs, garden cities, were all dealt with together; to him the issue at stake was that of house building 'in combinations to fit the allocation of the land to the best financial advantage without perhaps detracting from the pictorial point of view, which is fully recognised as an economic value'. His architectural views were rooted in the solution of immediate design problems rather than in any wider concern as to the social or cultural context that the cottage form should find itself in:

> it is clear that the governing principles involved in designing houses for these special purposes equally concern smaller undertakings, such as individual isolated cottages, or groups of small houses erected on separated sites by independent owners or landlords; and so far it matters but little whether cottages form part of a large estate of this sort or not.

He also ridiculed the stereotypical propagandist for the garden suburb and argued that the attitudes of such people created an unreal perception of the garden suburb, going so far as to call the term as a 'misnomer'. One cannot read Adams and remain unclear about his views:

> There is so much play made of the 'smock frock' and sun bonnet cult or 'simple life' figurings in the advertisements to be seen everywhere for the furtherance of such undertakings, with the skylark singing overhead and the rabbits frisking below, gambolling 'midst the heather in innocent ease', though

the sunflower of the aesthetic period of not so long ago has gone out of fashion.

Adams rejected any sort of ideological commitment to the notion of a social architecture. In reference to the Small Ownership Committee, one of many contemporary organisations whose aim was the establishment of a rational housing policy, he wrote: 'This committee's programme … is quite unhampered by socialistic short sightedness, and free of communistic ideals, which must be laid aside as impractical if success is to be ensured.'

The nature of the architectural environment, both natural and man-made, such a central issue of the period, was seen by Adams more in terms of a stylistic, rather than a practical necessity. In his view, it was the architect's job to manage the site, rather than to allow the site to determine the form and placing of houses. The environment was important primarily in terms of economic value, and then in visual terms.

> Proportionate use is made of the physical peculiarities of the estate and a due regard is allowed to the immediate environs of the property … [the environment] is an essential consideration but it can easily be overstated. In fact a 'garden like effect' in planning an estate through the judicious use of shrubberies is preferable to any disparity of treatment resulting from those gardens belonging to tenants.

What is also interesting here is his disregard of the tenant's right to determine his or her visual surroundings, whilst in architectural design the individual architect was seen as having total power. This ranking of the right to exercise design authority flies in the face of Morris's and Ruskin's theorising on the collaborative aspect of vernacular design. For Adams, design was fundamentally individualistic as opposed to collaborative, he valued the guiding role of the architect above all else in design methodology.

> The artistic or architectural fitness of every sort of garden dwelling must invariably be reliant upon the capability of the architect employed, not withstanding the socialistic ideals permeating such comprehensiveness. This fact brings into prominence in a remarkable degree how essentially individualistic good design always is and inevitably must be.

However in discussing the success of the cottage form, Adams substantially contradicts himself and argues the opposite point; that 'stylessness' of design, the result of vernacular development, is a benefit. It is at this point, in his appreciation of the cottage form and his evaluation of its worth, that Adams comes closest to the accepted ideals of the Arts and Crafts movement.[74] Adams saw two threads to the cottage form's adoption and success. Firstly an aesthetic one, with its origin in the drawings of Samuel Prout who popularised the cottage in picturesque works at the beginning of the nineteenth century,[75] and secondly through the spread of ideas surrounding the garden city.[76] He was at his closest to an Arts and Crafts aesthetic in his insistence that where possible local materials were used, especially where 'the temptation afforded by the facilities of railway transport for the implementation of "foreign" building materials furnishes too often an excuse for changing the old order of things'. Ultimately though, Adams can be seen as operating in an aesthetic area that had taken on ideological connotations for Arts and Crafts practitioners, and trying to establish its functional neutrality.

Ould and Adams can be linked together in their interpretation of the cottage form. The message conveyed through its styling – a reassuringly nostalgic image of stable rural tranquility – is however as far removed from the realities of a modern industrial state as is possible. It must be remembered that Port Sunlight village was built within sight and smelling distance of the biggest soap works in the industrialised world. Unlike the intentions for the cottage form that Morris had, Ould's and Adams's intentions were primarily aesthetic, with little or no interest in the relationship between the cottage form and its potential for social and cultural change.

These points are not made with any prescriptive purpose, but to indicate the gulf between the architects' own attitudes, and the way their work has subsequently been reinterpreted. It is worth reflecting at this point on the many differences in architectural styling in the village that have become combined in received attitudes into a single Arts and Crafts 'atmosphere'. The lack of coherence of just two of Lever's architects with regard to the cottage form when combined with Lever's view of the village suggests that the unifying architectural factor for the development of the estate lies in Lever's role as an architectural patron rather than in any underlying design philosophy. The predominance of black and white work in the village obscures the stylistic variety of the site. That variety of architectural form is the result of Lever's interest in architecture in itself, rather than in the role that architecture might play within a new design culture that stressed the importance of methodology. The elaborate quality of the housing form in the village still contributes to an atmosphere of aesthetic and physical well-being, and obscures any issues of architectural dysfunction. There is a considerable amount of 'facade work' on the estate, where the logic of internal planning in the cottages is sacrificed to external symmetry and formal coherence. In this and in the use of 'disguised' terraced housing form, much of the architecture on the estate lacks the functional honesty of later garden suburb work, although at first glance the bucolic styling appears to unite them.

With the negation of functional elements in these buildings, it follows that style must become the dominant feature, and the one that communicates most fully not with the users of the architecture but with its outside audience, which in an estate of the nature of Port Sunlight was a considerable one. This is significant because it reinforces the role for architectural form as a medium for the exchange of ideas. This however does not mean that any architectural forms so used have an objective or absolute value. As Ruskin observed, in order for this to happen architecture has to have a developed social and cultural context.

The architectural form of Port Sunlight village can be said to communicate the utopian ideal that was espoused by the majority of the advocates of the Arts and Crafts movement – that of egalitarianism achieved through hand labour. The material reality, however, was that the village's development was based upon wealth generation dependent on technologically advanced production methods. There is a profound contradiction between these two messages. One way of making sense of this is to say that the architectural form of Port Sunlight did not generate a new set of meanings, but rather used forms already potent in meaning. The conduct of the 1902 Liverpool Cathedral competition further indicates this idea that architectural style is an important signifier of social or cultural intention. In this case, the debate around architectural style was not obscured by the social function of the building programme, as was largely the case with regard to Port Sunlight. The issue of the cathedral's style – whether it should be Gothic or not – was of supreme importance. The adoption of architectural style was not simply a matter of choosing a physical appearance. There was an understanding that not only did the physical appearance of architecture convey certain information about attitudes and intentions, but that this ideological function of architecture was also of itself important.

In June 1903 the Church of England authorities in Liverpool announced the result of an architectural competition to build a new cathedral in the city. The winner was Gilbert Scott, but the competition saw many entrants of note such as Charles Rennie Macintosh and William Lethaby. The Church of England's decision to build a cathedral in the Gothic style met with passionate opposition in Liverpool and evolved into a national debate about how the new century was to be greeted

14 Charles Reilly's neo-classical design for the Cathedral for Liverpool
Competition, 1902, perspective drawing by S. D. Adshead (interior).

architecturally. It is the debate that surrounded the competition, rather
than the competition itself and its results that are relevant here. The
Gothic was still a potent populist style; it signified spirituality and
Englishness to important sections of the community. In Liverpool, with
its neo-classical architectural tradition and its increasingly influential
School of Architecture, the Gothic was seen as parochial and irrelevant.

15 Charles Reilly's neo-classical design for the Cathedral for Liverpool Competition, 1902, perspective drawing by S. D. Adshead (exterior).

After several false starts during the 1880s to build a Cathedral in Liverpool,[77] the appointment of a new Bishop[78] in 1900 saw the project take off. The first architectural action of the Cathedral Executive Sub-Committee[79] was to approach Professor Simpson, Director of the Liverpool School of Architecture and Applied Art, to ask his advice on the choice of architect and to enquire upon matters of style. Simpson did not reply personally, but through the Liverpool Architectural Society of which he was the current president. The Society's conclusions were that there should be an open competition, that 'the question of style be left open',[80] and that there should be a judging panel with a minimum of three members representing a cross section of contemporary architectural styles and approaches. During the previous attempt to build in the 1880s, a decision had been taken that the cathedral was to be Gothic in style, and the City's University's Principal, and its Professor of Fine Art, had made public their opposition to this idea. Their criticism was based on the idea that artistic form must relate directly to a social reality. In their opinion the Gothic had no relevance to the world as they perceived it. Professor Conway, like many of the city's intelligentsia, transitory or indigenous, travelled regularly to the United States and was well aware of architectural innovations on the American continent. Twenty years later, Professor Simpson had institutionalised American architectural educational ideas in his School, yet despite this immediate cosmopolitan cultural outlook, and the clear suggestions from the Liverpool Architectural Society, the Cathedral authorities wrote to the president of the RIBA, Sir William Emerson[81] (who 15 years earlier had been chosen to design the first attempted Liverpool Cathedral) and informed him that the style of the cathedral was to be Gothic.[82]

The man most directly responsible for the 'Gothic' decision, Robert Gladstone,[83] was not an architect but an Anglican – a devout one. It was his determination and doggedness in his role as Chairman of the Cathedral Building Committee that provided the internal drive for the style, backed up in committee by Bishop Chevasse and Lord Derby. Gladstone's argument was a predictable one, stemming from the ideas of Pugin. The Gothic was seen as an appropriate choice because: 'there could be no question whatever in the minds of thinking people that Gothic architecture produced a more devotional effect upon the mind than any other which human skill had yet invented.'[84] The decision to go for Gothic was widely known before its official pronouncement, and in September 1901 *The Builder* was to refer to the 'foolish and mischievous resolution that the style of the new cathedral should be Gothic.'[85] By October the national press had taken up the issue, and during the course of the month the whole set of arguments relating to the national and local design agendas were laid out for scrutiny.

It was Myddleton Shallcross, a Liverpudlian architect, who started the extended debate in the correspondence pages of *The Times*, a correspondence that was considered entertaining enough and of sufficient importance by *The Builder* to provide a weekly summary of the argument as it progressed. Shallcross called for a structure that reflected 'the science, the lives and environment, the pulse as it were, of the people of the period of its erection'.[86] This is hardly suprising considering the section of the city's culture that Shallcross came from. He was part of the city that was exposed to high technology and to the new initiatives in mechanising labour. His perception of the world was completely at odds with that of Gladstone who replied with an argument for the Gothic, but not before *The Builder* had called Shallcross's letter 'admirable … a matter of national and not merely local interest', and had subjected the Cathedral Committee to another dose of vitriol.[87] Reginald Blomfield then took up the cudgel. Blomfield was at this time a leading figure in advocating a baroque, neo-classical architectural design, but his criticisms were more wide-ranging than a simple battle of styles, dealing as he did with the wider idea of signification:

> Mr. R. Gladstone finds his devotions quickened by the pointed arch, but surely this is rather a slender foundation on which to raise a law that this, and no other, is to be the only possible type of building under which future generations may devoutly worship … Either the spiritual thought and feeling of modern Liverpool are the same as those of the cathedral builders of the thirteenth century, or they are not. If they are the same, no doubt the language of the builders of Salisbury will precisely express the aspirations of the Liverpool merchant and mechanic of this century; if they are not the same that language becomes meaningless as an expression of modern thought, and to insist on its use is to reduce the work of architecture to a sham.[88]

These attacks directed on the Cathedral Committee from all fronts were bewildering to Gladstone, who was unable to understand the arguments that were being laid before him. He was simply incapable, perhaps understandably, of seeing the argument against the Gothic in anything other than personal terms. Rather than reading the exchange of views as a dialogue in which architectural dogma was set against the idea of architectural fluidity, he read the situation as one of stylistic conflict. He replied to Blomfield: 'Can Mr. Blomfield suggest a nobler [style]. If he can, let him at once tell us what it is, and, in the interest not only of Liverpool but of our country, give us an opportunity to consider it.'[89]

Blomfield's answer, ('an excellent letter', said *The Builder*)[90] emphasised those architects who were 'sick of styles', and concentrated on the idea of architecture as the individual architect's struggle for expression. It is at this point, in which the individual takes precedence

over the collective expression of ideas, that the national debate differed
from the debate within the city. After a final retort by Gladstone,[91] the
correspondence in *The Times* was drawn to a close by an editorial article
which summarised the arguments put forward, placed them into a
historical perspective, and then found firmly in favour of those arguing
for an open competition: 'If architecture in the twentieth century is to
be alive, it must, like the great architecture of the past, be spontaneous.
Imitation is death, and life in any art is only to be found in the free
play of the artist's intelligence.'[92]

The closing of the correspondence in *The Times* was also marked by
The Builder in an article in which the opportunity was taken not only
to castigate the Cathedral Committee, but also to develop the idea of
a new socially generated architecture.

> The correspondence which has been going on in *The Times* in
> regard to the proposed Liverpool Cathedral ... must surely
> by this time [have] convinced even the fossil minds of the
> Liverpool Cathedral Committee that they have come near to
> making themselves a laughing stock ... While the artistic
> world has moved away from that position [the Gothic Revi-
> val], the minds of Mr. Gladstone and his colleagues seem to
> have remained just where the Camden Society was half a
> century ago. So much so is this the case, that they cannot even
> understand the existence of any architecture other than imi-
> tation; and when [exhorted] not to demand an imitation
> mediaeval cathedral, they cannot understand [the] argument,
> and reply in effect – 'What then are we to imitate?'[93]

The airing of views nationally had the effect wanted by Shallcross and
his colleagues in the Liverpool Architectural Society, and the Cathedral
Committee finally declared in favour of stylistic non-prescription. This
was duly reported in *The Times* of 29 October 1901.

By the time that the debate had emerged in the pages of *The Times*,
ideas had already been crystallised and the processes of their formation
obscured. Nationally, Blomfield's line reflected many of those who had
their design sensibilities formed under the ideas of the Arts and Crafts.
(Blomfield himself, whilst strongly advocating a neo-classical design
style had nevertheless been a member of the Art Workers Guild.) Those
designers whose sensibilities were influenced by Ruskinian ideas were
in the process of asserting the right of the artist and architect to express
themselves in a way that responded to the logic of vernacular materials
and social function. It was for this reason that the *Architectural Review*[94]
circulated a petition in opposition to the initial Gothic decision and
enlisted the support of a number of designers such as Walter Crane,

Thomas Jackson, C. F. Voysey and Philip Webb who, superficially, one might believe to be sympathetic towards the demands for a cathedral in Gothic style, but who were in fact quite virulent in their opposition to it. Jackson, who had given an important inaugural address at the founding of the Liverpool School, summed up attitudes well:

> Liverpool Cathedral ought to be Gothic – a thousand times 'yes'. But the point is, what do we mean by Gothic? By Gothic for English use I mean building with freedom, irrespective of precedent, conforming to the habits, climate, materials, and requirements of England and the English. I am almost afraid that this is not what the Committee mean by Gothic, but that they rather intend that blind imitation of mediaeval architecture which I should not call Gothic at all, but pseudo-Gothic.[95]

Nationally, a line was clearly drawn between the idea of the Gothic as a set of methodological devices, or alternatively as a style to emulate. Hence the 'sickness of styles', and the emphasis upon the vernacular. These ideas about a material and vernacular design process, based so fundamentally upon the ideas of the Arts and Crafts movement, were mutating in a number of European centres into a set of ideas that had begun to replace notions of a social design culture, by an emphasis upon iconoclastic individual expression. In Liverpool, despite possessing the UK's first integrated architecture and applied arts department, the Arts and Crafts legacy did not develop in the same way. Within the city's design culture it was the ideological motivation of the Arts and Crafts, those aspirations towards a collective and collaborative design that continued, whilst adopting a new stylistic form in which to express them; that of the Beaux Arts. A mutating baroque style was feeding the Liverpudlian move towards the Beaux Arts, and was seen by many in the Arts and Crafts movement as an abomination.[96] Curiously, since much of the criticism of the Arts and Crafts work at this time was its inability to give a cohesive range of meanings to buildings, the criticisms of the 'free baroque' centred around its lack of signification. Its complex variety of forms meant that it conveyed a set of values amongst which ostentation and extravagance were writ large. Perhaps those values it best represented are shown in the work of Aston Webb, whose constant change of architectural style in the service of ruling institutions militated against attempts to use neo-classical imagery coherently.

The first week of October 1901 saw Professor Simpson address the Liverpool Architectural Society.[97] He was at this time working with the architect William Willink on the construction of a set of laboratories for the University in a stripped down 'baroque' style. A modest building

(no doubt for financial reasons, but also I think because of its technological purpose), Simpson relied on its neo-classical elements for
connotations of restraint. He had already condemned the adoption of
a Gothic style for the cathedral, and an examination of his presidential
address shows the dilemma of a designer familiar with the Ruskinian
tradition attempting to reconcile the lessons taught by the Gothic and
its methodology, against its use as a fixed style.

In his first address the previous year Simpson had discussed the
development of the Gothic revival and its concern with restoration, and
how that had developed into a period of experimentation. He leant
towards aspects of the Gothic, particularly that aspect of it which meant
the full utilisation of craft skills in the construction of buildings. This
he placed in opposition to the 'desire for architectural expression in all
buildings, irrespective of the uses to which they were to be put …
without a recognised style, with no traditions to assist them, with an
absolutely uneducated set of workmen to carry out [the architect's]
ideas'.[98] This can be seen as a criticism of much of the labour-intensive
craft work needed for the baroque work being executed, as expressing
an antagonism towards the deformations of stylistic communication
caused by the indiscriminate use of Gothic styling. It helps to elucidate
Simpson's response to the Cathedral Committee. His argument identified the Committee's conception of the Gothic as something that was
essentially archeological in nature, rather than *methodologically* Gothic.

For Simpson the Gothic revival stood out as the 'most remarkable
feature in the architectural work of the last century', its success and its
importance were due to it being 'the democratic style', a style in which
'all worked, and from which no man dreamt of departing'. It should
not be difficult to identify the source of such ideas. He clarified the
somewhat suspect historical accuracy of this assertion by referring to
the notion of a cultural unity of purpose, rather than to an ideal derived
from an understanding (or misunderstanding) of medieval politics. It
is this issue of cultural and stylistic significance that was so important
to Simpson, and for those in Liverpool for whom he was acting as a
mouthpiece. The Gothic revival and enthusiasm for the Gothic were
waning. Architects were developing new approaches to design, and to
insist that those architects who wished to design a new cathedral should
work within a style whose cultural significance had been eclipsed
seemed an absurdity to him, particularly as a new approach to design
was something that occupied his professional life:

> In the large workshops there is no longer the enthusiasm for
> Gothic work which prevailed twenty years ago, and which
> made the Gothic revival more real than many have supposed.

> Of the men whose genius carried the revival to its height few
> survive … without the slightest exaggeration, it may be said
> that the greater number of architects now practising in Eng-
> land are seeking developments in other directions.[99]

Simpson expressed a conception of new architecture that was to be
responsive to the new age and its conditions:

> This is to be the first Cathedral of the new century. Is it to be
> merely the coping stone of the style of the last century, or is
> it to be the foundation of the style of the new? … [It] may
> take a quarter of a century to build; at the end of that time, if
> a dry as dust style is chosen, and the present architectural
> movement continues to grow as rapidly as it has done in the
> last ten or twenty years, it is probable that the first cathedral
> in the Twentieth Century when finished, will be as obsolete
> in style as an old East India-man is now.[100]

It can be seen quite clearly that the discussion concerning style developed beyond the rigid stylistic codification imposed by the Cathedral
Building Committee. Rather than the issue of Gothic versus the rest, as
it was perceived by the committee and voiced by Robert Gladstone
(and which was perhaps a substantial part of Blomfield's agenda),
Simpson was trying to address the question of suitability of style for
the cathedral in terms that related to the adaptability of a Gothic
methodology: 'It is possible that a building can be produced suitable
to modern requirements and yet Gothic in the true sense of the word …
If the term Gothic is used in its narrow sense, limitations will be placed
on architects which workers in no other art would tolerate for a
minute.'[101]

At the risk of oversimplifying the issue, the word 'Gothic' had ceased
to have the same meaning to different groups. As a style it had been
rendered impotent in the eyes of culturally progressive groups, such
as those in Liverpool who were centred around the School of Architecture and Applied Art, whilst it had become a symbol of cultural stability
in the eyes of those who were the representatives of established social
and cultural power, such as the Church of England.[102]

The final points concerning style that Simpson raised in his address
are less ideological in content and more pragmatically based, but again
related to the way that style signified something other than itself. One
point used the logic of his opponents, the other developed the idea of
modernity. Both are concerned with *appropriateness*. Inherent in the
argument of the Cathedral Committee was the assumption that the
Gothic style was the correct one, not only because it was a signifier of

spirituality, but also because it implied a cultural continuity.[103] Simpson pointed out a cultural continuity within the city that was more immediate: 'Against the style dictated there are certain local objectives. Liverpool has fine architectural traditions, but they are not Gothic. Its public buildings, and many of the fine blocks of city offices erected before the middle of the last century, are all Classic. So are the best recent buildings in the town.'[104]

This was not just an argument for the formal adoption of a classical style, but a request for an extension of an established cultural outlook.[105] This view of a flexible, responsive form of architectural expression would be as constrained by a dogmatic adoption of the Classic as by the Gothic. Within this document, a programme for further architectural development was in effect laid out. What is clear is the notion of an architecture fluid in form and style, responding to particular materials, functions and environments, and a groundswell in favour of the Beaux Arts revival which was to follow. Simpson was aware that the city's cosmopolitanism saw it looking to the American eastern seaboard for architectural solutions, where cities of the same vintage as Liverpool were establishing a civic architecture based on the best Beaux Arts practices. In the USA the Beaux Arts style was seen as a new international vernacular style rooted in egalitarian principles. It was a style, as Simpson was aware, that echoed the Arts and Crafts idea of anonymity, was able to absorb the new steel-frame building technologies, and yet still act as a vehicle for the other arts.

Because of the adverse publicity created by the national debate, rather than the intellectual opposition from within the city, the Cathedral Executive met again on 28 October 1901, rescinded their decision of 7 October, and withdrew the stipulation that the style of the entries should be Gothic. G. F. Bodley and R. Norman Shaw were appointed as judges and submitted their report on the designs submitted to the competition in August 1902.[106]

Notes

1 For biographical details of Lever's life see W. P. Jolly, *Lord Leverhulme: A Biography*, Constable, 1976.
2 S. Bayley, *The Garden City*, Milton Keynes: Open University Press, 1975, p. 16.
3 W. George, *Labour and Housing in Port Sunlight*, Alston Rivers, 1909.
4 Bayley, *The Garden City*.
5 Ibid., p. 16.
6 J. Ruskin, *The Stones of Venice*, George Allen, 1874.
7 The following list of significant dates gives some indication of the developments in the Arts and Crafts Movement's cultural social structures, and the way that these were to develop into the increasing power base that its practitioners had in educational establishments. This is not to suggest that it was a national movement

with a unified cultural or political policy, rather it was an informal grouping with a set of generally concurrent ideas: 'That the Arts and Crafts was not itself socialist is confirmed by the figures of Voysey, Baillie Scott, and Lutyens, all of whom remained quite aloof from this aspect, and were later outspoken politically in an opposite direction.' See J. D. Kornwolf, *Baillie Scott and the Arts and Crafts Movement*, Baltimore, MD: Baltimore University Press, 1972, p. 13.

1882, the founding of the Century Guild; 1884, the Art Workers Guild; 1888, the Liverpool, Birmingham and Edinburgh Art Workers' Guilds, also the founding of the Guild of Handicraft, first Exhibition of the Arts and Crafts Exhibition Society, with subsequent exhibitions in 1889, 1890, 1893, 1896, 1899. 1890, Kenton and Co; 1894, City of Liverpool School of Architecture and Applied Art, Lethaby appointed Art Advisor to the technical Education Board of the LCC; 1896, Lethaby appointed Joint Principal of Central College of Arts and Crafts; 1898, Crane appointed Principal of the RCA from his post as Director of Design at Manchester School of Art.

8 For a fuller examination of Morris's ideological motivation and his debt to Ruskin see M. Swenarton, *Artisans and Architects: The Ruskinian Tradition in Architectural Thought*, Macmillan Press, 1989, pp. 61–96.

9 C. Ashbee, Journal, 4 December 1887.

10 Douglas's buildings at Croxteth Hall consist of a bull box, bantam house, kennels, the laundry and a cottage. Nesfield (Norman Shaw's partner) was responsible for the dairy and the Dairy Manager's cottage built during the same period.

11 Architects used at Port Sunlight were; Maurice B. Adams (London); W. Naseby Adams (Liverpool); F. J. Barnish (Liverpool); H. Beswick (Liverpool); H. Bloomfield Bare (Liverpool); Bradshaw and Gass (Liverpool); Cleland and Hayward (Liverpool); C. E. Deacon and Horsburgh (Liverpool); Douglas and Fordham (Chester); Garnett, Wright and Matear (Liverpool); Ernest George, of George and Yeates (London); Grayson and Ould (Liverpool); Edmund Kirby (Liverpool); Lockwood and Sons (Chester); Lomax-Simpson (Liverpool); Edwin Lutyens (London); Maxwell and Tuke (Liverpool); Ernest Newton (London); Omrod and Pomeroy (Liverpool); William Owen, later in partnership with his son Segar (Warrington); Pain and Blease (Liverpool); T. Taliesin Rees (Liverpool); Charles Reilly (Liverpool); Jonathon Simpson (Liverpool); J. J. Talbot, of Wilson and Talbot (Liverpool); Lomax Simpson appointed Company Architect in 1910.

12 M. Morris, *Collected Works of William Morris*, London 1910–1915, vol. XXII, p. 329.

13 M. Morris, *William Morris, Artist, Writer, Socialist*, Oxford, 1936, p. 283.

14 Morris, *Collected Works*, vol. XXII, p. 429.

15 Bayley, *The Garden City*, p. 16.

16 Ruskin, *The Stones of Venice*.

17 J. W. Mackail, *The Life of William Morris*, 1899, vol. 1, p. 38.

18 W. Morris, Preface, in J. Ruskin, *The Nature of the Gothic*, Kelmscott Press, 1892.

19 Letter from Dr Furnivall, *Daily News*, 4 April 1899: 'through my sending him a prospectus of our Working Men's College, Ruskin kindly offered to help us and take the art classes ... So I got leave from him and his publisher, Mr. George Smith, to reprint this grand chapter, "On the nature of the Gothic"; and I had to add to it the subtitle "And Herein of the True Function of the Workman in Art", to how working men how it touches them.'

20 E. T. Cook, and A. Wedderburn (eds), *The Works of John Ruskin*, George Allan, 1904, vol. 10, p. lxi.

21 See the Preface, Ruskin, *The Stones of Venice*.

22 Cf. P. Stanton, *Pugin*, Thames and Hudson, 1971.

23 Cook and Wedderburn, *The Works of John Ruskin*, vol. 9, p. 438: 'But of all these fatuities, the basest is being lured into the Romanist Church by the glitter of it, like larks into a trap by broken glass … I know nothing in the shape of error so dark as this, no imbecility so absolute, no treachery so contemptible. I had hardly believed it was possible … until I came on this passage in Pugin's "Remarks on Articles in the Rambler" – "Those who have lived in want and privation are the best qualified to appreciate the blessing of plenty … Oh! then what delight! what joy unspeakable! when one of the solemn piles is presented to them in all its pristine life and glory."'

24 Cook and Wedderburn, *The Works of John Ruskin*, vol. 10, p. iv: 'Ruskin put the [Gothic] movement on a Protestant basis, and thus won for it a hearing in circles where it had hitherto been suspect. So again the movement had been mainly ecclesiastical. Ruskin made it civic.'

25 See the Preface, Ruskin, *The Stones of Venice*.

26 Letter from J. Ruskin, *Pall Mall Gazette*, 16 March 1872. Further to this, the following extract identifies the transitory nature of the contemporary use of the Gothic as perceived by Ruskin; J. Ruskin, *Sesame and Lilies*, George Allan, 1906, p. 104: 'The architecture we endeavoured to introduce is inconsistent, alike with the reckless luxury, the deforming mechanism, and the squalid misery of modern cities; among the formative fashions of the day, aided, especially in England, by ecclesiastical sentiment, it indeed obtained notoriety; and sometimes behind an engine furnace, or a railroad bank, you may detect the pathetic discord of its momentary grace, and, with toil, decipher its floral carvings choked with soot. I felt answerable to the schools I loved, only for their injury.'

27 T. Rickman, *An Attempt to Discriminate the Styles of English Architecture from the Conquest to the Reformation*, Longmans, 1817. See Q. Hughes, *Seaport*, Lund Humphries, 1969, pp. 136–44 as to Rickman's importance as a catalyst in the Gothic Revival.

28 Ruskin, *The Stones of Venice*, p. 172.

29 Ibid., p. 172.

30 Ibid., p. 178.

31 M. Mather, *John Ruskin: His Life and Teaching*, Warne, 1898, p. 25.

32 'We cannot say that a building is either Gothic or not Gothic in form we can only say that it is more or less Gothic.' Ruskin, *The Stones of Venice*, p. 205.

33 Ibid., p. 176: 'It is one of the virtues of the Gothic builders, that they never suffered ideas of outside symmetries and consistencies to interfere with the real use and value of what they did … [they were] … utterly regardless of any established conventionalities of external appearance.'

34 Ibid., p. 161. '[It is] the degradation of the operative into a machine, which, more than any other evil of the times, is leading the mass of the nations everywhere into vain incoherent, destructive struggling for a freedom of which they cannot explain the nature to themselves.'

35 W. G. Collingwood, *The Life of John Ruskin*, Methuen, 1900, p. 170.

36 Cook and Wedderburn, *The Works of John Ruskin*, vol. 10, p. 313.

37 Ruskin, *The Stones of Venice*, pp. 157–61.

38 For a full examination of this issue see G. Scott, *The Architecture of Humanism*, Oxford: The Architectural Press, 1980. See also Chapter six, note 23.

39 J. Ruskin, *The Two Paths*, George Allen, 1901, p. 18.

40 Ruskin, *The Stones of Venice*, pp. 170–78.

41 Ruskin, *The Two Paths*, 'The Deteriorative Power of Conventional Art', p. 41.

42 Ibid., 'The Influence of Imagination in Architecture' p. 137.

43 *Architectural Review*, July 1910, p. 45.

44 See W. L. Creese, *The Search for Environment*, NewHaven, CT: Yale University Press, 1966.

45 Profit sharing was a system developed in France by M. Leclaire in the mid nineteenth century as a means of increasing worker incentive and eliminating the antagonism between workers and owners. Employees are paid a share of the profits of their employer's enterprise, in accordance with agreements defined in advance. Such payments are distinct from and additional to regular earnings.

46 W. H. Lever, 'Prosperity Sharing versus Profit Sharing in Relation to Workshop Management', paper read before the Birkenhead Literary and Scientific Society, 19 November 1900, p. 9.

47 George, *Labour and Housing*, p. 5.

48 Ibid., p. 5.

49 Lever, 'Prosperity Sharing'.

50 W. H. Lever, 'Day Work or Piece Work, Which?' a paper read to the Port Sunlight Mutual Improvement Society, 13 January 1904, Published as a supplement to *Progress* [Lever Brothers' in-house magazine] February 1904.

51 Ibid., p. 3.

52 *Birkenhead News*, 24 November 1900.

53 Lever, 'Prosperity Sharing', p. 9.

54 Ibid., p. 10.

55 J. Ruskin, *Unto this Last*, Everyman, 1907, p. 185.

56 Lever, 'Prosperity Sharing', p. 10.

57 George, *Labour and Housing*, p. 87: 'There is a feeling that the company should defray the upkeep and expenses of the institutions'.

58 Ibid., p. 19.

59 Lever, 'Prosperity Sharing', p. 10.

60 Lever, *Day Work or Piece Work, Which?* p. 14.

61 George, *Labour and Housing*, p. 91.

62 Ibid., p. 105.

63 C. Wilson, *The History of Unilever*, Cassell, 1954, p. 150.

64 G. Darley, *Villages of Vision*, The Architectural Press, 1975: 'Life at Port Sunlight still bears the marks of an oppressively paternalistic regime ... that a man's house workplace, sport and entertainment are all provided by courtesy of one agent is suffocating and induces a depressing feeling of being bespoken for.'

65 Grayson and Ould's work at Port Sunlight; 1891, 85–88 Greendale Road; 1894, 8–14 Bridge Street, 2–8 Park Road, 97–100 Greendale Road; 1895, 27–55 Wood Street, 1–8 Riverside; 1898, 224–42, 288–92, 302–04, 310–26 New Chester Road, 55–59 Corniche Road, 12–20 Lodge Lane; 1899, 192–98 New Chester Road, 18–24 Greendale Road, 44–55 Bebington Road; 1900, The Bridge Inn; 1901, 37–45 Primrose Hill, 1–7 Lower Road, 6–10, 30–32, 40–43, 49–53 Greendale Road; 1902, Church Drive Schools, 6–18 Windy Bank; 1905, 3–11 Boundary Road, 13–33, 45–47 Boundary Road; 1907, 8–34 Pool Bank; 1910, 5–10 Lower Road.

66 Presidential Address to the Liverpool Architectural Society, reported in *The Builder*, 2 June 1900.

67 Ibid., p. 541.

68 E. Ould, *Old Cottages, Farm Houses and other Half Timbered Buildings in Shropshire, Herefordshire and Cheshire*, Batsford, 1904. The following extracts are from this work.

69 In talking of Cheshire timbering he mentions Speke Hall as amongst 'The finest timber mansions in the world' (p. 28). This is significant bearing in mind the importance of F. R. Leyland, the then owner of Speke Hall, and his role as a patron of painting in the city.

70 Maurice Adams's work at Port Sunlight: 1899, 59–63 Greendale Road, 52–56 Primrose Hill; 1907, 5–13 Central Road.

71 M. Adams, *Modern Cottage Architecture*, Batsford, 1904. The following extracts are from this work.

72 Ibid., p. 1: 'Cottage building is for many reasons a fascinating subject, possessing attractions peculiarly its own, while the planning of these small houses permits of so much ingenuity that the problem always seems to present some new scope for further improvement of fresh ideas. This interest is of course much increased when cottages of an artistically appropriate kind are intended to be built, without allowing bald utilitarian consideration to determine every detail.'

73 For example, Ashbee's mother's funding of his architectural endeavours in Cheyne Walk.

74 Adams, *Modern Cottage Architecture*, p. 15. '[And] it must be from the remains of vernacular work scattered up and down historic England that the best type and most suitable style of design will invariably be found … The absence of any affectation of style is one of the greatest reasons for the charm of historic buildings of the domestic kind to which I refer.'

75 Ibid., p. l4: 'Meanwhile the pictorial charms of many an old ruin of domestic origin and tumble down cottage became popularised by the delightful drawings of Samuel Prout, who, during the early years of the last century, opened up the eyes of the public to the beauties of the picturesque, which he so thoroughly appreciated himself, although without a notion as to the style or date or texture technically of the buildings he so lovingly depicted.' An appreciation of Prout's work was in turn encouraged by John Ruskin: see J. Ruskin, *Notes by Mr. Ruskin on Samuel Prout and William Hunt*, Fine Art Society, 1879.

76 Adams, *Modern Cottage Architecture*, p. 14: 'It may also be acknowledged that the garden city movement certainly has encouraged this development.'

77 See W. B. Forwood, *Liverpool Cathedral – the Story of its Foundation*, Liverpool: Lee and Nightingale, 1925.

78 This was Bishop Francis James Chavasse: his appointment meant a sympathetic ear for those who had long been lobbying in the city for a cathedral. The previous Bishop, John Rylle, had strong evangelic aspirations, and wanted a more dispersed church presence throughout the city.

79 On 8 March 1901.

80 Submission from the Liverpool Architectural Society to the Cathedral Executive Subcommittee, Liverpool City Library Archives.

81 President of the RIBA (Royal Institute of British Architects) 1899–1902.

82 Letter from J. Alderson Smith (Secretary, Cathedral Committee), to Sir William Emerson, 23 September 1901, Liverpool City Library Archives.

83 'I think it might be mentioned that it was by my earnest recommendations that 13th Century Gothic was adopted as the style of architecture for the cathedral'. From a manuscript book written by Robert Gladstone, 9 October 1908, F. M. Radcliffe Archive, Liverpool City Libraries.

84 Report of the Building Sub-Committee, 7 October 1901, Liverpool City Library Archives.

85 *The Builder*, 28 September 1901, p. 268: 'Here is the ecclesiological prejudice in church architecture in full blow again; a great chance for the production of a grand and original piece of modern church architecture is deliberately thrown away, and we shall have another specimen of imitation medievalism.'

86 Letter from T. Myddleton Shallcross to *The Times*, 8 October 1901.

87 *The Builder*, 12 October 1901, p. 308. 'A Liverpool Architect, Mr. Shallcross, writes an admirable letter in *The Times* attacking the action of the Liverpool Cathedral Committee in regard to what, as he truly says, is a matter of national and not merely local interest … In fact, the Cathedral Committee appears to consist of fossil ecclesiologists who are totally unaware of all that has been going on in the modern architectural mind during the last quarter of a century.'

88 Letter from R. Blomfield to *The Times*, 15 October 1901.

89 Letter from R. Gladstone to *The Times*, 17 October 1901.

90 *The Builder*, 19 October 1901, p. 331.

91 Letter from R. Gladstone to *The Times*, 21 October 1901: 'Is it not wiser to adopt the kind of architecture with which our devotional feelings are so closely entwined?'

92 Leader, *The Times*, 23 October 1901.

93 'The Ideal of the Modern Cathedral', *The Builder*, 26 October 1901, pp. 350–51.

94 T. G. Jackson, 'Liverpool Cathedral. A Protest and Petition', *Architectural Review*, November 1901.

95 Ibid.

96 See A. Service, *Edwardian Architecture*, Thames and Hudson, 1977, pp. 150–51, for an account of institutionalised Arts and Crafts opposition to the style.

97 F. M. Simpson, *Two Presidential Addresses*, Liverpool: University Press of Liverpool, 1901.

98 F. M. Simpson, *The Scheme of Architectural Education started at University College, Liverpool, in connection with the City of Liverpool School of Architecture and Applied Art*, Liverpool: Marples and Co., 1905, p. 12.

99 Ibid., p. 11.

100 Ibid., p. 11.

101 Ibid., p. 11.

102 A general point can be made here about the form that Church of England building took in Liverpool at this time. It showed a strong bias towards a vernacular Gothic style, whilst nonconformist churches opted for non-Gothic styling.

103 Cf. Minutes of the Building Sub-Committee, 7 October 1901. Here, Gladstone quotes Scott on Westminster Abbey as being of interest to 'everyman worthy of the name of Englishman'. He is also minuted as saying 'The great period of Gothic architecture was the hundred years which elapsed between 1220 and 1320, when the Early English entered upon the decorative period.' Liverpool City Library Archive.

104 Simpson, *Two Presidential Addresses*.

105 Ibid., p. 24: 'I am not protesting so much against the inclusion of Gothic, although I regard it as unsuitable, as the exclusion of other styles.'

106 Both Bodley and Shaw were at the end of their careers. Bodley was a veteran of the Gothic Revival and superficially was an obvious choice for judge. Shaw was less so, his work immediately prior to judging the competition was unsympathetic to a Gothic sensibility. In Liverpool he had acted as consultant for Doyle's Royal Insurance building, and as an advisor to Willink and Thicknesse's Parrs bank.

Chapter Two

The Origins of the
Liverpool School of Architecture
and Applied Art:
University College Liverpool and
National Design Culture

THE City of Liverpool School of Architecture and Applied Art was inaugurated in 1895. It has been briefly described by several authors in the past,[1] all of whom acknowledge that the School was an innovative episode in the history of architectural education, in part because of its alliance with the ideas of the Arts and Crafts movement. Its place in the history of architectural education is more easily established than trying to define the Arts and Crafts milieu in which it operated. It was not the first architectural course to be organised in Britain, although it was the first extra-metropolitan one. Nor was it the first full-time course – that had been established by Kings College London three years previously. What made the course unique was a combination of elements; its relative newness, its response to specific cultural circumstances, its funding in part by the municipal authorities, and its adoption of an integrated teaching programme that was briefly to become a teaching norm, principally under the direction of William Lethaby, firstly at the Central College of Arts and Crafts in London and then at the Royal College of Art.

The first architectural instruction in England was to be found at the Royal Academy Schools that were inaugurated in 1768. The value of such instruction was historically undistinguished until the Professorship of Architecture was awarded to Sir John Soane who held it from 1806–37. His commitment to his teaching at the Academy was the reason he felt unable to accept the Presidency of the newly founded RIBA in

1834. In 1870 the Academy set up a separate School of Architecture under Phené Spiers, a graduate of the Ecole des Beaux Arts.

The first certificated technical architectural education was offered by University College London in 1841 with the appointment of T. L. Donaldson (the first secretary of the RIBA) to the Professorship of Architecture. This took the form of a diploma offered by the Department of Civil Engineering and Architecture. The year 1841 also saw the establishment of an architectural course at King's College London. Both these courses were seen as supplementing, rather than supplanting, the process of office training.[2] During the 1840s the Government School of Design had architectural students in attendance, but there was no provision for an architectural education. Indeed, the Director of the School addressed complaints as to the lack of such provision; 'we do not profess to teach architecture, because it interferes with the right of private individuals'.[3] Barrington Kaye, in his book *The Development of the Architectural Profession in Britain*[4] suggests that this is a reference to the pupillage system. Pupillage meant that the aspirant school leaver was articled to an architect's office, where, on the payment of a premium he was trained from between three to five years. In 1891 three years of pupillage could cost the student two to five hundred guineas,[5] a useful source of income to the architect with a limited number of clients.

The Architectural Association was formed in 1847 as an alternative for those who were unable, because of the lack of required experience in practice, to become members of the RIBA. In 1865 George Gilbert Scott suggested in an address to the Association that a school of architecture should be established.[6] After some initial interest this idea faded, but in 1889 Leonard Stokes was made President of the Architectural Association and instigated a review of the Association's educational provision. By 1891 the mutual self help, guild tradition of the Association (which in the 1870s consisted of a fortnightly class in design) was dropped in favour of a formally taught, four year, part-time course.

The Royal Institute of British Architects, founded in 1834 as the Institute of British Architects, was essentially a metropolitan organisation and relied heavily upon the Architectural Association to provide any educational stimulus deemed necessary outside of pupillage instruction. In 1891 when the Architectural Association formalised its education programme, the Royal Institute of British Architects granted several endowments for the running of the scheme.

In 1892 King's College in London began a three year, full-time architectural course under the Professorship of Bannister Fletcher. In 1895 the Liverpool School was inaugurated, predating by a year its nearest equivalent, the Arts and Crafts orientated architectural instruction at the London Central College of Arts and Crafts, founded in 1896 under the directorship of William Lethaby.

Whilst in the past the importance of the Liverpool School as an educational institution has been emphasised in relation to its integrated teaching programme,[7] little examination of its origins has taken place. Frederick Moore Simpson, the first Professor, has generally been the focus of attention because of his success in establishing the School nationally. It would be wrong, however, to view its creation as solely related to a single person or issue. It can be seen, as can the subsequent founding of the Central College of Arts and Crafts, as the result of the culmination of a number of educational circumstances, and the ideological and cultural debates that resulted in the implementation of the Technical Instruction Act of 1889. The Liverpool School was jointly funded by the City of Liverpool and University College Liverpool. Without University College Liverpool, the creation of the School of Architecture and Applied Art would have resulted in an institution of a quite different character. The School was the result of much canvassing by the city's architectural community for a place of education, and by pressure from the Liverpool Trades Council for a thorough implementation of the Technical Instruction Act and the provision of skills training. What University College was able to supply was a cultural environment in which a vocational training system could be expanded. University College's aesthetic expectations enriched with a solid humanistic foundation what could have been a purely mechanistic training system. In this way the School was able to achieve what Matthew Arnold defined as a 'social idea' of culture, an idea of culture closely allied to those of Ruskin and Morris, where the educational struggle was one in which knowledge was systematically divested 'of all that was harsh, uncouth, difficult, abstract, professional, exclusive; [in order] to humanise it, to make it efficient outside the clique of the cultivated'. [8]

In the event the School was, albeit briefly, the focus of national attention with regard to the training of architects, and a precursor of similar establishments. The ideological foundations of the School can be split into two parts, the internal cultural base in University College Liverpool, and the external circumstances that made the architectural community in Liverpool wish to gain access to it. It is obvious that the issues surrounding the development of the Liverpool School are far more complicated and wide-ranging than those around the development of Port Sunlight, though both can be seen as operating within the same general cultural paradigms.

The first important individual contribution to this unique cultural environment was that of Gerald Rendall, appointed in 1881 as the first Principal of University College Liverpool. It was he, along with Alderman Philip Rathbone, who ensured that the new university was to have some form of aesthetic education. The structure that it was to take was governed by the establishment of the Roscoe Professorship of Fine Art. Rendall's principalship saw considerable collaboration with the civic authorities,[9] and perhaps this very act of cooperation (whilst obviously part of the survival process of the college in difficult times) was a demonstration of his commitment to a democratic conception of the process of education. This educational notion lent itself to the principles of collaborative working practices espoused by the School of Architecture and Applied Art. Given this, it is worth looking at two public (and subsequently published) addresses by Rendall, in which his cultural attitudes and aspirations can be quite clearly distinguished. One is the inaugural address presented at the opening of University College Liverpool in 1882,[10] the other a lecture at Liverpool College given in the same year of the foundation of the School of Architecture and Applied Art in 1894.[11]

The Education Act of 1870 acts as a convenient focus for Rendall's inaugural address, establishing the fundamentals of a national educational system. It was Rendall's starting point in arguing for the further development of local educational provision: 'Yet there inhers in the nature of things no reason why [to pursue their training] the engineer should migrate to the Clyde, or why the Liverpool Artist should learn his craft in Manchester'.[12] This local provision (in part established)[13] was to be open to the secular and the religious in all their manifestations. Women were particularly welcomed as members of the new establishment by Rendall.[14] His conception of the role of education was a socially empowering one; 'The best and noblest spirit of democracy … now claims that in education the old disabilities of poverty shall be done away; that defect of opportunity shall no longer imprint on the less favoured its indelible stamp; that the child of low degree shall not perforce go ill-schooled.'[15]

If we can read this as a programme for action, then it is evident that any initiative within the University that can be identified as 'progressive' or 'innovative' must have enjoyed the approval of Rendall, if not his active support.

Rendall's next published pronouncement on education was not for another 12 years. In his address at Liverpool College in 1894, Rendall related education to its two polar conditions – education as an end in itself, and as an applied vocational process. Both conditions, Rendall argued, were present when education is seen as having a social value.[16] A large part of Rendall's address was given over to an examination of the work of the city's Technical Instruction Committee. This is particularly relevant given that it was with this committee's direct assistance that the School of Architecture and Applied Art was set up. In the light of Rendall's expressed views on the interrelationship between education and vocation, the School acts as a paradigm for this principle, linking vocational training with studies in design aesthetics.

The Roscoe Professorship was an important stage in the emergence of the School of Architecture and Applied Art. Rendall publicly identified the lack of art practice in the new college as being a major omission in 1882,[17] and it was with Philip Rathbone's active support within the city[18] that sufficient funds were raised to pay for the first appointment in this area. However, it was in March 1881 that Rendall, newly appointed to the Principalship, mentioned to William Martin Conway that there was to be a Professorship of Art at Liverpool. Conway was at that time writing a book on the woodcutters of the Netherlands with the aid of a grant from Cambridge Library.[19] He was a protégé of Henry Bradshaw, the University Librarian at Cambridge, and it was through this connection that Rendall knew of him, as he was at that time Gladstone Professor of Classics and Ancient History at Cambridge.[20] Conway wrote in his memoirs:

> He [Rendall] mentioned that there was to be a Professorship of Art. A peculiar expression passed over his face, and for once in a while I was observant and gave it what I am sure was the correct interpretation. Knowing that I was working with Colvin and Bradshaw he was on the point of saying to me, 'You might perhaps get the post', but he, being a very cautious and wise person, thought silence safer and said nothing.[21]

In September Rendall contacted Conway to tell him that the creation of the Chair was imminent, and in October when the Chair of Art was formally nominated, Rendall wrote to Conway: 'We this week decided that the chair was to be one of lecturing on the History, Theory and Practice of Art, and that the function of the professor was to be to enlighten the public rather than to train artists … Five years tenure was fixed upon, and residence during term is obligatory.'[22]

In April 1882, Conway applied for what was then the Roscoe Professorship of Fine Art, and in June was to hear of his rejection. The Chair remained unfilled. We do not know on what grounds he was rejected. It cannot have been too serious because in August the following year he was invited by the University to give a brief course of lectures along with two other lecturers whom it is reasonable to assume were also considered for the Chair; these were Barclay Day and W. G. Collingwood. Conway accepted this invitation[23] and in 1884 lectured on Flemish painting. The lectures must have been considered capable, or more, because in March 1885 Conway was offered the post of Roscoe Professor of Art.[24]

On his own admission Conway's lecture courses were not a great success.[25] They were never part of any programme of certification, and he lectured on what interested him, rather than in populist subjects. It is probable the lecture programmes were abandoned when there was no enrolment for them. In his years at Liverpool he lectured,[26] or proposed to lecture, on the Italian Renaissance (spending a substantial part of one term on Raphael, and another on Leonardo); the art of ancient Egypt, Chaldea and Assyria and 'Phoenicia and her dependencies'. A course centred around some lectures on the paintings in the Liverpool Royal Institution Gallery, was turned into a book.[27] Whilst his lecture programme was not necessarily a success, Conway's intellectual activities do provide us with a sort of paradigm of the cultural expectations of the University and its Senate. For an institution to support a Professorship of Art that had so singularly failed to produce any tangible evidence of educational success indicates, if nothing else, a determination that the original intention to 'enlighten the public' was worth dogged pursuit. (He was thought of well enough by the University for them to offer him the principalship when it became vacant in 1899.)[28] Whilst in Liverpool Conway visited John Ruskin[29] in the Lake District in order to gain his support for his Liverpool education projects. This too speaks of a position in line with a didactic, cultural role for art.

Conway's interest in architecture was a small part of his aesthetic outlook, though when he touched upon it he was astute in his observations.[30] Whilst Roscoe Professor his only public pronouncement about architecture was in an open letter[31] to the Bishop of Liverpool co-written with Gerald Rendall. This, as we have already encountered, was during the first attempt to build a Gothic cathedral in Liverpool in 1886. Because Conway wrote so little on architecture it is impossible to tell whose is the dominant personality in the writing. Certainly the main thrust of the piece, the notion that artistic form must relate directly to a social reality can be found in other aspects of Conway's writing at the time. In his lecture *The Succession of Ideals*,[32] Conway laid down a very clear argument relating artistic production to material conditions in a manner that paralleled the outlook of William Morris.[33] Further intellectual parallels with an Arts and Crafts sensibility[34] can be discerned in the emphasis that he placed upon the role of hand crafted objects. He was to write: 'An honest carpenter may continue the influence of his honesty long after his death, if the work he has done be respected by those privileged to use it. If they wilfully destroy it, the good man's influence is at an end.'[35]

Rendall's involvement in the letter to the Bishop of Liverpool suggests two things. Firstly, it makes sense to suppose that Rendall concurred with Conway's general cultural position. Secondly, it indicates a shared attitude to architectural design and its social responsibilities within the University. In so doing, it establishes an identifiable cultural stance that can be associated with later developments within the School of Architecture and Applied Art. Rendall and Conway argued against a Gothic cathedral because 'imitative forms of expression necessarily lack that free life and adaption which attest living faith ... Cathedrals of the twelfth and thirteenth centuries can furnish no type for the cathedral of today.'[36] The new social and cultural patterns of contemporary society should determine new architectural forms. The Gothic cathedral 'was built to supply a set of social needs which no longer exist; its forms were developed in response to those needs; it follows that a modern cathedral being required to fulfil quite different functions should be built on an entirely different plan'.[37] This critical attitude towards a simplistic Gothic revivalism and the similarity of these arguments to those that were presented 15 years later by Professor Simpson, does suggest that the cultural environment within the University was well prepared for what was to emerge in architectural training.

Conway resigned his position as Roscoe Professor in 1888, having organised, with Philip Rathbone, the formation of the National Association for the Advancement of Art and its Application to Industry and oversaw its first congress in Liverpool (the consequences of this will be examined in detail in chapter 3). On his departure the chair was awarded to R. A. M. Stevenson in circumstances that are not at all clear, but he was a friend of Conway's and a fellow member of the Saville Club; in Conway's words 'one of the very best talkers of his day'.[38] Stevenson's enthusiasm for the post was not great,[39] and his contemporaries were well aware of his discomfort. Twenty years later Walter Raleigh was to write in recollection of Stevenson that: 'Stevenson was frightened by the University of which a strange accident had made him professor – frightened as a woodland creature is frightened by a steam plough.'[40]

Conway's concerns were with the evolution of cultural ideas, but Stevenson was primarily a painter. He held only two advertised classes, one a practical art class,[41] the other a course on classical architecture that had been requested by the Liverpool Architectural Society.[42] He resigned in 1892, having first put forward to the University his ideas regarding the Professorship. He thought that the role of the Professorship as originally conceived was unproductive in an environment such as Liverpool's, and that the Professorship should be associated with a specific artistic discipline such as a Life School or a School of Architecture. It was this last sentiment, undoubtedly the result of his response to the demands for an architectural history course, that endeared him to the city's architectural community.[43] With his departure from the Chair in September 1892, two possibilities were considered by the University; the development of the Chair as a Chair of Fine Art, or its transformation into a Chair of Architecture. One last attempt to keep the Roscoe Professorship as one of Fine Art by combining the Directorship of the City Museum with the existing University responsibilities fell through when the prospective Professor, Lionel Cust, declined the offer. He was shortly afterwards to become Director of the National Portrait Gallery.[44]

In 1892 (before Stevenson's departure) the University Senate had set up a committee to investigate the possibility of architectural teaching in the University. The Architectural Society of Liverpool had already made advances to Rendall requesting some form of architectural teaching.[45] It is difficult to pinpoint a specific date, but the first instance of architectural instruction within the University was in the academic year 1888–89, when an evening class looked at the stylistic variants of construction.[46] I have already mentioned the later architectural classes of Stevenson in the academic year of 1891–92. Circumstantial evidence suggests that within the University a substantial contribution to the idea of architectural education was made by Professor Mackay, holder of the Chair of History. Mackay had a vision of a School of Fine Arts at Liverpool, of which architectural study was to be a component part. He considered himself (in 1892) to have been largely responsible for the element of architectural instruction already given by Stevenson, and actively encouraged the Liverpool Architectural Society in its discussion with the University about the development of architectural study.[47] In 1914, Charles Reilly, the then Roscoe Professor of Architecture, was to write: 'That architecture is a full subject in the academic curriculum of the University of Liverpool, with a chair devoted to it, is largely due to Professor Mackay.'[48]

Unfortunately, Reilly's flamboyant character and his willingness to entertain does cast doubt on his role as a completely reliable witness in the absence of corroborating evidence. What these sentiments do indicate is Mackay's enthusiasm for the project of architectural education and the willingness of the University to cooperate in demands for it. In 1894 the Roscoe Professorship was duly transferred to Architecture and Frederick Moore Simpson was its first incumbent. When the post was advertised nationally *The Builder* was: 'glad to notice, among the advertisements for display amongst our columns this week, the one from University College Liverpool, inviting application for the position of Professor of Architecture to the College. This is an excellent step … forming a precedent which may be followed elsewhere.'[49] As indeed it was.

There were influences, apart from the University, that contributed to the founding of the Liverpool School of Architecture and Applied Art. These ideas can be divided into two groups: the increasing national demand for a system of technical education, with its local architectural manifestations; and the decision by the RIBA in 1891 to establish a series of membership examinations.

There had been a Mechanics Institute in Liverpool since 1825. Its original intentions encapsulated in its motto, 'Knowledge is Power', had by the early 1890s been considerably modified (in art education), by its involvement in the national South Kensington System of Art Education. The national art education system was a graded one of seemingly endless, self-referential skill-based tests.[50] It is worth quoting a passage by George Moore, whose contemporary criticism of the organisation of the arts in Britain was based on his cosmopolitanism, and vented on the 'brewer or distiller',[51] whom he saw forming the parochial aesthetic of the British. In describing the South Kensington System he is summarising the attitudes not only of those involved in his immediate circle, such as Whistler and the New English Art Club, but also those like Walter Crane and William Lethaby who were attempting to establish a new conception of design education:

> In England it is customary for art to enter by the side door, and the enormous subvention to the Kensington Schools would never have been voted by Parliament if the Bill had not been gilt with the usual utility gilding. It was represented that the schools were intended for something much more serious than the mere painting of pictures, which only rich people could buy; the schools were primarily intended as schools of design, wherein the sons and daughters of the people would be taught how to design wall papers, patterns for lace, damask table cloths, etc. The intention, like many another was excellent; but the fact remains that, except for examination purposes, the work done by Kensington students is useless. A design for a piece of wall paper, for which a Kensington student is awarded a medal, is almost sure to prove abortive when put to a practical test. The isolated pattern looks pretty enough on the two feet of white paper on which it is drawn; but when the pattern is manifolded, it is usually found that the designer has not taken into account the effect of the repetition. That is the pitfall into which the Kensington student falls; he cannot make practical application of his knowledge ... So complete is the failure of the Kensington student, that to plead a Kensington education is considered

to be an almost fatal objection against anyone applying for work in any of our industrial centres.[52]

If one allows for hyperbole in the last sentence of the above passage, it indicates well the lack of regard which was given to the South Kensington System by British design circles.

The concerns expressed by Moore about art education are often overlooked by writers examining the effects of the Technical Instruction Act of 1889.[53] What was evident in Liverpool – artistic education taking advantage of the new circumstances afforded by the Act – was later to be the case with London's Central School of Arts and Crafts.[54] The Liverpool School (or more correctly the Applied Arts Section) was funded from the city through the rating powers that the Act gave the municipal authority. Given this fact, the issue of technical education assumes an important role, particularly when the motivation for the Act can be seen coming from progressive elements within the British intelligentsia. Furthermore, the prime mover of the act in Parliament was Sir Henry Roscoe, of the Liverpool Roscoes, who whilst lecturing in chemistry in Manchester must have retained some contact with the Unitarian community in Liverpool that was funding the Roscoe Professorship.

The issue of technical education was not a new one in Britain at the time. For many years concern had been expressed at the poor quality of British design compared to her European competitors,[55] but it was brought into focus by the Royal Commission on Technical Education 1881–84. The Commission's recommendations for modest improvements in general education in order to stimulate industrial growth were not substantial contributions to the development of technical education, but the report was important because, according to Roscoe, it created a good deal of interest in the press which stimulated public discussion and concern.[56]

In 1887 the National Association for the Promotion of Technical Education was formed with the express purpose of pressing the government to instigate a coherent technical education programme. Prominent amongst the members was T. H. Huxley who had spent many years arguing for an objective, rational, secular education system which was to be 'a sort of neutral ground on which the capitalist and the artisan would be equally welcome'.[57]

Huxley and his associates' expectations were that extra-metropolitan communities would tax themselves in order to fund educational schemes specific to their communal and industrial needs. This was, as far as Huxley was concerned, a basic principle of democratic organisation. Speaking at the inaugural meeting of the National Association for the Advancement of Technical Education at Manchester Town Hall in 1887, Huxley laid down this axiom:

> I believe it sound doctrine that a municipality – and the state itself for that matter – is a corporation existing for the benefit of its members, and that here [the issue of technical education], as in all other cases, it is for the majority to determine that which is for the good of the whole, and to act upon that.[58]

The importance of this issue to the Liverpool School of Architecture and Applied Art was that (on the passing of the Technical Instruction Act) it was to be funded through local, rather than national taxation,[59] and that educational initiatives would no longer need to be funded through private endowment, as had been the the case with the Roscoe Professorship of Fine Art.

In its first annual report[60] in 1888 the National Association for the Advancement of Technical Education recorded its successes in meetings in Liverpool, Manchester and other northern cities. That 300,000 of its leaflets were distributed gives some idea of the success of its public relations effort at least. Sir Henry Roscoe introduced the Association's Technical Instruction Bill in the same year, and after a series of modifications it was passed in 1889.[61]

It was not only national pressure that forced the pace of change. The campaigning by the Liverpudlian architectural community has already been discussed. In addition it is worth noting the importance that the University community gave to Trades Council activities in the city. In an article 'Liverpool Workmen and Technical Education' in *Sphinx*, the University College magazine, a detailed examination of the campaigning by the Liverpool United Trades Council and the Workmen's Technical Scholarship Committee was made.[62] When the School of Architecture and Applied Art was finally inaugurated in May 1895 it was under the management of a joint board consisting of University College, the City's Technical Instruction Committee, the Liverpool Architectural Society, and the Master Builders' Association amongst others. Without the Act the Liverpool School of Architecture would have been a very different educational establishment. The School's importance is all the more astonishing when Huxley's last piece of propandising is considered. Shortly before his death Huxley sent the Vice-Chancellor of the University of London a plan for the reorganisation of the University into a number of colleges providing 'professional education in a) Law, b) Medicine, c) The Industrial Professions, d) The Scholastic Profession, e) Painting, Sculpture and Architecture, f) Music'.[63] These constituent colleges were to be organised on a federal basis, organising their own professional certification. The plan was not accepted, and because of Huxley's death remained undeveloped. In Liverpool, because of the lack of traditional educational structures and a consequent lack of vested interest in maintaining the status quo, the possibilities that Huxley envisaged under the new Act were fulfilled, especially in Education, Engineering, and Architecture and Applied Arts.[64]

Before looking more specifically at the local cultural roots of the architectural and design ideology of the new School, one last national institutional mechanism needs to be examined briefly, the decision of the RIBA to instigate a programme of professional examinations, beginning the process of making architecture a closed society of registered practitioners. As the direct consequence of a Parliamentary Bill wishing to do the same on a state basis, this move caused considerable friction in the national architectural community, mainly because it took away the aspect of architecture as a fine art which was so highly valued at the time. In a letter to *The Times*, opponents of both state and RIBA control of the profession wrote: 'Architecture has for some time been less constantly associated with the sister arts of Painting and Sculpture than, in our opinion, is desirable, and we think that examinations and diplomas, by raising up artificial barriers, would have a tendency still further to alienate these branches of art.'[65]

The RIBA's advocacy of certification can be summarised as that of an Institute that wished to become more powerful,[66] and whose advocacy genuinely reflected a legitimate concern that the new building technologies resulting from the processes of industrialisation needed a new form of administration. The new building technologies of the period were eroding not only the traditional forms of building construction, but also the traditional role of the architect.

There were objections to the RIBA's proposals; a resentment towards the power that the Institute would be seen to hold, a lack of confidence in the quality of the proposed exam (this is unsurprising given the lack of educational provision provided by the Institute), and finally a reluctance by a generation of architects immersed in the principles of the Arts and Crafts and vernacular traditions to see a diminishing role for architecture at the core of the fine arts.

T. G. Jackson, who opened the Liverpool School in May 1895, was the national focus of opposition to the RIBA proposals. He, along with Richard Norman Shaw, edited a key text in the debate, *Architecture: A Profession or an Art?*[67] in which opponents of the RIBA aired their views in a series of essays. Jackson was not a member of the Institute (neither was Shaw), and in his introduction to the book he becomes a de facto spokesman for such figures as George Bodley, William Butterfield,

William Lethaby, Philip Webb, Walter Crane and William Morris who were signatories to *The Times* letter of 3 March 1895, and who were also members of the Art Workers Guild. Jackson, in characterising the RIBA's moves as concerned with 'the professional advancement of the architect', then proceeded to paint a picture of the sort of architect that he would wish to see; a picture that fits well into the Arts and Crafts conception of design practice:

> The architect suffers at present through his isolation from the sister arts of painting and sculpture; to tighten the bonds of professionalism would be to shut him up off from them entirely and to smother what little of the artist is left in him. Our proper field is not consigned to the office; we are, or should be, still more at home in the workshop or building sheds; our brethren are not the lawyer and doctor, but the craftsman and the artisan.[68]

Norman Shaw, whose work was increasingly using a neo-classical design vocabulary, objected to what he saw as the inability of a scheme of certification to produce the sort of training that was necessary. By concentrating on the skills issues of construction and technique, the notion of design becomes a subsidiary one:

> The insinuation occasionally made that architects who have made design their first consideration are deficient in practical attainments or knowledge of construction is opposed to all experience ... who ever heard of a clerk of works being an authority on architecture, or ever desiring to be thought one? ... It is the architect we want, the man who has in addition to all necessary practical knowledge the power of design.[69]

The conception of education for the architect was seen by those writing in the book *Architecture: A Profession or an Art?* [70] as one of union with the other visual arts, rather than one in tandem with a technological or technical education. This view is expressed in *The Times*'s letter and finds a constant echo throughout the chapters.

Frederick Simpson was one of the seven members who resigned from the Institute over the matter of certification. (Five others, Reginald Blomfield, G. C. Horsley, Mervyn Macartney, Ernest Newton and Edward Prior were all members of the Art Workers Guild and all contributed to Jackson's book.)[71] What Simpson was able to do at the Liverpool School was to codify the educational concerns of the group with whom he was associated – all of whom were working in different styles but with a shared methodology – and to legitimise another route to architectural practice than that proposed by the RIBA. Already in Liverpool alternate routes to the RIBA were being considered, the Liverpool Architectural Society talked of the first ad hoc architectural education programme at University College as being an amalgam of RIBA examination demands and the Architectural Association's scheme of studies.[72] Architects outside the Institute saw the codified means of instruction administered by RIBA as potentially stultifying as the South Kensington System – Lethaby talked of:

> The so-called training of architects at the present time [consisting] not in being taught their art, but in learning more or less by rote out of books some facts about it … the study of 'architecture' now is the study of lists of old buildings and their parts, classified and tabulated under every conceivable cross-indexing of features, style place and date.[73]

His solution, as exemplified by the London Central School of Arts and Crafts, for so long seen as being innovatory, can be seen in the light of the Liverpool experiment as being part of a larger evolutionary process within design education. However, the fact remains that the fruition of such ideas in Liverpool places the courses at Liverpool at the centre of a national focus.

Notes

1 R. Bisson, *The Sandon Studios Society and the Arts*, Liverpool: Parry Books, 1965; L. Budden, *The Book of the Liverpool School of Architecture*, Liverpool: Liverpool University Press, 1932; Q. Hughes, 'Before the Bauhaus'; *Architectural History*, vol. 25, 1982; T. Kelly, *For Advancement of Learning*, Liverpool: Liverpool University Press, 1981; J. Willet, *Art in a City*, Methuen, 1967.

2 B. Kaye, *The Development of the Architectural Profession in Britain*, Allen and Unwin, 1960, p. 134. 'Even the elaborate courses at Kings and University Colleges were intended to supplement, rather than supplant, office training.'

3 *The Builder*, 1864, note 4, p. 465.

4 Kaye, *The Development of the Architectural Profession*, p. 9: 'These private individuals were presumably those architects who found in their pupils their chief source of income.'

5 J. Clayton, 'The Isolation of "Professional" Architecture from the other Arts', in R. Shaw and T. Jackson (eds), *Architecture: A Profession or an Art?*, John Murray, 1892. 'Thus to architecture, as an art, the terms of pupilage are as unwarrantably accommodating as they are cruelly misleading. Early pledges of artistic genius, essential to the other arts, are dispensed with in architecture, for the practice of which ordinary education and presumable common sense are thought sufficient. These qualifications are, on fulfilment of the prescribed brief course of a three years pupilage in an "office", at a cost of from 200 to 500 guineas, expected to bear fruit in the acquisition of a profundity in scientific construction and a knowledge of business, which are supposed to be hopelessly beyond the grasp of painters and sculptors. Further, as is now proposed by the Institute, the warrant for "practice"

in the profession shall, as in divinity, Law and Physic, be by diploma only, independently of any natural gifts or qualifications for art on the part of the student.' As this demonstrates, the system of pupillage was not greatly liked by certain sections of the profession.

6 J. Summerson, *The Architectural Association* 1847–1947, Pleiades for the Architectural Association, 1947, pp. 18–19.

7 Principally by Quentin Hughes – see Q. Hughes, 'Before the Bauhaus', *Architectural History*, vol. 25, 1982.

8 M. Arnold, 'Culture and Anarchy', see J. Bryson, (ed.), *Matthew Arnold Poetry and Prose*, Rupert Hart Davies, 1967, p. 493.

9 Gerald Rendall was Principal of University College Liverpool from its inauguration in 1881 until his death in 1898. See G. Rendall, *Education in Liverpool Past and Present*, Liverpool, 1894, p. 4: 'Few, I may suppose, have served on more committees, few have had more happy and frequent chances of seeing and understanding the work of secondary schools in Liverpool, than have fallen to my lot in the past thirteen years in Liverpool, in which the advancement of education in this place has been the capital desire and preoccupation of my life.'

10 G. Rendall, 'Inaugural Address', Cambridge, 1882.

11 G. Rendall, 'Education in Liverpool Past and Present', Liverpool, 1894.

12 Rendall, 'Inaugural Address', p. 8.

13 Albeit precariously; 'Now, more than ever in the past, permanence of endowment is needful for stability of life. Amid the rapid modern fluctuations of opinion, of population and of the market, no young centre of higher education can count upon long life unless it is able calmly to face all temporary ebbs and flows of popular caprice. But such sense of security, such guarantee of survival, University College possesses in the solid endowment with which it begins life.' Ibid., p. 4.

14 'It may be said that the higher education of women has not yet passed the experimental stage. Yet, in so far as it has been tried, even those who instinctively distrust it cannot allege failure. Therefore has the unanimous sense of the directors of this movement willed that students of either sex should find equal favour, and that our infant college should not close her doors on those whom the ancient universities are already giving access.' Ibid., p. 15.

15 It is worth noting, in order to gauge the radical nature of the educational enterprise in Liverpool, that the 1870 Education Act caused much acrimony in its secularising approach. So much so that Disraeli's attempt in 1874 to 'denationalise' endowed schools caused *The Times* to comment; 'It is difficult to find precedent for it – a bill proposing the wholesale redelivery to one religious body, of schools which, founded for national purposes and endowed with national property, have been set free for the use and education of all Englishmen', *The Times*, 22 July 1874. Rendall can be seen as being in the same progressive educational camp as occupied by Matthew Arnold (cf. W. H. G. Armytage, *Four Hundred Years of English Education*, Cambridge University Press, 1970, pp. 135–65), and engaged as deeply with education in Liverpool as Randall was, it is likely that he met Arnold on his frequent trips to Liverpool in his role as HMI. Certainly Arnold was personally delighted by the creation of the new University Colleges at Liverpool, Manchester and Leeds. (Cf. A. L. Rowse, *Matthew Arnold, Poet and Prophet*, Thames and Hudson, 1976, p. 128.)

16 G. Rendall, 'Education in Liverpool Past and Present', Liverpool, 1894: 'The pressure and temptation to remove boys early from school proves irresistible, though the policy often turns out "penny wise and pound foolish" ... partners did not take their own sons from school or college, and put them in the office at the age

of 14 or 15; for this good reason, that it would fit them only for the menial lower walks, and not train them to the larger outlooks or the balanced judgments of mercantile responsibility … A boy, it is said, came to Euclid, the philosopher to learn. At the end of the first proposition, he asked. "what shall I get for it?" "Give the boy three halfpence", was the philosopher's reply, "and send him away; for he asks what he will get for it." By that tale take counsel. If distrustful of education you seek the quick return, take the pittance, go away, and be three half-penny boys for the rest of your careers.' p. 15.

17 Rendall, 'Inaugural Address', 'looking forward to what the first imperfect commencements adumbrate, should the college justify its existence and extension, we can discern that neither language, nor philosophy, nor art, nor science will be disenfranchised of their rights.' p. 8.

18 J. Evans, *The Conways: A History of Three Generations*, Museum Press, 1966, p. 69: 'At the end of September [1881] Conway had definite news of the Liverpool Art Professorship from Gerald Rendall, who had gone into residence as the first Vice Chancellor of the University. Its endowment had been fixed at a capital of £10,000 but only £6,000 has so far been promised or paid, though Philip Rathbone, Its chief promoter, hoped to have the fund complete by the spring of 1882'. Philip Rathbone was to personally contribute £1,000.

19 W. M. Conway, *Woodcutters of the Netherlands*, Cambridge: Cambridge University Press, 1894.

20 Bradshaw also endowed at this time a lectureship in Classical Archeology. (Cf. G. W. Prothero, *A Memoir of Henry Bradshaw*, Kegan Paul, 1888.

21 W. M. Conway, *Episodes in a Varied Life*, Country Life, 1932, p. 83.

22 Evans, *The Conways*, p. 70.

23 In November Conway wrote to his father-in-law, Manton Marbles; 'I spent all last week in Liverpool and had a great time of dinners and the like – now happily over … I stopped at four different houses and dined and receptioned with I don't know how many, and can't remember any of their names.' Ibid., p. 82.

24 At £400 p.a., resident for Spring and Winter terms only. In November the Conways took up residence at 25 Princes Avenue.

25 See Conway, *Episodes in a Varied Life*, p. 84: 'I may as well confess the fact that I never enlisted a single student. My public lectures were well enough attended, and with that my employers were content. I was used as a kind of freelance, and sent to address meetings (with a view to raising money), to reply at public or semi-public dinners on behalf of the college, to give away prizes at Schools and Institutions, to run the local art club, and generally make myself useful.'

26 For a full list of Conway's advertised teaching commitments see University College Liverpool Calendar, for Sessions 1883–84, 1884–85, 1885–86, 1886–87, 1887–88.

27 W. M. Conway, *Liverpool Royal Institute Gallery of Art*, Seeley, Jackson and Halliday, 1884.

28 He turned them down, though was later M. P. for Liverpool University.

29 See Evans, *The Conways*, p. 113: 'he visited Brantwood and obtained the aging Ruskin's blessing on his projects'. It is interesting to speculate as to whether the introduction to Ruskin was effected by Collingwood.

30 By way of illustration in the chapter 'The Succession of Ideals' in W. M. Conway, *The Domain of Art*, John Murray, 1901, p. 148, substantially based upon a previous paper (see note 33), Conway introduces a new section which includes some thoughts on the relationship between material and structure, in this case steel. 'Steel is becoming the important structural material in large modern buildings. The steel girder is now revolutionising architecture. The new style has not yet emerged.

At present metal structures are in the experimental stage. before long perhaps we shall see the metal displaying itself, when a satisfactory method has been invented for preserving the material from injury by atmospheric action. A new style is undoubtedly in process of formation. It will produce a new architectural epoch.' How much of this thinking was the result of Conway's eight years experience away from Liverpool, and how much of it was current in intellectual circles in Liverpool at the time of his stay it is impossible to tell. He was a frequent visitor to New York, and it is interesting to note that the first steel-frame buildings in England were soon to be built in Liverpool (Aubrey Thomas's Tower Building and Liver Building). Conway must have been aware during his stay of the legacy of cast iron structures in the Liverpool townscape.

31 G. Rendall, and W. M. Conway, 'Liverpool Cathedral: A Letter to the Lord Bishop of Liverpool', Liverpool, 1886.

32 W. M. Conway, 'The Succession of Ideals', an address delivered in St George's Hall, Liverpool at the opening of the College Session, 2 October 1886, Liverpool: Thompson, 1886.

33 '… neither again are the social and political conditions ever twice the same and the spiritual and intellectual ideals of a day are always functions of the actual conditions of life'. Ibid., p. 5.

34 Even in discussion of the collection of the paintings at the Liverpool Royal Institution Conway relates the political economy to artistic production; 'The revival of art towards the close of the thirteenth century was … a consequence of the great social and religious revival.' Conway, *Liverpool Royal Institute Gallery of Art*, p. 4.

35 Ibid., p. 8.

36 Rendall and Conway, 'Liverpool Cathedral: A Letter', p. 3.

37 Ibid., p. 10.

38 Conway, *Episodes in a Varied Life*, p. 255. Conway also said of Stevenson; 'He … had acquired [his ideas concerning art] at Barbizon in the entourage of Corot, where he worked for many years without ever becoming a successful artist. "Style" was the war cry of Barbizon, and Bob Stevenson was its English prophet.' Ibid., p. 257.

39 W. H. Low, *A Chronicle of Friendships 1873–1900*, Hodder and Stoughton, 1908, p. 467: 'I held out for as long as I could and then simply cut it, for no human being could have stood it any longer.'

40 W. Raleigh, 'John MacDonald Mackay', p. 2, in O. Eton, *A Miscellany Presented to J. M. Mackay*, Liverpool: Liverpool University Press, 1914.

41 University College of Liverpool Calendar Session 1891–92, p. 117: 'Students … have an opportunity of doing some practical work … and receiving some guidance from the Professor.'

42 Ibid., p. 118: 'The course … expressly arranged, after consultation with the Liverpool Architectural Society to meet the needs of candidates entering for the qualifying exam for the RIBA.'

43 J. M. Mackay, 'The Teaching of Architecture in the new University: A School of the Fine Arts' in Eton, *A Miscellany*: 'We had both a very high regard for the Professor of Art, R. A. M. Stevenson.' (p. 355); 'The late professor's legacy to his colleagues was, "Establish either a School of Architecture or a Life School on our chair of art."' (p. 361).

44 T. Kelly, *For Advancement of Learning*, Liverpool: Liverpool University Press, 1981, p. 117.

45 Mackay, 'The Teaching of Architecture' in Eton, *A Miscellany*: 'He [T. Harnett Hartley] had interviews with the Principal and some Professors, "What can

University College do for Architecture, what teaching can it give? – these were his persistent inquiries."' p. 355.

46 University College of Liverpool Calendar Session 1888–89, p. 132: Evening Class in Architectural Construction. Lecture followed by a drawing class. Instruction given by J. Battye ARIBA 'The construction of buildings will be explained … and will be further illustrated by examples in detail of parts of buildings in some of the different styles of architecture.'

47 Mackay, 'The Teaching of Architecture' in *A Miscellany*, p. 355.

48 Ibid., p. 146.

49 *The Builder*, 16 January 1894.

50 See S. Macdonald, *The History and Philosophy of Art Education*, University of London Press, 1970, pp. 226–52.

51 G. Moore, *Modern Painting*, The Walter Scott Publishing Co. Ltd., 1893, p. 146: 'The general art patron in England is a brewer or distiller.'

52 Ibid., p. 64.

53 S. F. Cotgrove, *Technical Education and Social Change*, Allen and Unwin, 1958.

54 See G. Rubens, *William Richard Lethaby*, The Architectural Press, pp. 173–99.

55 Cotgrove, *Technical Education*, p. 14.

56 H. E. Roscoe, *The Life and Experiences of Sir Henry Enfield Roscoe*, Macmillan, 1906, p. 214.

57 See T. H. Huxley quoted in C. Bibby, *T. H. Huxley: Scientist, Humanist and Educator*, Watts, 1959, p. 130.

58 C. Bibby, *T. H. Huxley on Education*, Cambridge: Cambridge University Press, 1971, p. 202.

59 The Local Government Act of 1888 was also to facilitate this process. See Armytage, *Four Hundred Years of English Education*, pp. 171–72.

60 *First Annual Report of the National Association for the Promotion of Technical Education 1888*, Co-operative Printing Society, 1888.

61 *Third Annual Report of the National Association for the Promotion of Technical Education 1890*, Co-operative Printing Society, 1890, p. 9.

62 Bibby, *T. H. Huxley: Scientist*, p. 142.

63 *University College Magazine*, vol. 5, 1890, p. 99: 'The Liverpool United Trades Council … have petitioned the corporation to put in force the Technical Education Act … It will thus be seen that the labouring classes are moving. A definite object is set before this committee [Workman's Technical Scholarship Committee] … the realisation of which will give them a deep and permanent interest in all educational developments in the future.'

64 See Kelly, *For Advancement of Learning*, 1981.

65 *The Times*, 3 May 1891.

66 See Ely J. Wilton, 'The Rise of the Professional Architect in England', p. 202, in S. Kostof (ed.), *The Architect. Chapters in the History of the Profession*, Oxford University Press, 1977: 'By the end of the 19th Century still only 10% of the profession belonged to an organisation which the *Times* had dismissed in 1870 as "a highly respectable Trades Union".'

67 T. Jackson and R. Norman Shaw, *Architecture: A Profession or an Art?*, John Murray, 1892.

68 Ibid., p. xxix.

69 Ibid., pp. 11–12.

70 For example J. Clayton, 'The Isolation of "Professional" Architecture from the other Arts' in ibid., p. 126: 'It is a common complaint with architects, even those of undoubted ability as artists, that they, unlike painters and sculptors, have no

standard reference as to "style" and method in their work, by direct appeal to nature. The reply to this is conclusive. The arts of all countries and epochs show that architecture preserved its touch with nature solely, but surely, by joining hands with painting and sculpture.'

71 The seventh architect was E. J. May.

72 See Mackay, 'The Teaching of Architecture' in Eton, *A Miscellany*, p. 356. Whilst no date is attributable to Mackay's address, his comment 'the Institute and the Association kissed each other', implies a date after 1891 when the RIBA was funding the formal teaching programme of the AA.

73 W. R. Lethaby, 'The Builder's Art and the Craftsman', p. 151, in Jackson and Norman Shaw, *Architecture: A Profession*.

Chapter Three

The Origins
of the Liverpool School of
Architecture and Applied Art:
Design Culture in Liverpool

NATIONAL initiatives, such as the Technical Instruction Act, enabled the development of ideas about architectural education in Liverpool, but were it not for its own vigorous cultural life the city would not have been able to capitalise upon the events taking place. The city had its own institutions and a number of powerful figures who were eager for cultural change. In examining their attitudes it is possible to see where Liverpudlian intellectual life meshed with national preoccupations and where and how the local initiatives developed. The interlocking web of personalities and the organisations created a cultural environment in Liverpool that contained the ingredients necessary for the instigation of the new venture in design education, and the political will to put it into operation. This sense of a city culture is important because it militates against the idea (as has been suggested in the past) [1] that the founding of the Liverpool School can be attributed to a specific individual, or to a single set of ideas. To do so is to neglect the wider cultural sphere with all its complications and contradictions, and to make the supposition that the concurrence of ideas by different protagonists also means their active collaboration. The city's institutions were neither self-sufficient nor self-enclosed. Institutions, whether the existing School of Art, the city council's Technical Instruction Committee, or the Liverpool Architectural Society were in constant negotiation with each other and with national bodies. Sometimes in agreement with each other, sometimes not, these multiple acts of institutional negotiation created the intellectual and practical environment in which the Liverpool School of Architecture and Applied Arts was conceived and founded.

Conway's last act in Liverpool, in partnership with Philip Rathbone, was the formation of the National Association for the Advancement of Art and its Application to Industry. He was acting outside his role as Roscoe Professor, although one must assume it was his status as professor that enabled him to gain the support of so many eminent practitioners. The Liverpool Congress of the Association was the first of three, the other congresses were held in Edinburgh and Birmingham, and Conway's resignation as secretary to the Association led to its ultimate demise.[2] Examining the Liverpool Congress enables us to do two things: place the debate concerning the Gothic within the city into a national perspective; and bring the issues of design education into focus. A summary of national arguments about design practice put forward during the congress elucidates the Liverpool context. The cultural intention of the congress was spelt out quite clearly: 'Machinery, by making less immediate the contact of the artisan with the object of manufacture, and by its tendency to specialise the artisan's work, has rendered obsolete ... the old traditions of design, and these have not yet been replaced by new.'[3] In setting the agenda, and avoiding prescriptive solutions, the congress can be seen as a genuine, if unwieldy, mechanism attempting to come to terms with the new conditions defined by aesthetic and industrial practitioners. The dilemma of contemporary practitioners was the attempt to reconcile the methodology and design ideology of the Arts and Crafts with a new architectural style which was able to communicate those ideas in a fresh and culturally invigorating way. Whether the congress and the association achieved their declared aims is outside the scope of this book, the relevance of the events here is the way in which the Liverpool Congress acts as a paradigm of social and aesthetic discourse. Nevertheless it is worth quoting the forlorn comment from the section of the congress's transactions; 'The Practical Outcome of the Art Congress'. It reads, 'No paper received from the author.'[4]

The congress was divided into nine sections, mainly Painting, Sculpture, Architecture, and Applied Art with other hybrids. It was an event that attracted the most prestigious of British practitioners: Lord Leighton as President of the Association gave it establishment status; Walter Crane and others as vice-presidents gave it intellectual credibility. In all, 58 papers were read at Liverpool. Of these, a dozen can be seen as directly applicable to the concerns which were current in Liverpool at the time, the establishment of a city 'School of Design', equipped to confront the reality of industrial and 'fine' design in all its forms. The views expressed in these papers were in opposition to the South Kensington System which was seen as stultifying local and personal achievements.[5] A view of the international inferiority of the South Kensington System was common throughout the papers given[6] and forms an interesting backdrop for the several examinations of continental systems of design education. Before looking at these it is worth returning to the analysis of the problem facing art and design practitioners of the time – how to reconcile machine production with a set of design principles rooted in a pre-industrial age.

The powerful legacy of John Ruskin's ideas is evident throughout the congress papers, and as Patrick Geddes observed; 'It is not a little noteworthy that Mr. Ruskin has been speaking to us through a score of voices, since it shows how the most unpopular ideas of one generation become the convictions of the next.'[7] 'The Machine' however is not generally seen as the threat as it was by Ruskin, and apart from a handful of contributions – most noticeably William Morris's – the assumption was that industrialisation was a permanent phenomenon, out of control, but ultimately controllable. Rather than its banishment, a solution was seen as emerging from new thinking about, and approach to, industrial design and design education. It is this latter pragmatism that can subsequently be seen as the motivation for the Liverpool School of Architecture and Applied Art.

J. D. Sedding's paper 'Things Amiss with our Arts and Industries' acts as a useful pivot around which the handicrafts argument runs. The agenda was set through Ruskin's demand for enriching working conditions,[8] and then developed. 'Let us not be too hard upon the machine', Sedding said, 'after all [it] has no volition of its own, but is merely a dead, passive instrument.'[9] Sedding's way forward was not a critique of the contemporary processes of design or of the shoddy goods that these produced, but rather of that class who produced them, the capitalist class. His argument was undeveloped, and implicit in his text was the assumption that all that was needed structurally was a change of proprietor of the 'design' shop, rather than a reexamination of the nature of retailing. He acknowledged the role of Morris, paying him fulsome tribute,[10] and made much of the Gothic revival – 'It has been the health giving spark – the ozone of modern art.'[11] Morris's own paper 'Art and its Producers', was more rigorously intellectual. As he said himself, it was an 'often told tale'.[12] In it he rehearsed the arguments that he spent much of his life promulgating; that production should be for use and not profit, and that to achieve this aim, a reconstruction of society and a rethinking of the role of the state was necessary. Detectable in the paper is the weariness that Morris was feeling in attempting this transformation, and the limited tools at his disposal.[13] He might well feel discouraged and talk of the Arts and Crafts Society as 'petty and unheroic'[14] if one considers his allies in the Guilds, and the performance given by the Master of the Art Workers' Guild in Liverpool, G. Harvey Garraway who spoke pessimistically of art, architecture, Liverpool, and Britain generally, in language that was as banal as it was unconstructive.[15]

One third of the speakers at the congress were from the Art Workers' Guilds.[16] They were there at the express wish of the promoters, Conway and Rathbone, and their contribution must have been substantial, but delivered in their status as individuals rather than under the blanket designation of Guildsmen. It is significant given the lacklustre performance of Garraway that the Art Workers' Guild in Liverpool played no formal part in the formation of the Liverpool School of Architecture and Applied Art, despite the obvious sympathies that key personalities and institutions must have had for it. Bearing this in mind, Crane's presentation must be seen as operating theoretically, for he made great claims as to the vitality and solidarity of the Guilds. It could be argued that the Guilds were useful in maintaining a form of communication between like-minded people, and as such were productive in ensuring that ideas became widespread amongst practitioners, but their value in instigating activity in the wider social arena must be assumed to be minimal, and if considerable, the result of strong personality rather than organisational strength. The Liverpool Architectural Society that was to play such an important part in the formation of the School of Architecture and Applied Art undoubtedly had members of the Art Workers' Guild amongst their membership, but their success in instigating the debate about design education in the city was the result of their membership of the Liverpool Architectural Society rather than the Art Workers' Guild.

What was important about Crane's address was the central issue of education for craft workers. His concern was that the further the artefact moved from handcrafting the more impotent it became.[17] Because of its relation to the education of craft workers this issue becomes central. The majority of speakers on education systems were in agreement that there was a desperate need for new technical and design education practices. The congress's debate revolved around issues such as: how far should practical skills be taught? What emphasis should be placed upon expression and style? What models should replace the discredited South Kensington System?

T. G. Jackson played an important role in putting the Liverpool School into a cultural context seven years later, which is discussed further in Chapter Four. He saw an obstacle in a workforce which was skilled technically, but had no cultural traditions.[18] He proposed that the architect should control all aspects of the building's design. This was a considerable move away from Ruskin's emancipated workforce embellishing a building collectively as it was constructed! Whilst Jackson touched on the need for training, he proposed no models other than affirming that the architect should be sufficiently familiar with sculpture so he could 'correct the models in the clay'. His later writings developed this stance into an educational system that endorsed the aims and objectives of the Liverpool School. The attitude that demanded the acquisition of hand skills in the fine arts as well as the decorative arts, whilst rooted in the Gothic revival (Jackson was a member of the Art Workers' Guild) also has its parallels in the Beaux Arts tradition. Other papers presented to the congress concentrated upon architecture as the unifier of the arts,[19] bemoaning loudly the specialisation in the South Kensington System. The proposed way forward was the unification of the arts in education and the further reinforcement of this under the stewardship of architecture.

The final issue pertinent to the development of design education in Liverpool was the form it was to take. Two prominent members of the Liverpudlian intelligentsia spoke on the issue, H. Bloomfield Bare and Philip Rathbone. Bloomfield Bare's contribution is probably the best bridge between the issue of the unifying quality of architecture in the arts and the issue of design education. He was an architect (who designed a set of houses for Lever in Port Sunlight in 1906); a designer (who designed the wrought iron gates for the Philharmonic public house, two minutes walk from the art school) and spent at least a year editing an Arts and Crafts magazine in the USA in the early 1890s.[20] He was to play an important role in publicising the Liverpool School in the pages of *The Studio* in the late 1890s. He is important because in his congress contribution he referred specifically to the Liverpool context.[21] He echoed the many voices in the congress that called for a unified approach to artistic education, but he went beyond them in proposing a solution, and one that was to later take form in the Liverpool School:

> The problem before us is this: How to bring the decorative arts out of their present disorganised, feeble condition into conformity with the parent art of architecture ... I should urge, therefore, as essential to the scheme of training, some form of instruction which should combine the studio, the lecture hall and the workshop.

Bloomfield Bare pointed out that the basic provision for the next step in design education was already provided in the Roscoe Chair at

University College and made demands for the creation of a 'Chair of Architecture and Applied Arts'. This, as far as I am aware, was the first public demand in the city (and perhaps nationally) for the specific educational pairing of Architecture and the Applied Arts. Bloomfield Bare set out a general programme of study that in its emphasis upon drawing and the combination of studio and workshop closely prefigures the form that teaching at the Liverpool School was to finally take. The proposals that he put forward as a designer in Liverpool were also echoed in a paper which came to similar conclusions after a study of the German systems of art education.[22]

A close study of Industrial Art Schools in Dresden and Munich suggested a course of education that relied heavily upon multi-disciplinary study and general instruction in drawing delivered by a national system of locally constituted art schools. Throughout Magnus's paper it is clear that despite the efficiency of the German system it is the French Beaux Arts that he favoured; 'Students who are being trained to become trade designers are taught art. Their eyes are saturated with nature, and their hands are taught to represent it'.[23] It is ironic that the views represented here, which could so easily be from a passage by Ruskin, should be an observation of a state system of education, particularly when the indigenous South Kensington System was so constantly reviled. One aspect of the German system that can be seen later in the Liverpool School is the extension of the Atelier system from the sphere of the fine arts into that of applied arts. Another examination of technical education in Munich and Stuttgart talked approvingly of the excellence of the standard of instruction derived from employing 'men who can not only teach but practise applied art in its highest forms. [And who] have ateliers within the walls of the schools'.[24]

It was Philip Rathbone who extensively examined the system of French education. Because his conviction was that the UK system lacked not designers but gifted artisans, he examined the French National School of Decorative Art and the municipal Schools of Art, rather than the Ecole des Beaux Arts. His examination rested on the Ruskinian assumption that an emancipated workforce equals good architecture. More important to him than a successful industrial art was the success of that art in reflecting the fulfilled lives of its workers. Rathbone proposed a system of teaching galleries and museums in Liverpool whose function was an actively didactic role rather than passively storing precious objects (a position derived from the public acquisition of connoisseurs' collections).

It is illuminating that both Bloomfield Bare and Rathbone should be so clearly in favour of creating a local rather than a national alternative to the South Kensington System. It is obvious why such a stance was productive; they were lecturing to a largely local audience, and they were influential locally, if not holders of great administrative power. Finally and most importantly, the metropolitan emphasis of power within the national system meant nothing could be achieved except through regional activity that bypassed, rather than modified, the existing system.

Just as it would be a distortion of the truth to say that there was a single contemporary Arts and Crafts voice, so too, there was no single voice from the congress arguing the course that education in the arts should take. All that was unanimous about the amorphous collection of ideas and attitudes represented at the congress was the perception that change was needed. A sizeable section of the Arts and Crafts movement saw the need for formal technical education in order to cope with new working conditions, both to ensure the production of quality work, and to enhance the quality of life of the artisan. This attitude was quite distinct from those held by Ashbee and the Gimsons who saw the answer as lying solely in the revival of handcrafts. It is unsurprising that in a complex urban environment like Liverpool, the latter was considered irrelevant. The emphasis upon the central role of architecture in the fine and applied arts came from two sources, the Ecole des Beaux Arts and the German Industrial Art Schools. The Liverpool School was to take elements from both, and further enrich them with Simpson's knowledge of educational practice in the United States of America. The booming economy of Liverpool and its constant building programme meant that there was pressure from the architectural community in Liverpool for a skilled workforce to ensure good quality building, in order to secure further commissioned work for local architects. This pragmatic and economic motivation for a locally constituted art education must not be overlooked. One of the problems of the South Kensington System was that it was unresponsive to local demands. By arguing for the establishment of a local school, a system of fine tuning for local demands in training could be readily made.

The Liverpool Architectural Society [25] played an important part in the lobbying for an educational architectural institution within the city. Whilst many issues concerning architectural education were discussed privately and publicly by the Liverpool Architectural Society and its members, its role was primarily as an association of professionals banded together to promote their skills, and to educate their students. The size of the architectural community in Liverpool, its ability to organise, and the potential generated wealth that it represented makes it easy to understand why an experiment in architectural education should take place in the city. It also makes it understandable why aesthetic architectural debate should be so strong in the city, for only in an architectural environment in which there is constant building work can the luxury of architectural aesthetic debate flourish.

The Liverpool Architectural and Archaeological Society was founded on 1 March 1848, after a public meeting held to discover whether there was sufficient interest in the formation of such a group.[26] The 'archaeological' in its title can be seen as a contemporary signifier of erudition and scholarship, rather than indicating an interest in the purely historical, for the Society's declared aims were very much architectural. The Society's intention was to agitate for the improvement of architectural taste and construction, the improvement of the town environs, the formation of a library, and the provision of facilities for students. (These facilities were unspecified but it it is reasonably safe to assume, given the city's cultural climate, that they were educational rather than recreational.) That the Society was not one of gentlemen connoisseurs, but of men active in their profession with an interest in new ideas and technology, is clearly indicated by the 'Exhibition of Electric Light', held at the Society's first annual soirée at the Liverpool Academy.[27]

The formation of the Society was amongst the first extra-metropolitan grouping of architects. The Royal Institute of British Architects, founded in 1834, was still essentially a regional association having emerged from the London Architectural Society. Likewise, the Architectural Association, founded in 1847, was also a London-based, rather than a national organisation. By the end of the Liverpool Society's first year there was a membership of 120, and consideration began to be given to the admission of Master Masons into the Society. The Society's size, and its relative importance in establishing a national architectural professional association was recognised by the RIBA in 1851 when formal discussion between the two organisations was established.[28] Liverpool's first formal contacts with the Association began in 1855, when the Architectural Association wrote to the Society canvassing support for requests to the RIBA for the instigation of an architectural diploma. The following year the Society passed a resolution calling for formal certificated education in architecture. Subsequent correspondence from the RIBA indicated it was thought premature.

In 1862 the Architectural Alliance was formed, and the Liverpool Society was to play a dominant role in its affairs. The Alliance was a federation of the country's architectural societies, other than the RIBA and the Architectural Association. Its aim was to present a unified stand on architectural issues, primarily those of education. The RIBA almost immediately called upon the Alliance to affiliate itself to the Institute but the request was declined.[29]

In 1871 a division within the Alliance emerged when T. H. Wyatt, President of the Royal Institute of British Architects, addressed the Liverpool Society and requested cooperation between the three architectural organisations; the RIBA, the Architectural Alliance and the Architectural Association. The Liverpool Society saw the way to achieve its own educational aims by allying itself to the metropolitan, as opposed to extra-metropolitan groupings. The subsequent result was that the Liverpool Society sent delegates to the next Architectural Alliance AGM with instructions to urge the organisation's dissolution and to encourage the union of the Architectural Societies with the RIBA. This was to be the first of several such attempts by the Liverpool Society which took 20 years to become a reality. The next formal application for alliance with the RIBA took place in 1888 after several of the Society's members successfully took the RIBA exams. It would appear that the RIBA wanted the whole of the Alliance, rather than a single Society. The application was rejected and no further movement was made until 1892.

In April 1892 a national conference was convened in Liverpool by the Liverpool Architectural Society which was attended by delegates from most of the Alliance societies as well as, at the specific request of the Liverpool Society, representatives of the Royal Institute of British Architects. What was proposed was the formal division of the country into 'architectural provinces', linking the various architectural societies with a local centre and 'uniting them directly with the heart of the system, the chartered body in London'.[30]

There is insufficient documentary evidence available to determine how much of the conference was stage-managed by the RIBA and how much the Liverpool Society used its power and prestige within the Alliance to court the RIBA. Certainly, the acquisition of the Alliance's administrative network was a prize the RIBA had long looked for, and within six months of the conference they had drawn up detailed plans as to its future organisation under its administration. That the RIBA was also in the middle of the national 'Profession or an Art' debate, and was vigorously pursuing its aim of becoming the architectural profession's sole representative should not be overlooked, neither should its recent endowment in 1891 to the Architectural Association to fund a formal educational programme. These facts suggest a manipulation of events by an increasingly powerful and ambitious RIBA. Alternatively, it is possible to see a powerful Liverpool Society delivering the Alliance to the RIBA in order to gain access to its newly established educational programme, something the architectural community in Liverpool had long wished for. Certain facts are incontrovertible: the Liverpool Society called the conference in April 1892, when it was reported in the *Royal Institute of British Architects'*

Journal.[31] At the first general meeting of the RIBA in 1893 the President, J. McVicar Anderson, presented a formal scheme for the implementation of the proposals put forward at the Liverpool Conference.

Two resolutions amongst many passed at the conference deserve closer attention. One requested seats on the council of the RIBA for regional Presidents – this was to be rejected by the RIBA as 'impracticable'.[32] The rejection of this demand, which would have ensured the continuation of the federal structure of the Architectural Alliance, indicates two things. Firstly, the strength of the RIBA, in that it could annex the existing structure of the Alliance, with no concessions made as to its own internal structuring. Secondly, and more importantly for the current argument, the lure of formal access to the RIBA's certification programme overrode any issues about the autonomy of regional architectural groupings. It is reasonable to assume that the Liverpool Society, a prime mover of this set of circumstances, was powerful enough to maintain a sense of cultural identity in the face of a possible centralised bureaucracy administering an exam system with all the disadvantages of the South Kensington System. Subsequent events in Liverpool support this argument.[33] The Liverpool Architectural Society needed the RIBA's approbation more than it needed the support of the Architectural Alliance in its demands for an architectural education system. The instigation of the Liverpool conference can be seen as the Liverpool Society publicly demonstrating this, though there was no great affection for the RIBA if the Liverpool Society's President can be seen as representative of the city's opinion. Addressing the Society at an open meeting [34] Henry Hartley preferred, in the words of the RIBA's journal's reporter 'not to enter into the controversy as to whether Architecture was a profession or an Art',[35] and gave a strong indication that the Royal Institute of British Architects was an organisation that was suffered as a means to an end, rather than an end in itself:

> Who knows whether the advance of architectural education
> in provincial centres may not one day assist in the erection of
> local barriers to metropolitan aggression … and show that a
> result so desirable for local enterprise was attained partly by
> its wise endeavour.[36]

There can be no denying the Liverpool Society's constant innovative attitude towards lobbying for architectural education. This was recognised by the RIBA, who, from the 1892 Liverpool conference on, reported regularly on the educational achievements of the Liverpool Society.

A further resolution was carried at the conference referring to the advantages of the RIBA's recently established Progressive Examinations, affirming that they would 'raise the standard of architectural education in all parts'.[37] The issue of education was fundamental to most of the Liverpool Society's activities at the time. T. Harnet Harrison, who was the President of the Liverpool Architectural Society 1891–93, had conducted extensive negotiations with University College[38] about the possibility of architectural education, and it was at the request of the Liverpool Architectural Society that Stevenson, the Roscoe Professor, lectured on classical architecture, specifically to aid candidates for the Royal Institute of British Architects' exam. Henry Hartley, President of the Liverpool Society 1893–95, presided over the instigation of classes funded with the assistance of the Liverpool municipal authorities. The structure of these classes and their success was noted in the Institute's journal.[39] The course of instruction was for the society's student members entering the Intermediate Examination of the Institute. There was a formal syllabus consisting of weekly lectures and project assignments for homework, all of which, according to the Institute's Journal afforded 'good evidence of the vitality of the society'.[40]

By this time (November 1893), the Society was close to concluding its negotiations with the City and the University over the proposed new school. Hartley reported to an open meeting of the Society,[41] that a petition signed by the architectural practitioners of Liverpool had been presented to the Technical Instruction Sub-Committee of the City Council 'begging' for their further assistance and cooperation in proposals for architectural education within the city, intimating that in the event of the establishment of a School of Architecture, they were prepared to promote its success even to the extent of inserting a clause in the articles of their pupils enabling them to take advantage of the special training that such a school would provide. In the event this was precisely what happened.

The Liverpool Society, predictably, gave the formation of the Liverpool School of Architecture and Applied Art its wholehearted support. The pragmatic demands of the Liverpool Society for student architects' education had been fulfilled and the new school would be welcomed. The architectural culture of the city was of considerable sophistication, and the policy of the new school was every bit as important as its existence. The lack of complete records of the Society prevents accurate statements about its aesthetic position, but certain attitudes can be divined from the surviving evidence.

There was a high public profile for adherents to those ideas emerging from the writings of Ruskin and Morris. It was not merely a single dominant individual who was important in the architectural community, but rather a series of personalities espousing similar (but not identical) ideas in separate, but overlapping, areas of the City's cultural life. The complete absence of records for the Liverpool Art Workers'

Guild makes it impossible to tell authoritatively how influential that organisation was within the Liverpool Architectural Society, although from the examination of other areas it is possible to say the influence of the ideas of the Art Workers' Guild was substantial. Exhibitions by Guild Workers were formal excursions for the Society's members [42] and Rathbone addressed the Society [43] on the need to develop skilled artisans within the building trades in order for the symbolic role of architecture to be fully exploited. [44]

Bloomfield Bare, a Society member, as we have already seen, was a prominent local figure at the 1888 congress in Liverpool. George Grayson who was President of the Society 1886–87 and Edward Ould who was president from 1899–1900, were prominent architects for Lever in the initial stages of the development at Port Sunlight. T. Harnett Harrison, President of the Society 1891–93, was active in negotiations with University College. The capable W. E. Willink, President 1897–99, was a key figure on the City Council's Technical Instruction Sub-Committee and his partner, P. C. Thicknesse was President of the Society 1904–06. The urbanity with which Frederick Simpson was welcomed by the Society [45] on his arrival in Liverpool was further underlined by his election to the post of President 1900–02, and his architectural work with the above-named architects.

In the years prior to the founding of the Liverpool School of Architecture and Applied Arts the then president of the Liverpool Architectural Society, Henry Hartley, made two nationally reported speeches in which the voice of Ruskin is clearly heard again. [46] Hartley asserted that architectural education should be a balance between artistic imagination and technical skill, [47] and interestingly in the light of the 'Profession or an Art' debate, argued that the simple passing of an exam was not in itself valuable without a fuller conception of education. Neither could an architectural education be complete until it fully justified Ruskin's vision of architecture as 'the mother of all the arts.' [48] In his Presidential Address in 1894, [49] Hartley returned publicly to these issues but with the knowledge that the local efforts of the Society had helped to initiate the new School. He discussed the issues raised by the RIBA exam, pointing out, presumably to those members who were unsure as to how the new School would effect the pupillage system, the positive advantages of the new institution. [50] In praising the new School he emphasised its relevance to the Institute's examination structure at the same time indicating that its aims far exceeded the narrow confines of the exam.

Conceptually and culturally, one half of the Liverpool School of Architecture and Applied Arts, the architecture half, came from University

College and the Liverpool Architectural Society. The other half, the applied arts part, had its roots in the Liverpool Institute and School of Art in Mount Street. It had been a part of the city's cultural life for a lot longer than University College, and was part of the day-to-day artistic culture of Liverpool.[51] The School of Art was initially planned as the site of the applied art section of the new venture, but this was not to happen until 1905, after further national art education legislation. This issue is a complex one, and one that I shall discuss in more detail in Chapter Four. The School of Art was intimately bound up with the dreaded South Kensington System, and its relationship with the Department of Science and Art, and the Liverpool municipal authorities, casts an interesting light on the eventual decision to create a new municipal School of Design, (which was effectively what the applied art section was), rather than use the School of Art as a base for further developments.

Art classes at the Liverpool Mechanics Institute were recognised by the Department of Science and Art in 1854, although drawing classes of varying types had been undertaken at the institution since its inception in 1825. Drawing instruction fell into two categories; 'artistic' and vocational. It was this latter aspect that ensured its approval as part of the Government's strategy for a national network of Schools of Design, but ironically it was the former which ensured its survival as an institution during the course of the nineteenth century. Luke Fildes, for example, started his eminent career as a student at the Mechanics Institute. The recognition of the Institution in 1854 was part of a plan for three Schools of Art in the City. The Mechanics Institution was to be the Liverpool South Branch School of Art; a North Branch was to be based at the Liverpool Collegiate. A third, central, school was to be funded by the municipal authorities.[52] In the event the municipal school was not created and the directors of the new institution decided to call the school the Liverpool Institute and School of Art.

John Finnie, who was to be later known as a distinguished landscape artist,[53] was appointed headmaster of the new School, and was to remain so until 1896. His first act was to formalise the variety of art classes into a coherent suite of rooms with a sculpture gallery, picture gallery and a museum. The teaching at this time involved mainly drawing exercises in perspective, and copying from drawings, engravings and from casts. Life drawing was introduced after the appointment of E. J. Poynter in 1875 which liberalised the South Kensington System to some degree. The School of Art became separated from the Institute in 1883, when it moved into a purpose-built building designed by Thomas Cook, the winner of an open competition. It was the first such building in the city, and further distinguished itself with the institution of a specialist library. It can be seen as part of the wider process of consolidating the culture of the city in tandem with the founding of University College.

Finnie's artistic interests can be seen to be at odds with many of the training concerns of the Department of Science and Art, whose concern was with the instruction of artisans. From the 1860s onwards, Liverpool was considered by the Department to be one of the less successful of the art schools because of the paucity of its students gaining national medals. The training of artisans was not of prime importance to Liverpool at the time, as the trading wealth of the city was commercial in character rather than industrial.[54] Art instruction in the city was to train artists who could satisfy the demand for paintings set by the local merchant community.[55] Because of this, the form of art instruction given at the school was not solely geared to the training of artisans to improve their market value as a skilled workforce, but more to the production of professional artists.[56] Finnie attempted to boost student attendance which had fallen (due to the competing attraction of the classes in drawing given by Stevenson at University College) by giving a series of lectures on landscape 'as an inducement to a good attendance'.[57] This was not the kind of artistic education envisaged by the authorities at South Kensington.

In association with the rise of art practice, as opposed to skills instruction, at the School, there was an increase in candidates for the Department of Science and Art's 'Design' exams. Within the School of Art, design practice's definition was broad and primarily interpreted as decorative composition. Design was the only South Kensington subject at Liverpool that could be studied at honours level, all other examinable areas such as still life, freehand, plant drawing etc. were at either elementary or advanced level only. Because of the School's success in this particular area, in 1891 it was suddenly ranked fifth in the Department of Science and Art's national league table. In attempting to direct this success in 1892 the Technical Instruction Sub-Committee of Liverpool City Council set up a scholarship for successful students at Liverpool to study principles of ornament, design, modelling design and architecture.

This was a positive aspect of the Technical Instruction Act (1889) for the School. A negative aspect was the subsequent withdrawal of funding for technical instruction by the Department of Science and Art, as the Act required that the provision of maintenance for the national art schools should be the responsibility of the municipal authorities. In Liverpool, negotiations between the City Council and the Art School fell through when the City Council finally decided to fund technical education in association with University College. The School was only able to continue as an institution by drastically reducing its staff. John Finnie formally retired on 27 February 1897, though his duties had ceased the previous year.

The City Council played an important part in the administering of monies and institutions through its committees. This world of filing cabinets and minute books hidden beneath the glamour of bohemian artistic life was far more influential in enabling artistic activity than is often acknowleged. The Technical Instruction Sub-Committe which was so instrumental in curtailing the activities of the School of Art for a decade and for establishing the Liverpool School of Architecture and Applied Arts, was selected at a meeting of the Library, Museums and Arts Committee convened by Philip Rathbone on 12 February 1891. Its first Chairman was the architect William Willink. One of the first acts of the Sub-Committee, as already described, was the setting up of a scholarship for the study of the applied arts.

In April 1893 Willink invited proposals from interested bodies as to how architectural education could be developed within the city. Invitations were sent to both Gerald Rendall and Professor Mackay. In May an informal meeting took place between Willink, T. Harnett Harrison and Mackay. As the representative of University College, Mackay assured the Technical Instruction Sub-Committee of financial support for the idea of a School of Architecture and Applied Arts. The School of Art was approached with the request to organise a Department of Applied Art. By the end of the year however the Technical Instruction Committee had proposed that the applied arts section in the new school was to be under the direct control of the Professor of Architecture. From this point on the development of the School of Art was no longer seen as one of the options open to the Technical Instruction Sub-Committee. Apparently politicking by University College in the form of its representatives was probably responsible for this, as the early actions of the Technical Instruction Sub-Committee indicated a willingness to use the School of Art. In May 1894 the Technical Instruction Sub-Committee produced a report, the 'Amended Report on the Proposed School of Architecture and Applied Arts', in which the project was formally envisaged without the participation of the School of Art. This report contained the structure of the new school which was to be implemented by F. M. Simpson.

Whilst the importance of institutional mechanisms and discourses cannot be underestimated, it often obscures the role of individuals who acted as catalysts between institutional bodies. A player in the city's culture who constantly emerges at key points as a man who, through collaboration with others, ensured the smooth running of a number of artistic projects was Philip Rathbone. He was largely responsible for the Roscoe Professorship, and its subsequent development into the City of Liverpool School of Architecture and Applied Art was considerably helped by his promotion of technical education. His collaboration with Conway in the formation of the National Association for the Advancement of Art and its Application to Industry reflected his views on the subject and was a success because of his energies. He was important in the development of the collection of paintings at the Walker Art Gallery and turned the Liverpool Autumn Exhibition into a national event. Rathbone's artistic promotions were not always successful; his problems over the commissioning of Stirling Lee's sculptural panels for St. George's Hall [58] were, nevertheless, national news. [59] As a man he was generally liked, though he was thought absurd by some, and vilified by a few. *The Porcupine* [60] advised Rathbone not to 'fill a popgun with spluttering theories, and go firing them about for the amusement of himself, the gratification of his opponents, and the disgrace of his friends'. [61] Despite this, on his death, Lund's brief, admiring, biography of him, *The Ideal Citizen* [62] went into several editions.

Philip Rathbone was the youngest son of William Rathbone. In 1846 he went to study in Geneva, and was witness during the next two years to the social and political revolutions in Europe. In 1848 he left Europe for China and the USA for a year. He then returned to England, first working in London for a firm of underwriters and spending considerable amounts of his spare time at the Great Exhibition. He came home to Liverpool in the early 1850s to take up a position as an underwriter with the family firm. During this time he built up his power base in Liverpool through his successes as a committee man. [63] He was elected to the council as a Liberal in 1867. The year 1871 saw the first of his artistic endeavours when he reestablished the Liverpool Autumn Exhibition through the Library, Museum and Arts Committee. From this time until his death in 1895, he wrote and lectured on art and its social functions and tried to further, in a most disinterested way, the cultural life of the city through his role as elected representative.

He must have had much to do with Gerald Rendall in the first years of University College, for Rendall wrote his obituary in *Sphinx* [64] in a way that can only have been the result of considerable respect, talking of his broad mind, his erudition, and his concern for the necessity of a form of 'civic expression'. Certainly Rathbone shared the views of Rendall with regard to the emancipation of women. In one lecture [65] he connected the 'prudish prurience' of the English attitude to nudity with the view, commonly held, that a wife was the husband's property. In allusion to the act of wife beating he said; 'In many cases only

Mr. Whistler could do full justice to the charms of English wives by painting them as arrangements in black and blue'. By this simple public pronouncement he allied himself with the social progressives of the time, who saw the educational possibilities of a municipal and public role for the arts. His stance can be separated from those successful aldermen who used the arts, and their promotion, as a means to public self assertion.[66] (This of course is not to ignore the traditional role of the arts within the city, as in any other, to act as a private focus for the patron.)[67] Rathbone's personal wealth and power was put behind the promulgation of a conception of art that was broadly educative in its aims, rather than specific in its style.

To Rathbone, art was at its best when it expressed 'the common mind of the community'[68] in a permanent form available to public access, and its main object was to 'do whatever we have to do so as to be of most use and give most pleasure'.[69] Given the speed of its visual assimilation, and presumably its ubiquity, Rathbone envisaged civic sculpture acting as a means of social cohesion, summarising communal history and giving voice to it.[70] Rathbone saw art as a purely material activity, 'there can be nothing mysterious in Art, and ... it can only teach what it learns from outward nature, but surely that is enough'.[71] He viewed attempts to elevate it to a spiritual level with suspicion.[72] Art was for him a practical human activity that served a role as a medium for the exchange of social ideas. The applied arts also served this purpose but had the material bonus of enriching the material lives of both producers and consumers.[73] Perhaps because of this pragmatic view of art he was able to convince those in positions of municipal power to implement his schemes. As a successful merchant he could say, with only the minimum of ridicule: 'The cultivation of artistic taste is well worth the statesman's serious attention',[74] referring to both the social and economic function of artistic taste.

Not only was the creation of art, and art objects, a life-enhancing activity in Rathbone's eyes, so was the study of past art and artefacts. This enabled communities to understand their historical as well as their immediate social context, and also to enrich the meaning of their own contemporary art. Art was considered to be more than mere decoration by Rathbone, and he echoes Morris's position when he talks of art used as a luxury, corrupting rather than emancipating.[75] Rathbone wrote and spoke on the role of galleries and museums as tools of cultural exploration as opposed to repositories of valuable objects. On a more pragmatic level, of course such collections would be teaching aids for the training of artisans.[76] His vision of the galleries of the future encompassed new technology with the bravura that much of his pronouncements had – 'Photographs on glass exhibited by the oxyhydrogen lantern may be used with great effect … and what may be in many ways of still more value to the professor of art, a collection of autotype and permanent photographs of the principal pictures of the European galleries.'[77]

Rathbone used the forum of the free library and the art gallery for lectures (as well as attending more prestigious congresses), leading from the front in his concern to establish a broad based audience for the arts within the city. His promotion of the Roscoe Professorship must be seen in this light. His vision was not of an isolated connoisseur, but of an active agent within the community promoting aesthetic and artistic education. Conway's attitude to the didactic role that Rathbone adopted must have been one of cooperation, but was not one of unconditional support. When he wrote of Rathbone that 'He trundles the Art Machine around Liverpool',[78] it is not said with any great affection.[79] In his pamphlet, *The Object and Scope of an Art Professorship*,[80] Rathbone talked of a proposed professor taking two possible routes to achieve a single aim, the flourishing of the arts in Liverpool. Rathbone proposed either a professor who trained artists to produce, or one who stimulated public discussion necessary for that production.

Rathbone's didactic concern was with artistic intention rather than a sense of stylistic correctness. He started his career as spokesman for art education with an approval of Pre-Raphaelitism,[81] seeing in its programme of 'truth to nature' a base upon which the development of art could continue. One of the man's most endearing qualities was his refusal to accept that there was only one solution to a problem. His constant presence around the discussion of the role of the Roscoe Professorship is ample evidence of this. Towards the end of his life he was able to absorb the developments in English painting that encompassed Impressionism, writing reviews for *Sphinx*, writing programme notes for the Liverpool Autumn Exhibition catalogues and delivering lectures at the Walker Art Gallery. His artistic views were measured and calm. In *The School of English Impressionists*[82] he explained the intention of the school clearly and offered no personal comment other than to warn against the danger of stylisation, as one would expect from a man who envisaged art relating as directly as possible to human experience.[83] In *Impressionism in Art*[84] he again talked of the development of the movement's aesthetic, speaking approvingly of Steer and Whistler, and of the 'fortunate introduction' of Japanese art into Britain. His conclusion was to hope that the public would find a 'representative collection which will enable you to form your own opinion on their respective merits'.[85] This approach, where information was presented in an even-handed manner in the hope, often forlorn, that the 'correct' path would be chosen, is typical of the man.

The *Liverpool Review* published an article, 'The Apostle Philip',[86] which was typical of the sort of response that he was to receive from traditional quarters – a bemusement at his antics, with the tacit assumption that he meant well. The article's summary of his 'progressive ideas' are modified by the use of words such as 'extreme' and 'curious', which indicate a mixed response to his idea of a gallery in which paintings are seen as objects of cultural, rather than aesthetic value.[87]

> Alderman Rathbone is regarded as an oracle on all matters of art, and dilettante and professor alike are united in their admiration of his profound knowledge ... true, he has occasionally been responsible for importing curiosities in art work which have caused considerable controversy, but this has been due to his extreme desire to make Liverpool representative of every school of painting and to encourage originality of design and execution.[88]

His views on art were broadminded, pragmatic and constructive, rooted in an appreciation of the work of Ruskin,[89] as were his pronouncements on technical education. While Rathbone cannot be said to be representative of any particular social or cultural grouping within the city, his links with disparate elements in the artistic community such as University College, the Art Workers' Guild and the Ruskin Society are indicative of a body of opinion whose aims he came to represent. He wished to ensure that art and its processes were to be a fundamentally liberating experience. Once more, this is not to suggest that such views were consistent, or necessarily homogeneous, but rather that they indicate an identifiable ideological approach to general issues in art and design. What makes Philip Rathbone unusual, and special, in this situation is his role in administering the political system that many art practitioners were unable to gain access to, and his willingness to put their ideas into action in an enthusiastic and disinterested manner.

Rathbone was just one of many individuals who were part of the interlocking web of personalities and the organisations that created a socially and intellectually progressive cultural environment in Liverpool. He is often neglected because of his bureaucratic rather than artistic personage. However the municipal bureaucracies must also be considered in their role as the administrators of a corporate culture that was to promote and encourage a civic vision of architectural modernity that the Liverpool School of Architecture and Applied Art was to develop.

Notes

1 Q. Hughes, 'Before the Bauhaus', *Architectural History*, vol. 25, 1982. Hughes lays great, and I think undue, emphasis upon the role of T. G. Jackson in the formulation of the ideas that were to motivate the School, thus distorting the value of subsequent events. These are examined in more detail in Chapter Four.

2 An autobiographical account of Conway's involvement in the Association can be found in W. M. Conway, *Episodes in a Varied Life*, Country Life, 1932.

3 'Transactions of the National Association for the Advancement of Art and its Application to Industry: Liverpool Meeting 1888', 'Objects of the Association', p. viii.

4 Ibid., H. Sumners, 'The Practical Outcome of the Art Congress', p. 205.

5 Ibid., E. Seward, 'The Development of Local Influences for the Advancement of Art', p. 322: 'South Kensington has practically been for more than thirty years the one state aided organisation for the promotion of national training in art over the country, our admiration or appreciation of some of the work it has been doing ought not to be too great to prevent our inquiring if that system is being everywhere applied in the best way.'

6 Ibid., G. Simonds, 'Sculpture in its Relation to Architecture', p. 375.

7 Ibid., P. Geddes, 'Economic Arguments for the Encouragement of the Fine Arts', p. 337.

8 Ibid., J. D. Sedding, 'Things Amiss with our Arts and Industries', p. 347: 'All the lecturings and teachings, and prizes and principles of art in the world are of no use so long as you don't surround your men with happy influences and beautiful things.'

9 Ibid., pp. 344–45.

10 Ibid., p. 349: 'The one man who above all others has inspired hope and brought life and light into modern manufacture is William Morris. And this because, a very giant in design, cultured at the feet of antiquity, learned in the history of art, rich in faith, prodigal of his strength, he has united in his own person the two factors of industrial art which before were divided.'

11 Ibid., p. 354: 'And yet, remember that if we have misled you in the art revolution of this half century, there are aspirations behind revolutions. The results may not be satisfactory, yet the motives which actuated us were good. Our Gothic revival has been a solid, and not a trifling, transient, piece of art history. It has enriched the crafts by impetus and initiation. It has endured two generations of art-workers with a new passion. It has been the health giving spark – the ozone of modern art.'

12 Ibid., W. Morris, 'Art and its Producers', p. 238.

13 Ibid., B. Champneys, 'Style'. In his discussion of style, and the Gothic in particular, 'the only real and true style which the modern world has seen' (p. 173), Champneys discusses Morris's 'pessimistic view of the prospects of architecture' (p. 172), demonstrating the bewilderment that many in the Arts and Crafts movement felt about Morris's move away from the assumption that the arts underpinned all cultural activity. Morris's gradual disengagement from the arts, brought into focus by the Bloody Sunday debacle of a year previously, and the decline of the Socialist League from a radical working class organisation to a debating club, far from disillusioning Morris in terms of politics, galvanised him to greater political activity at the expense of aesthetic activity. Cf. P. Thompson, *The Work of William Morris*, Quartet, 1977, pp. 227–32.

14 'Transactions of the National Society for the Advancement of Art', W. Morris, 'Art and its Producers', p. 235.

15 Ibid., G. Harvey Garraway, 'The Liverpool Art Workers Guild'. Garraway's contribution could be characterised as trite and negative, a good example of the sort of analysis presented by him is the following; 'It is a truly frightful thing to see the rows upon rows of ugly houses, built by uneducated builders, which deface this town wherever you go.' (p. 244).

16 According to Walter Crane; ibid., W. Crane, 'Address'.

17 Ibid., 'I hold that the true root and basis of all art lies in the handicrafts, and that artistic impulse and invention weakens as it loses its close connection and intimate relationship with them.' (p. 215).

18 Ibid., T. J. Jackson, 'The Obstacles Opposed to the Advancement of Architecture by Architects Themselves'. In his presentation Jackson prefigures two important areas of discussion which were to bear heavily upon the formation of the Liverpool School of Architecture and Applied Art seven years later, that is; the training of architects and the way that this issue was bound up with the registration of architects by a professional body, in this case the RIBA.

19 Ibid., Simonds, 'Sculpture in its Relation to Architecture', pp. 369–74; J. Belcher, 'The Alliance of Sculpture and Architecture', pp. 375–80.

20 Bloomfield Bare edited the magazine *Arts and Crafts* published by the Art Workers' Guild of Philadelphia for the year 1893.

21 'Transactions of the National Association for the Advancement of Art', H. Bloomfield Bare, 'A School for Artistic Handicrafts', pp. 266–68.

22 Ibid., P. Magnus, 'Some Notes on the Training of Industrial Artists', pp. 248–55.

23 Ibid., 'The Art School of Munich is itself a university of applied art ... The School in Vienna is very similar ... The instruction throughout is essentially practical' (p. 251).

24 Ibid., A. Harris, 'The Development of Modern Industrial Art in Germany', pp. 398–406.

25 Unless stated otherwise information concerning the Liverpool Architectural Society comes from the holdings of the Society's proceedings in the Picton Library. These unfortunately are not complete, as the documentation covering the years 1888–1915 is missing. This means that a full investigation of the Society's role in the formation of the Liverpool School of Architecture and Applied Arts cannot be undertaken. However, enough information about the activities of the Society is available from other sources to piece together an objective narrative. The Liverpool Architectural and Archaeological Society was to become the Liverpool Architectural Society in 1875.

26 That the meeting was held at the Lyceum has importance because it suggests two things: firstly, erudition, as the Lyceum had a substantial lending library and an intellectual reputation dating back to the days of William Roscoe; secondly it is suggestive of status and power, as it was a social centre for wealthy merchants.

27 On 28 March 1849.

28 See F. J. M. Ormrod, 'The Development of the Liverpool Architectural Society over the last One Hundred Years', *Royal Institute of British Architects Journal*, June 1948.

29 Ibid.

30 *RIBA Journal*, vol. I, 1893, p. 4.

31 *RIBA Journal*, vol. IX, 1896, pp. 310, 343.

32 *RIBA Journal*, vol. I, 1893, p. 8.

33 That is, the collaboration with the University and municipal authorities to provide formal architectural education at The City of Liverpool School of Architecture and the Applied Arts.

34 On 16 November 1893.

35 *RIBA Journal*, vol. I, 1893, p. 60.

36 Ibid., p. 62.

37 Ibid., p. 8.

38 J. M. Mackay, 'The Teaching of Architecture in the New University: A School of Fine Arts', p. 355, in *A Miscellany Presented to J. M. Mackay*, Liverpool: Liverpool University Press, 1914.

39 *RIBA Journal*, vol. I, 1893, pp. 7, 60, 185.

40 Ibid., p. 185.

41 As reported in *RIBA Journal*, vol. I, 1893, p. 60.

42 An exhibition at the Art Club, 30 March 1886 or 1887, by members of the Art Workers' Guild was the subject of a formal visit by The Liverpool Architectural Society.

43 P. Rathbone, 'Architecture as a Necessary Element in National Economy', paper read to the Liverpool Architectural Society, 3 December 1894.

44 Ibid., 'The future greatness of cities will be in proportion to the skill of their artisans' and, 'Be it well understood that architecture is almost the only means of enforcing a visible and unmistakable impression of the greatness and intellectual superiority of a town.'

45 *RIBA Journal*, vol. II, 1894, p. 30.

46 *RIBA Journal*, vol. II, 1893, 'Report of H. Hartley's Address to the Liverpool Architectural Society 16th November 1893', p. 60.

47 Ibid., p. 60.

48 Ibid., p. 62.

49 *RIBA Journal*, vol. II, 1894, 'Report of Hartley's Address', p. 30.

50 Ibid., p. 32; '... to return to the School of Architecture. Although the School has not been established with the sole object of preparing pupils for the [RIBA] examination the educational course will include ... the necessary subjects to enable young men to qualify for admission to the Institute examination. I trust you are able to realise the importance of the advantages. In past years our society has endeavoured, and I may say has, to an extent, successfully endeavoured ... to provide courses of lectures to students so as to help them qualify for their examination; but the new school will provide a more complete and more perfect curriculum of study, and will give our future students advantages that few, if any provincial towns enjoy.'

51 Significantly, Lily Day, who had studied at the School of Art was to teach in the Applied Art section of the new institution.

52 Annual Meeting, Liverpool Mechanics Institution, 14 March 1855.

53 Brief biographies of Finnie can be found in B. G. Orchard, *Liverpool's Legion of Honour*, Birkenhead: published by the author, 1893; H. C. Marillier, *The Liverpool School of Painters*, John Murray, 1904.

54 C. Petrie, *The Victorians*, Eyre and Spottiswood, 1960: 'There was probably no city of equal size in the world in which, in 1901, so small a proportion of the population was maintained by permanent and stable industrial work ... the principal occupation of the city and the basis of its prosperity was the handling of goods in transit' (p. 79).

55 Cf. J. Willet, *Art in a City*, Methuen, 1967, pp. 23–42.

56 Nationally, students of the Liverpool School of Art such as Sidney Sime, Charles Mackenzie and Warren Williams all pursued respectable careers as landscape painters. Details of successful artists working locally can be found in Marillier, *The Liverpool School of Painters*.

57 Minutes of the School of Art and Evening School Committee, 1 May 1890.

58 For a brief review of this event see Willet, *Art in a City*, pp. 49–50.

59 *The Builder*, 15 June 1895, p. 446.

60 A Liverpudlian weekly satirical paper.

61 *The Porcupine*, 18 July 1874. In the same issue the journal's editorial said; 'Mr. Philip Rathbone whines and groans like a discontented peasant who has touched his hat to the squire and got no recognition.'

62 T. W. M. Lund, *The Ideal Citizen*, Liverpool, 1896.

63 Rathbone was, whilst working for Rathbone, Martin and Co., Chairman of the Commercial Laws Committee, Chairman of the Salvage Association, and President of the Chamber of Commerce. He was for seven years a member, and for three years Chairman, of the Liverpool Committee of Lloyds Register of Shipping.

64 G. Rendall, 'In Memoriam' *The Sphinx*, vol. 3, 1895–96. Also reprinted as a pamphlet. Conway on the other hand had little time for Rathbone, finding him an earnest, posturing, well-meaning buffoon; 'a queer man … always trying to be epigramatic and sometimes succeeding (tho' seldom); a lot of common sense loaded with the unpleasant cant of continual posing for effect.' Quoted in J. Evans, *The Conways: A History of Three Generations*, Museum Press, 1966, p. 42.

65 P. Rathbone, 'The Mission of the Undraped Figure in Art', Liverpool, 1878. Paper read at the Social Science Congress of that year.

66 Such as the much vilified John Lea;

    'ART's a fine thing and its all very well,

    But COMMERCE is greater – its harder to spell,

    So we'll hang up the works that are likely to sell,

    Lea, – lie – low!'

C. W. Sharpe, *The Sport of Civic Life, or Art and the Municipality*, Liverpool, published by the author, 1909.

67 The merchant F. R. Leyland is a good example of this. Referred to as the 'Liverpool Medici' by Whistler, he followed aesthetic fashion assiduously buying, for example, Speke Hall and renovating it with much use of Morris and Co. wallpapers. See Willet, *Art in a City*, pp. 44–46, H. Taylor, *James NcNeill Whistler*, Studio Vista, 1978, pp. 86–90; Walker Art Gallery, *Whistler*, Exhibition catalogue, Liverpool, 1976, pp. 30–38.

68 P. Rathbone, *The Political Value of Art to the Municipal Life of a Nation*, Liverpool, 1875, p. 44.

69 P. Rathbone, 'The Place of Art in The Future Industrial Progress of the Nation'. Paper read at the Social Science Congress, Birmingham, 1884, p. 4.

70 Rathbone, *The Political Value of Art*, pp. 38–41.

71 P. Rathbone, *Realism, Idealism, and the Grotesque in Art: Their Limits and Functions*, Liverpool, 1877, p. 25.

72 Rathbone, *The Political Value of Art*, p. 35: 'I do not wish to attribute to Art any supernatural qualities, or speak of it in that vague and mystical language which does so much mischief.'

73 Rathbone, 'The Place of Art'.

74 Ibid.

75 Rathbone, *The Political Value of Art*, p. 11; 'borrowed Art, especially when employed as a luxury, not infrequently corrupts; it becomes the expression of an unreality instead of the visible form of the deepest feeling.'

76 P. Rathbone, *Lessons from France as to Imperial and Municipal Encouragement of National Art*, Liverpool, 1888.

77 P. Rathbone, *The Object and Scope of an Art Professorship*. Sole extant copy of the

above without its cover. Liverpool? Early 1880s? p. 4. Liverpool City Libraries Archives.

78 Evans, *The Conways*, p. 85.

79 Conway's accounts of his dealings with Rathbone in his autobiography, *Episodes in a Varied Life*, Country Life, 1932, are quite supercilious in tone.

80 Rathbone, *The Object and Scope of an Art Professorship*.

81 Ibid.

82 P. Rathbone, *The School of English Impressionists*, Liverpool, 1883, p. 2: 'The new school do not profess to paint the whole, but, as I gather from an examination of their work, the impression received from a scene or an object at a given time and under certain states of the atmosphere, and with the eye and attention directed to given points.'

83 P. Rathbone, 'Art Department', n. d., pp. 6–7.

84 P. Rathbone, *Impressionism in Art*, Liverpool, 1890.

85 Ibid., p. 13.

86 *Liverpool Review*, 18 March 1893, p. 9.

87 After Rathbone's death his enlightened exhibition policy was reversed. See Willet, *Art in a City*, pp. 42–43.

88 *Liverpool Review*, 'The Apostle Philip', 18 March 1893.

89 Willet, *Art in a City*, p. 43.

Chapter Four

The Inauguration and Evolution of the Integrated Course at the Liverpool School of Architecture and Applied Art

IT should not suprise us that when the aims and objectives of the new Liverpool School of Architecture and Applied Art are scrutinised, a number of contradictions emerge. Neither should it be a suprise to find those contradictions have already been identified in the wider aspects of design culture within the city. A body of opinion sees the Liverpool School of Architecture and Applied Art as a paradigm of Arts and Crafts education;[1] yet even a cursory comparison between Jackson's inaugural address, and Professor Simpson's first scheme of work, shows substantial differences in expectation for the course. Jackson looked to a national vernacular design rooted in the past; Simpson looked to the new experiments in architectural education in the United States. What links the two men was their interest in methodology. If the early American influence on design thinking in Liverpool is emphasised, it fundamentally alters the traditional perception of the evolution of 'Beaux Arts' training in Britain, placing its origins in Liverpool a decade earlier than has previously been thought. It also alters the ideological perception of the Beaux Art style as practised at Liverpool in the early twentieth century, because the style emerged from *within* the Arts and Crafts debate, and was not solely a reaction *against* its ideas.

The Liverpool School was formally opened by the Lord Mayor of Liverpool in the University Arts Theatre on 10 May 1895. His views on architectural education are not of quite the same authority as those of T. G. Jackson, who gave the inaugural address, but are worth a glance in order to gauge the local establishment's opinion of the experiment which was taking place in the city. In his opening speech[2] the Mayor talked of Liverpool's 'civic love of art',[3] and painted a picture of slow cultural progress from the instigation of the Society for the Encouragement of Designing, Drawing and Painting in 1768 to its culmination in the municipal funding of the School of Architecture.[4] Philip Rathbone's role in helping to establish the School was formally acknowledged, and the man himself spoke with the cultural emphasis that would be expected from him. The *Daily Post* reported him saying that: 'it was only right and fair that they should help skilled labour to become more common. In the future there might possibly be a great glut of cotton and other produce, but there could not possibly be any glut of beauty.[5]

After the opening the municipal authorities provided a sumptuous banquet at the Town Hall[6] where further speeches took place. The Lord Mayor obviously relished the attention that was focused on the city, noting 'the warmest congratulations on the object of their gathering' that had come from all over the country. Even Jackson was not immune to the heady atmosphere of the day and compared the municipal promotion of art in Liverpool to that of 'the municipalities of the middle ages'. The last toast of the evening was from Rathbone – 'Decorative Arts in Liverpool' – where architecture was toasted as the means of achieving a union between the arts.

That the municipal authorities had invested money, and time, in the founding of the school is obvious. That the School had considerable national prestige is evident from the the reports of its opening from the architectural press. The *RIBA Journal* said; 'One of the most gratifying results of the educational movement which, during the last quarter of a century has taken place in this country is the establishment of a School of Architecture and Applied Arts in Liverpool'.[7] *The Builder* referred to the opening as 'an event of considerable importance'.[8] Both journals reported extensively on the structure of the course and on the inaugural remarks of T. G. Jackson.

We do not know who invited Jackson to inaugurate the new School; it could have been either Philip Rathbone or Frederick Simpson. Thomas Graham Jackson was articled to G. Gilbert Scott in 1858, at a time when Gilbert Scott's office was heavily engaged in Gothic Revival work. Jackson was later to say that Morris 'had grasped the truth which the new gothic school ignored – that what is really of value to us moderns in the bygone styles is not their letter but their spirit'.[9] Nevertheless his training in such a successful practice enabled him to set up his own in 1862. In 1873 he published his book *Modern Gothic Architecture*,[10] and in the 1880s was active in the Art Workers' Guild.

The Art Workers' Guild was the result of the development of the

St George's Art Society, a mutual self-help group made up of those who had been trained by Richard Norman Shaw, and who took the new name when membership was extended beyond Norman Shaw's pupils in 1884. In 1888 the Art Workers' Guild became part of the Arts and Crafts Exhibiting Society. Jackson's own description of the activities of the Art Workers' Guild demonstrates the Arts and Crafts principles of cooperation that were to be formalised into an educational system by the Liverpool School of Architecture and Applied Art:

> The Art Workers Guild, a fraternity which unites in a common brotherhood artists of all kinds – architects, painters, sculptors, designers, stained glass men, printers, book binders, cabinet makers, paperhangers, and still others. They meet once a fortnight, if I remember. Someone reads a paper on his own craft, which is followed by others and a brisk discussion in which all join at their pleasure, whatever their own pursuit may be. It is understood that everyone freely reveals all he knows and keeps back no secrets. The usefulness of this interchange of information is beyond price. Whatever one might want to know about any process one was pretty sure to be able to learn from a brother worker in that craft, and the methods of the different arts so freely discussed could not but have a harmonising result, bringing together those decorative arts which had so long been sundered.[11]

In 1892 Jackson was elected to the Royal Academy and in his election address spoke of his hope to see a 'reconciliation' between painting, sculpture and architecture.[12] The above points are enough to place Jackson within an Arts and Crafts sensibility, and would make him suitable for the opening of an institution like the new School. However his invitation carries with it further ramifications. In his very vocal opposition to the RIBA's attempt in 1891 to make 'architecture a closed profession of registered practitioners, accessible only by passing examinations and obtaining diplomas',[13] he acquired the status of a national figurehead proposing an alternative vision of an architectural profession. As we have seen in a previous chapter, the RIBA's position was concerned more with the smooth running of the vocational aspects of architectural practice, rather than the broader issues of the nature and role of architecture. What Jackson brought into focus with the publication of *Architecture: A Profession or an Art?* was a conception of architecture operating within a cultural and social arena, referring to issues and skills other than those which were intrinsic and self-referential. And so, in commissioning articles from architects opposed to the RIBA's proposals, he gave voice to a further development in

those ideas with regard to architectural design that were generated by
John Ruskin.

Jackson's own contribution to *Architecture: A Profession or an Art?*,
'On True and False Ideals in the Education of an Architect', is important
for two reasons. Firstly because he refers to it in his inaugural speech,
and secondly because it relates so clearly to the scheme of studies
at the Liverpool School. Jackson envisaged the architect as a 'master-
workman ... a handicraftsman as well as a designer',[14] a person familiar
with the materials that he or she is working with so that when designing, to use Jackson's example of sculptured decoration for their
buildings, they are aware of how it could be put into operation through
either modelling, moulding, or through carving. This view of a working
architect was one that Jackson knew was not necessarily appealing to
the profession or to the lay public. In fact it was one that was not
completely realistic given the technological demands that new building
methods were creating. (*The Builder*, which otherwise was wholly sup-
portive of Jackson's stand with regard to architectural education found
it necessary to be distanced from the idea of an architect liberated from
the drawing board and his office.)[15] Unrealistic as these ideas may
seem, they are nevertheless an important link in the ideological chain
that connected the educational experiment in Liverpool with the Arts
and Crafts movement.

The first issue of *Architectural Review* in 1896 carried a lead article
'Architecture as an Applied Art'[16] and a lengthy article on the 'Work
of T. G. Jackson R.A.', in which Jackson's work was examined and placed
alongside that of Webb and Bodley. This indicates the esteem that
Jackson was held in by some of his contemporaries, a man who con-
formed to the English predilection for dependable empiricism. In his
own words, 'I regard all buildings which conform to the conditions of
English climate, material and habit as Gothic'.[17] As far the editorial board
of *Architectural Review* was concerned, Jackson was one 'of the few
modern artists who are today creating in England work of distinction
and interest – work, in a word, whose influence is likely to live.'[18]

Jackson's address 'Some Thoughts on the Training of Architects',[19]
started, and ended, with an emphasis upon the national importance of
the School. He placed the School within the national trend for technical
education, then distinguished it from the pack by identifying its radical
break from the increasingly formalised and abstracted system of technical education in the UK.[20] Part of the necessity for a new national
system of technical education in the UK was the decline of the apprentice
system in skilled trades. The contemporary Arts and Crafts approach
to this problem was to form guilds, and to attempt to re-establish a
traditional set of master–apprentice relationships. In so doing the old

tradition of skills education was continued, albeit in a truncated form. Jackson pointed out the innovative nature of the educational approach of the new School, where the master–apprentice relationship was to develop to a new stage. He argued that the continuity of ideas in art practice was maintained through traditional methodology; 'Art has its traditions and its canons, the result of the gathered up experience of ages, all of which must be learned and obeyed'.[21]

What was to happen at Liverpool was the traditional master–apprentice relationship was to be codified within a formal institution. Architecture was to be taught as a traditional handcraft, rather than just as a formal academic skill. It was to be learned primarily from the interaction with materials, rather than from textbooks. This was in line with the ideas of those architects writing in *Architecture: A Profession or an Art?* who advocated a 'hands on' approach to architectural training. However, within the new school organisation this idea was to be taken further. It was to be removed from the hands of self-help groups and placed under the control of a cultural institution. Thus, the traditional 'one to one' approach (although in practice it was rarely so intimate), was mutated into a formalised group.

This teacher–class relationship as elaborated by Jackson, and implemented by Simpson, was not new in municipal and state education. What was to be innovative was the approach within the group, where the instructor was also a practitioner. Again, this in itself is not unusual, for artists and architects had a long tradition of running ateliers, especially within the Beaux Arts system. The system of pupillage can be seen as a debased version of this, and just as the function of the pupillage system was primarily a financial one, subsidising lean times for the architect, so too was the traditional artist's atelier. The creative work of the 'master' was seen to be dominant, the 'apprentice' fitted in around it. Within the Liverpool School, perhaps for the first time in the UK, the artist's creative work was seen to be bound up intimately, and equally, with his or her formalised educational role. This was what separated the School from so many other technical institutes. Jackson stressed the need for teachers to be practitioners so that the student was 'trained by an individual and not by an abstraction'. This unusual balance of practice with theory, and group education with personal creativity, was also to be conducive to the integration of different art disciplines, an issue which was at the forefront of the 'Art or Profession' debate. Jackson argued the case, as he often did, against the sterility of office practice:

> There is yet another evil in the seclusion of the architect's office: it shuts him up not only from practical acquaintance

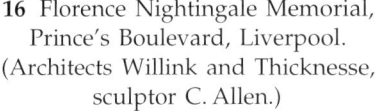

16 Florence Nightingale Memorial,
Prince's Boulevard, Liverpool.
(Architects Willink and Thicknesse,
sculptor C. Allen.)

17 Rupert Boyce Memorial,
University of Liverpool.
(Architects Willink and Thicknesse.)

with the building trades, but also from all intimacy with the
sister arts, and what is as bad, it shuts out the painter and
sculptor from all chance of establishing a sympathy with the
architect with whom they are inevitably from time to time
called upon to cooperate.[22]

The argument for this particular issue of 'policy' is best understood,
not just through a position of ideology, but through an analysis of the
methods of construction that the Arts and Crafts movement favoured.
The demand for an integration of the fine arts in architecture was not
an abstract, ideological goal, but a demand rooted in a view of architectural construction that was craft skill-based, where the building
was at the centre of the arts, acting as a vehicle for their display.
This was to be the norm of architectural practice rather than its exception. If, as the dictum ran, architectural ornamentation was an integral
part of building and not a surface decoration applied at a later stage,
then it was important that practitioners were aware of the limitations
of both the skills and materials they were using, and the relevance of

18 Unveiling of the Queen Victoria monument, Derby Square, 1906.
(Architect F. M. Simpson, sculptor C. J. Allen).

their own skills with regard to their collaborators. Jackson's summary of the School's programme focuses on this point:

> It will ... be an understood thing that every architectural student shall, as a necessary part of his training, pass through the modelling school, and learn to finger the clay ... And in the same way, I would have every young sculptor thoroughly trained in the School of Architecture. [They are] fields ... which lie side by side, and which have ... no fence or boundary line drawn between them.[23]

This attitude logically leads towards the adoption of an approach to architecture that encompasses the builder as well as the architect and the artist. The builder is intimately connected in the construction of the building and needs to understand the same issues that are open to the architect or artist; this was particularly important as Jackson remarked, when the majority of buildings were 'unarchitected'.[24] Building skills, carpentry, masonry, plastering and plumbing would be integrated into the teaching programme in the same way as the fine arts.[25] For this reason, and in opposition to the idea of a closed profession of architects,

Jackson called for a School of *Architecture* rather than of *Architects* to be implemented by first-hand experience of building and artistic practice, rather than the abstracted learning that that was currently prevalent.

In Jackson's analysis architectural style stems from two sources: from an interaction with materials, a familiarity with which precludes their inappropriate use, and through the study of the history of architecture. This latter study, which was common at the time, resulted too often in a conception of architectural style as a dry exercise in historicism. Jackson's argument that 'a man may be an admirable archeologist without a spark of that creative instinct which makes the artist', did not blind him to the importance of style. As style springs from an understanding of function, and its interrelationship with materials and its manipulation by the architect,[26] Jackson considered it necessary to understand the interaction of all these issues. He argued that the innovative was relevant, and that this point could be vindicated through the examination of the art and artefacts of the past, where 'changes were brought about, not so much by any mere aesthetic impulses, as by suggestions of construction, of economy of material, of increasing skill in the working of stone and wood'. The history of architecture was to be a tool for understanding this process, because it helped to determine the root cause that forms the structure. This is distinct from the revivalist position, where neglect of the examination of motivation for style led to the assumption that style itself was the driving force in architecture. Jackson argued that reasoned design led to a style that reflected the making of object. The superficial adoption of style leads to an architecture that makes no cultural sense, that becomes in his words, 'fictitious'; 'We should not have plain useful sashed windows pretending to be mullioned lights, with useless half mullions masking the wooden frames; we should not see honest brick walls bedizened with thin boards nailed on and plastered between, to try and make the world believe the building a half-timbered house like Speke Hall.'[27]

When Jackson says that the old should be valued for its role in determining the new, but has no intrinsic value, he is setting a scenario that permits the introduction of new building technologies in a way that the simplistic return to handcrafts as envisaged by some in the Arts and Crafts movement never could. His views also cast an interesting light on the domestic architecture of Port Sunlight which could easily be considered as a work of fiction.

Jackson concluded his address with a quotation from his essay in *Architecture: A Profession or an Art?* [28] In it he laid down guiding principles for an ideal School. It was to be a school without formal barriers of profession or class, where practising artists and architects contributed to the educational process, creating their own works alongside those of their students. The students were to be exposed, through first-hand experience, to those creative and pragmatic processes that reflected upon their future practice. In this ideal School the student never fully graduated, but came back as a practitioner and thus continued and enriched the structure from which he emerged. In his last paragraph Jackson finally wore his heart on his sleeve:

> Such was my dream of an ideal school of architecture and applied art three years ago, an Utopian dream as it then seemed. And such is the ideal school which I hope and venture to believe it is your intention to create here at Liverpool. It is a scheme to which every true son of art will, from his heart, wish a successful issue, and on which, if it succeeds, cannot fail to have an abiding influence on the history of art in England.

Thus a programme was presented, and policy stated. It seems unlikely that such a detailed and wide-ranging discussion of the issues involved at the new School would have been undertaken without the collaboration of Simpson, whose formal scheme of architectural education was published for the commencement of the new term in October 1895. If the scheme of work presented by Simpson is compared to Jackson's address, however, it is possible to find the two men going in different cultural directions.

In 1895, presumably in time for the autumn term, Frederick Moore Simpson, Roscoe Professor of Architecture, published *The Scheme of Architectural Education Started at University College, Liverpool, in Connection with the City of Liverpool School of Architecture and Applied Art*.[29] In it he laid out his aims and objectives for architectural education and presented a formal plan of study for those enrolled at the college. The pamphlet covers the same area of discussion as that covered by Jackson, and comes to the same conclusions, but there is a different emphasis which makes its close examination necessary. In his inaugural address, Jackson laid out a cultural paradigm, the result of an analysis which was rooted in his own specific aesthetic origins. His ideas can be seen as a preface to Simpson's own, rather than a summary of them, for Simpson sets out a precise programme of study drawn from the same ideological base as Jackson, but presents not only a *methodology* for implementing them, but also suggests a *form* that the resultant architecture might adopt.

The main body of Simpson's writing is the presentation of the course's formal structure. Because of the breadth of study involved at the School,[30] Simpson emphasised the systematic nature of the course's organisation,[31] presumably to still any doubts from those who assumed that because of the 'art' affiliation that the college was to have that it would be run on bohemian lines. He also went to great lengths to reassure those in the profession who might see the School as a potential threat to the pupillage system that the course would fit into the un-folding career of the architect without substantially disrupting any existing structures.[32] As would be expected given his cultural position, Simpson explained the structure of the course in terms of the integration of theory and practice at all levels, and repeated the 'Gothic' litany of methodology:

> He [the architect] should be a master builder in all; able to guide and direct the workman under him, and should under-stand, not only the practical, but also the aesthetic use of materials. In the case of some crafts, such as wrought iron work and stone and wood carving, he should himself be able to bend the iron or carve with the tools.[33]

Once beyond the issue of methodology, Simpson's stance entailed a move away from a vernacular solution. The move away from a verna-cular style in practice was not abrupt, and involved a period in which a mixture of styles can be seen. Ideas about Beaux Arts styling that were to gradually gain favour in Liverpool emerged against a backdrop of decorated neo-baroque work. (The work of the City Surveyor, Thomas Shelmedine, shows this transitional stage quite clearly.)[34] A number of points in Simpson's pamphlet articulate this change. His conception of the integration of construction, architecture, and the fine arts, rooted in the Arts and Crafts movement can be seen as taking a new direction. He enumerates precisely the American and French sources which were the models for the School, and for the form of architecture that was later to emerge.

It seems quite clear that the French Beaux Arts tradition and the way that it was revolutionising American architectural practice was one that was uppermost in Simpson's mind at the time that the School was being organised. Simpson was an advocate of the atelier system where architectural students in the ateliers received 'up to a certain point, exactly the same training in freehand drawing as sculptors and painters.'[35] In the Liverpool School this was to take the form of figure drawing, a radical break from the Kensington System of cast drawing. This, combined with the determination that the student should be fully aware of the possibilities of modelling and carving, can be interpreted as a move from the simple issue of education in decorative handcrafts, towards a conception of architecture as a grand union of all the fine arts. It is illuminating here to draw a parallel with John Clayton's chapter in *Architecture: A Profession or an Art?* In 'The Isolation of Professional Architecture from the other Arts' Clayton spends some considerable time examining the French system of architectural education, and arguing that it was directly responsible for the

> coherency of the associated arts [which] may be seen throughout France – in Paris for example. Here brief reference may be made ... to the National Opera House, where the architect Garnier, the painter Baudry, and the sculptor Carpeaux, worthily represent the unity of the arts. By such harmony of expression, and freedom from imitative archeology, architecture evidences its ceaseless vitality and touch with nature.[36]

This is a different conception of the form of the unity of arts that one associates with the Art Workers' Guild. It is a view proposing a new conception of style. Clayton goes on to say:

> To the superficial observer there may appear in France little development or originality in its architecture of to-day. But it is this very undemonstrative and unconscious quality of its movement, linked as it is with modern life and the other arts, that testifies so consistently and surely to its vitality and progress.[37]

This point of view can be seen as running parallel to the conception of 'anonymous' architecture that was so valued by the Arts and Crafts practitioners. But rather than the anonymity of the English vernacular, what was being proposed was the anonymity of an urbane and cosmopolitan style (that could readily absorb the emergent steel-frame technology, an issue ignored by Jackson), and yet still act as a vehicle for the other arts. It was a style that was internationalist rather than national. Simpson regarded the Beaux Arts style as a 'vernacular style' that was infinitely preferable to the contemporary English stylistic confusion.[38] What was also attractive to Simpson about French architectural education was not just the conception of the unity of the plastic arts, nor that the training was 'both long and severe', but rather that it enabled the French to maintain an unbroken architectural tradition[39] in which a subtle and sophisticated architectural language was developed. With this in mind it is interesting to note the emphasis that Simpson placed upon American architectural education. This was undoubtedly because it followed the same sort of principles for its architectural courses as the French, and was to all extent and purposes universal in its application in the USA. Two American colleges were specifically cited as models to follow; Columbia College, New York, for the thoroughness of the course it operated, and the University of Pennsylvania as an example of how successful such courses could be.[40]

Simpson was quite clear in distinguishing between what he considered successful work – that based on the Beaux Arts traditions – and other less disciplined methods of architectural practice:

> The American architects have in their huge blocks of offices, very difficult problems to solve. It is no wonder that they do not always succeed. It took centuries to perfect the Greek temple, notwithstanding the fact that the work was done under most favourable circumstances. The Americans have their future before them, and, considering the training their architects receive, it ought to prove a successful one.[41]

What was particularly attractive to Simpson about the American system was that it was university-based, and validated through degree. That Simpson ultimately planned a School of Architecture modelled upon the American system is without doubt. His respect for the course at Columbia University '[it] seems to be the most thorough', is further reinforced through his acknowledgement of the receipt of 'much valuable information', from its Professor, William Ware. Whether this exchange of information was purely formal or more personal in its nature it is not possible to tell (if personal it was through correspondence as Simpson had not visited the United States). But it does give clear indications of the direction that Simpson wished the School to go in terms of architectural instruction. Simpson quoted in his *Scheme* from Ware's address to the Alumni Association of Columbia University.[42] Elsewhere in this address, not quoted by Simpson, is the following paragraph:

> There is not time, in school, to acquire a working familiarity with more than one set of historical traditions, and there can be no question to my mind [that] the Greek and Roman styles are more important than any others on account of their unique historical positions … Without this knowledge the history of architecture is unintelligible … These styles are, in all the more important elements of composition, singularly flexible, as is abundantly witnessed by the whole course of their history.[43]

I do not wish to suggest that this quote reflects the complete design philosophy of Simpson, but what it does do is to indicate that the Liverpool School's stylistic direction can be given a tangible starting point. The more one examines the teaching philosophy of Professor Ware, the closer the conceptual associations between the courses at Columbia University and University College Liverpool become.

Ware started his Architecture course from within the School of Mines[44] at Columbia University in 1881 with two students. He quickly disposed of a large part of the scientific study initially imposed on him by the institution and substituted lessons in drawing and design. Facility in design was considered by Ware to be the most important of the architect's accomplishments, and Ware 'felt with William Morris that the true incentive to useful and happy labour [was] and must be pleasure in the work itself'.

In 1882 Ware was given an assistant, A. Hamlin, who lectured in ornament and who had spent time in the office of McKim, Mead and White. Ware did not follow a prescriptive Beaux Arts course at Columbia, but rather took the principles of the Beaux Arts, well aware that a comprehensive curriculum could only give a superficial training, and that students should be allowed and encouraged to devote themselves to the studies which they felt they needed. Ware was never a great architect, but he was a great educator, his teaching inspirational rather than institutionalised. He believed that the background for architectural practice was of necessity comprised of a knowledge of history, poetry, and 'all art and learning'.

By 1896, when Ware's department formally became the School of Architecture, he had 89 students. Simpson was aware of the successes at Columbia, and given the differences between the two courses – the Liverpool School was weighted in student numbers towards the Applied Art section, and came from an immediate Arts and Crafts cultural environment – the similarities must be stressed. In common was an insistence upon drawing and designing, the open form of study, and the emphasis upon the arts as the natural environment from which the architect should work.

The Americans, Simpson argued, had no architectural traditions,[45] but he then linked American educational practice with that of the French. This raises an approximation of the two cultures as different but of comparable status, whose architectural concerns and educational methodology were similar. It further implies that the Americans would eventually share a similar architectural form to that of the French. This was Simpson's aspiration too as his major architectural essay in Liverpool, the Queen Victoria monument in Castle Street, shows.

It need not appear surprising that such architectural innovation should be fermenting in Liverpool, given its American connections and its record in developing cast iron building technologies. Within a dozen years of the opening of the School, Britain's first steel-frame and reinforced concrete buildings were built in the city. These emerged from within the dynamics of an expanding and successful city rather than from the Liverpool School, but indicate nonetheless why Simpson felt able to say that 'Liverpool is, in many respects, a first rate centre for a School of Architecture ... and in the Liverpool Free Library there is perhaps the largest and most complete architectural library out of London.'[46] This was not merely self-aggrandisement, for *The Builder* reviewed the architectural room at the Walker Art Gallery Spring Exhibition suggesting it was 'a step in the right direction, and we only wish the Royal Academy would take a hint from it.'[47]

It should be clear that the intention of the course at the Liverpool School was the integration of the applied arts with architecture, but this integration whilst so carefully theorised and promulgated never took place fully. The Liverpool School essentially operated as an institution with two sections, the School of Architecture funded by the University through the Roscoe endowment, and the Applied Art section funded by the City Council through the Technical Instruction Committee. This arrangement, with changes in the status of the Applied Art section to be discussed later, was to continue from 1895 until 1905, when funding was finally withdrawn from the Applied Art section by the Technical Instruction Committee and put back into the Art School at Mount Street. In creating a Municipal Art School from the Mount Street School, the reputation of whose students' work was becoming increasingly prestigious nationally, the City Council severed its links with University College, and the Liverpool School of Architecture and Applied Art ceased to exist in its old form. The School became one solely of Architecture in 1904.

Frederick Moore Simpson was Roscoe Professor and Director of the School of Architecture and Applied Art until 1904 when he took up the Professorship at University College London. He was succeeded by Charles Reilly, who, when appointed to the Roscoe Chair had no jurisdiction over the Applied Art section. It was to function another year in the limbo of the university precinct before its formal transfer to the School of Art.[48] The initial enthusiasm in the architectural and art journals for the integrated nature of the course, so evident on its inauguration, was to gradually diminish. A number of factors were responsible for this slow loss of interest in the course. Ironically it was the conditions that allowed Liverpool to acquire a cultural autonomy and independence, that militated against the success of its cultural initiatives.

The staff were never really a coherent body adhering to a defined aesthetic approach. Despite the fact that Simpson, Richard Anning Bell (in charge of painting and drawing),[49] and Charles Allen (in charge of modelling and sculpture),[50] were all members of the Art Workers' Guild, it was only Anning Bell whose formal aesthetic sensibilities really belonged to the Arts and Crafts. Simpson's and Allen's tastes were more those of the Beaux Arts, and even Anning Bell did not exhibit exclusively with the Arts and Crafts Society. In 1893 he exhibited both in the Arts and Crafts Exhibition and with the New English Art Club. Anning Bell's replacement in 1898 was Herbert McNair, who was always considered to be part of the Glasgow School and never ceased to be associated with it despite his years in Liverpool. The 'spook style', as the English Arts and Crafts characterised the work of 'The Four', was never fully accepted into mainstream English design life, and it is not surprising that McNair's work in Liverpool should have so little impact outside the city.

Whilst initially there was considerable talk from Jackson and Simpson about the interrelationship between architectural and applied art practice, there is little evidence of this happening in the School curriculum. In part this was due to the imbalance of numbers between architectural students and applied art students. Architecture students were in a minority and the applied art students continued with their own studies physically unconnected with the other half of the school. This schism was also partly due to the personality-based teaching that was a result of the School's teaching methodology.[51] This dependence upon a series of highly individualistic, highly stylised approaches to design in the Applied Art section was bound to work in opposition to a set of architectural design principles based, no matter how loosely, upon Beaux Arts practice. The legacy of student work from the Applied Art section demonstrates little connection with an integrated practice.[52] It shows a wide range of stylistic influences, largely Art Nouveau, each directly attributable to the teaching of individual staff members. The works' relationship to architectural practice is, on the whole, limited.[53]

The main architectural drift of the School towards the Beaux Arts and American educational practice, which had no contemporary parallel in England was largely ignored until Reilly made the School one with an international reputation. The cultural position that enabled Liverpool to look actively to the United States of America rather than London for cultural affiliation, also meant that Liverpool's cultural neglect of the national centre isolated itself. Information about the course, and interest in its success and failure was negligible in national terms. Initially the course operated outside the South Kensington System. This meant it was essentially excluded from national peer group pressure and responded only to local demands. When in 1902 the Applied Art section was obliged to affiliate to the South Kensington System, further dividing the sense of unity in the Liverpool School of Architecture and Applied Art, its established idiosyncratic qualities meant a disadvantage in conforming to established examination practice. This was made still more evident by the considerable, and ever increasing, national success of the School of Art at Mount Street within the exam system. The Applied Art section's 'late start' in conforming to established art education practice put it in a weak position for funding purposes.

By 1900 the Liverpool School of Architecture and Applied Art was offering a degree in Architecture. In order for architecture to be seriously considered as an academic subject it had to conform to the structures of University instruction. For the first year of the degree the curriculum was substantially that taken by students studying for a non-vocational arts degree.[54] Architectural instruction increased in the second and third years of the degree, but it is clear that by 1900 the Applied Art section had become a subsidiary part in the educational process rather than an equal partner. This situation was inevitable given that Liverpool, unlike Birmingham and Manchester whose municipal advances in design education were becoming artistic news,[55] was not a manufacturing town. The economic infrastructure that would have enabled students who so wished to enter into design for manufacture, simply did not exist in Liverpool. Students from the Applied Art section from both the Liverpool School of Architecture and Applied Art, and the Liverpool School of Art worked, if they managed to work at all, as private crafts people[56] or in association with architects in embellishing buildings. This was recognised by the City Council which in a new policy set aside monies for commissioning artists in the decoration of municipal buildings. Graduate architects of course had no problems in ensuring they were taken up into a booming local construction industry.

There is little documentary evidence to be found concerning the administration of the course, so it is difficult to separate the educational intention of the course from its actual instruction. What there is however, is a wealth of evidence about contemporary *attitudes* towards the course. Examining these, it is possible to make sense of the received responses to the design teaching programme at the Liverpool School. Despite T. G. Jackson's enthusiasm at the inauguration of the course, when he grandly predicted that the scheme of work proposed at the School of Architecture and Applied Arts was 'a scheme that cannot fail to have an abiding influence on the history of art in England',[57] by the time he wrote his autobiography,[58] the events at Liverpool did not merit a mention from him. The course received a good deal of coverage from the architectural press in the first few years of its existence; the demise of the integrated course however met with little response as it had ceased by 1905 to be of any interest to the architectural community at large.

The Builder covered the events in Liverpool in 1895 in great detail. It welcomed the opening of the Liverpool School of Architecture and Applied Art in May, and reported Jackson's inaugural speech in detail.[59] More than this however, it reported Henry Hartley's (President of the Liverpool Architectural Society) enthusiastic response to the opening of the school,[60] and the first public outing of Professor Simpson with his students to the Walker Art Gallery Spring Exhibition. It describes Simpson's main teaching theme on this particular occasion.[61] He apparently drew attention to the role of sculpture within architectural schemes and the role of painting within decorating interiors. The journal helps to establish a view of the cultural direction of the School and its director. Four months later another article in *The Builder* acted as a form of editorial advertisement for the course at Liverpool; 'The especial boldness of the scheme lies in the provision of a course of education for architectural tyros prior to their entry into an office, which is, as far as we know, the first attempt in England to place architectural education in line with the system universally adopted on the continent and in America.'[62]

The *Royal Institute of British Architects Journal* reported the inauguration of the new school as thoroughly as *The Builder*, but in a more restrained way. This is unsurprising given the response of some of the RIBA's senior members to architectural instruction outside of the Institute's control. (Professor Aitchison of the RIBA was to later say witheringly that 'amongst some the idea of teaching is almost a mania'.)[63] Nevertheless the journal reported the events in Liverpool on three occasions, and reported verbatim Jackson's lengthy inaugural address.[64] The journal was willing to concede that: 'One of the most gratifying results of the educational movement, which during the last quarter of a century has taken place in this country is the establishment of a School of Architecture and Applied Arts in Liverpool.'[65]

The opposition of both Jackson and Simpson to the educational plans of the RIBA makes this coverage by the *RIBA Journal* all the more remarkable, and suggests that the inauguration of the course was widely considered of importance in the architectural community. Richard Anning Bell's address to the Liverpool Architectural Society, *The Training of Workers in the Applied Arts*,[66] was next reported in detail by the journal, and so conveyed the School's educational ethos to an audience not necessarily in touch with the broad based design issues of the day. In his address Anning Bell said the sort of things that would be expected from him. He discussed the integration of the artistic disciplines, and poured scorn on individuality and elitism in the arts. How novel such ideas were to the readership of the journal it is difficult to gauge. His ideas justifying the validity of the educational practice at Liverpool however, must have caused some discussion, although it was not reported in the pages of the *RIBA Journal* but in those of *The Builder*.

We have seen in previous chapters how the debate for architectural education became largely polarised between the Royal Institute of British Architects' attempts to centralise the process, and the Liverpool architectural community's determination to go it alone as far as possible. We have seen also how this debate was characterised by a division between architectural education as hands-on, and abstracted rote learning. In an article on the Royal Institute of British Architects' examination structure, *The Builder* reported a speech by George Bradbury, (the Liverpool Architectural Society's President 1896–97). The article, mainly a verbatim report of Bradbury's views, was prefaced with an editorial comment suggesting that Bradbury's views reflected wider concern about the Institute's work.[67] His views, forcibly expressed, were that the Institute's exam was 'capable of very great improvements', and rather than national, was London based. It is interesting that *The Builder* was prepared to give so much space to his unsubstantiated claims about the Liverpool course. Bradbury was quoted as saying, 'I am not sure, gentlemen if we cannot boast of having in Liverpool a School of Architecture established at the University, that gives to our students a superior system of education than that given by the associates of the Institute in London.'[68]

True or not, such opinions framed as they were by an editorial voice, and expressed in the pages of a national journal have a tendency to be accepted as fact. A sympathetic report[69] on work from the department published in *The Builder* suggests that the journal at least, was inclined to think it was all true. Three years later in a review of the first exhibition devoted solely to work by students of the School at the Walker Art Gallery[70] *The Builder* was still as enthusiastic about the work produced at the School,[71] but was not to mention the course again until brief items reported the resignation of Simpson and the subsequent appointment of Charles Reilly in 1904. The last mention of the course was in 1905, with a brief report of the Liverpool Education Committee's decision to transfer all its funding to the newly established Municipal School of Art.[72] What makes this interesting is that the official demise of the School's Applied Art section did not merit a review of its achievements or of its original aspirations. What *The Builder* reported were accusations of profligacy and incompetence, where the education of 135 students at the Liverpool School was costing £2,000 per annum, compared to the Mount Street Art School's 357 students costing an annual £200. The Architectural Department of the School was secure in the face of this report having had the first degree students graduating in this year (1905), and the continuing support of the architectural community in Liverpool, but it could not have reflected well upon Simpson.

As far as the architectural press was concerned the death of the integrated course was not worth an obituary. It is impossible to say why, but two possible alternatives present themselves. Firstly, its local achievements did not live up to national expectations. The policy of educating craftworkers and architects together made only a small impact upon the fundamental nature of building practice in the city – the new building technologies made far more – but perhaps it was sufficient that the city's architectural community was able to draw upon indigenous craftworkers, whose skills were considerable. The legacy of the school's educational policy was still to be found in the 1930s with architectural sculptors like Herbert Tyson Smith and Edward Carter-Preston who were trained in the Applied Arts Section, continuing to work intimately with the architects of the city.[73] Secondly, the course had simply outlived its time. As I have already argued, the genesis of it lay in Ruskin's arguments which, by the time the Applied Arts Section closed, were nearly half a century old. The importation of new building technologies from the United States of America rendered labour-intensive building methods redundant, and what was required in the new building style was not decoration that was an integral part of its construction, as had been envisaged by Arts and Crafts advocates, but decoration that was applied to the skin of the structure. This form of architectural embellishment was dependent upon the traditional skills of sculptor and painter rather than the idealised emancipated artisan.

There is little evidence of any interest in the educational events in Liverpool in the art journals of the period. Indeed, were it not for the regular reports of Herbert Bloomfield Bare in *The Studio*,[74] the evolution and achievements of the course would be unremarked. This was not because of any notion of metropolitan indifference to provincial cultural activity, nor the status of Liverpool itself, which had a high artistic profile. The Autumn Exhibition was a notable event in the national artistic calendar, and there were many wealthy patrons in the city who ensured a living for an equal number of artists, some of whom, like Robert Fowler,[75] were national celebrities.

Neither was this lack of interest because the staff at the School were unsuccessful or unknown; Richard Anning Bell, lecturing at the Royal College of Art before his appointment, was already widely known in the national art world and his work was often reproduced in the art press. Charles Allen, though less well known nationally, was nevertheless a successful sculptor, exhibiting regularly at the Royal Academy and later gaining some recognition for his work in France. It was their very successes as artists that ensured Allen and Anning Bell their original appointments. The School's policy was that only active practitioners could drag art education out of the rut that career teachers in the South Kensington System had pulled it into.[76] It was not even a case of the course being ignored by the art press because it was seen as belonging to the applied, rather than to the fine, arts. *The Studio* supplies the only consistent record of events, but only because of Bloomfield Bare's articles. *The Studio* was a great promoter of the work of Anning Bell prior to his appointment to the Liverpool School, when even his designs for Lord Leighton's bookplates were considered newsworthy.[77] Yet his appointment to Liverpool was not mentioned, and when Anning Bell exhibited a frieze worked collectively with his students at the 1896 Arts and Crafts' Exhibition, its radical collaborative nature was ignored and the work attributed to an institution that did not yet exist, the 'Liverpool Municipal School of Art'.[78]

Because the Liverpool School was initially outside the South Kensington System there was no formal structure, or informal grapevine for information about its progress to be transmitted. It was a school concerned with the transmission of ideas and skills, its *methodology* could not be exhibited, and so at important exhibitions, such as the 1899 Arts and Crafts Exhibition, when there was a strong Liverpool presence in the form of Anning Bell's painting and reliefs; Harold Rathbone's Della Robbia Works pottery (designed in main by students from the School); and Richard Rathbone's metalwork, individuals were identified, not their working methods or the institution to which they were associated.[79] To all intents and purposes because the School was independent, affiliated to no centralised educational structure, it existed in an extra-national limbo. In 1896, in a short aside in a regular satirical column in *The Studio*,[80] talk of the possible establishment of municipally funded art schools independent of South Kensington was reported and encouraged. Had the establishment of the Liverpool School been widely known at the time, the impact of such gossip would have been negligible, for the Liverpool School *was* an independent, municipally funded art school, and the first national example of one. It is interesting that the Liverpool School of Art which operated within the South Kensington System, albeit reluctantly, received much wider coverage. Initially, before Burridge's teaching successes, this was simply because it was within that national system and was thus known to art educators outside Liverpool who would act as external examiners.

Because of the diligence of Bloomfield Bare's reporting, there was considerable coverage in *The Studio* of artistic activity in Liverpool.

Whilst Bloomfield Bare's reviews were written for a favourably disposed audience, it must be borne in mind that his views are equally important in expressing the attitudes of the artistic community in Liverpool, or at least that portion of it which helped to create the School in the first instance.

The first public showing of the work of the Applied Arts section was in an exhibition organised by the Liverpool Architectural Society at the Walker Art Gallery in the spring of 1898, The Spring Exhibition of Arts and Crafts. Work from students at the Mount Street School of Art was also on show. Bloomfield Bare reviewed it favourably for *The Studio*, mentioning the directorship of Simpson and the work of Anning Bell, Allen and Platt (the wrought iron teacher.) [81] From this point on constant reference to the work of individual students, and brief asides about the work at the School were made in *The Studio* column, 'Studio Talk' under the initials H.B.B., until the demise of the School.

There were two further substantial reviews of exhibitions of work by students in 1899 and 1900. The show at the Walker Art Gallery of over 350 works in June 1899 was the official debut of the School. The exhibition was given a three page review [82] with a large number of photographic reproductions of the work. The underlying message was similar to that of *The Builder*'s,[83] that the School was a radical innovation in educational practice and was producing high quality work as its reputation was growing. The following year the annual exhibition of the Liverpool School was treated to the same sort of extensive and enthusiastic coverage, with Simpson given fulsome praise in promoting excellence of design and craftmanship.[84] Despite this glowing assessment, this was the last mention of the School in any detail. Its activities and those of its students continued to be mentioned, but only as peripheral information to the developing reputation of the Liverpool School of Art under Frederick Burridge. This was a probable response to the start of the financial troubles at the Applied Art section which led to its enmeshment in the South Kensington System and its ultimate demise.

If we look at what *The Studio* had to say about the Liverpool School of Art at Mount Street it reflects upon the Liverpool School of Architecture and Applied Art in a number of ways. In concentrating upon the work produced at Mount Street, Bloomfield Bare, who had been so closely involved with the Liverpool School of Architecture and Applied Art, was discreetly abandoning his first allegiance. The Liverpool School of Art certainly achieved a success that always eluded The Liverpool School of Architecture and Applied Art, and Bloomfield Bare was one of the first to acknowledge it: 'There is further reason for congratulating Mr. Frederick Burridge ... upon the result of [his] painstaking efforts to advance this school in the direction of the applied arts in the fact that out of the five gold medals awarded to Great Britain at the Paris exhibition ... Liverpool [Mount Street] has been awarded one.'[85]

Further reviews[86] followed, written with the enthusiasm he once used to reserve for the Liverpool School of Architecture and Applied Art. Further ignominy was to be heaped upon the reputation of the Liverpool School of Architecture and Applied Art when Bloomfield Bare argued that Lethaby's vision of a new revitalised workforce that would rejuvenate British industry could be found already at the Liverpool School of Art.[87] Frederick Burridge was later to succeed Lethaby as head of the London Central School of Arts and Crafts.

The demise of the integrated course at the Liverpool School in 1905 was not mentioned directly by Bloomfield Bare. His enthusiasm for the new municipal status of the Liverpool School of Art (which since around 1901 had become known colloquially as '*the* Liverpool School', another reflection on the locally waning prestige of the Liverpool School of Architecture and Applied Art) obliterated its memory. The reader unaware that the funding of Mount Street meant the demise of the Applied Art section at University College would be none the wiser from this cryptic passage. To those aware, its omissions could communicate a good deal: 'This [excellent] quality places the Liverpool School upon a high plane amongst the art schools of the country, and has gained for it a reputation which attracts students from an increasing area. Under the proposed new organisation and increased financial support from the municipality which it promises, there is every good prospect for its growing influence as an art centre.'[88]

That the Liverpool School of Art was rapidly gaining in prestige and status can be seen from a quick glimpse at its profile drawn in the pages of *The Studio*. Besides Bloomfield Bare's reports the Mount Street School was discussed by other writers. Its successes in teaching needlework saw an article[89] arguing that radical teaching methods, involving a suppression of issues of technique in favour of those of expression, was sufficiently successful to merit description as a 'school of needlework'. A ten page review of students' work in 1902[90] saw it compared with the work produced in the Glasgow School of Art. Despite the presence at the Liverpool School of Architecture and Applied Art of two of the Glasgow 'Four', Herbert and Frances McNair, their successes in Vienna and Turin made little impact on the reputation of their teaching nationally.[91] The last couple of years of the Applied Art section saw the advantages of the Liverpool School of Art's long-term involvement in the South Kensington System, as Mount Street figured prominently in reports of the National Competition of Schools of Art for 1902 and 1903.[92] By 1903 *The Studio* was talking of its 'excellent' reputation.[93]

It is ironic that one of the ambitions of the Liverpool School of Architecture and Applied Art, which was to educate artisans in the hand crafts, should be achieved through the diligence and personal charisma of one man, Burridge, at the Mount Street School, working through the despised South Kensington System. Simpson, on the other hand, who had unprecedented national coverage for the inauguration of the integrated course at the Liverpool School of Architecture and Applied Art, the backing of prestigious figures in the Art Workers' Guild, the backing of the architectural community, the University *and* the municipality left Liverpool with the Applied Art section in disarray.

In part Simpson suffered from cultural isolation as his architectural ideas were at odds with the wider national architectural community. A still greater form of cultural isolation was the School's lack of contact with the national structures of art education that were so vital in ensuring the success of Burridge's venture at Mount Street, in spite of his opposition to the system. Anning Bell's later administrative success at Glasgow also came from within the system. The other great artistic personalities of the School, Herbert McNair and Augustus John worked on the periphery of established art education networks, and no matter how successful or radical their teaching, it had to remain unremarked because it existed in an enclosed city culture.

At its inception the Liverpool School of Architecture and Applied Art was wary of the South Kensington System, seeing it responsible for the stultified nature of much contemporary design work in its cramped educational practice, limited to self-referential exam schedules. Because of this, the School was initially independent of the South Kensington System. This independence began to be eroded after 1900 because of economic difficulties. An extra grant was required from the municipality to cover a financial deficit at the end of that academic year.[94] The academic session was extended to 40 weeks a year,[95] but this and the active recruitment of more 'young ladies from Sefton Park making pretty things',[96] was still not enough to balance the books for the School. The municipality, as the founder of the Applied Arts section, insisted that further financial support be linked to the affiliation to the Board of Education grants scheme. This meant the School's involvement with the much despised South Kensington System.

The Board of Education had been founded in 1899 through the merging of the then Education Department and the Science and Art Department. Its foundation meant a national system of grants for institutions of secondary education administered by local authorities, providing certain educational conditions were met and confirmed by a system of inspectors. It also meant the establishment of a national register of teachers. The advantage to local authorities of the new national structure was further grant aid for educational provision already established.[97] To the staff and students of the Liverpool School there were only disadvantages evident in being part of a long dis-credited national system, but without such affiliation there would be no funding. What might have ensured its continuation would have been measurable success in terms of the national recognition that the Mount Street School was acquiring. However, this would be impossible with-out first gaining access to the national network of the South Kensington System.

In 1902 the Applied Art section was formally part of the South Kensington System offering instruction for its exams. This has to be seen as the end of the original conception of the course, as this year also saw the formal acknowledgement by the Royal Institute of British Architects that the School's Certificate exempted its holders from the Institute's own Intermediate Exam. The 'Art or Profession' debate of a decade previously had thus been shortcircuited. The School, whose Director had played such an important role in the 'Art' camp, had seen its success as an institute of architectural education vindicated but at the price of absorption by the very institutions it had originally set out to side step. Its original intention, the notion that the applied arts and architecture were intimately connected, was also negated by these events as they became formally separated into distinct areas of examination.[98]

The same year, 1902, saw further developments in the erosion of the integrated course. W. Hewitt, the Director of Technical Education in Liverpool reported to the Technical Instruction Committee,[99] reviewed the possibilities for art education in the city and proposed a 'Municipal School of Art'. This must be seen in the light of the 1902 Education Act which enabled Local Education Authorities to establish post-elementary school institutions helped by a grant and by a direct capitation grant from the new Board of Education. In his report, Hewitt remarked that the fragmented nature of the organisation of the 'artistic crafts' in the city,[100] was not sufficiently successful in directing the 'streams which should flow towards it from the lower sections'. This observation reflects on the lack of success of the Liverpool School's original intention to train artisans alongside architects.

The Beaux Arts model adapted by the Liverpool School provided a solution for the architect who wished to enrich his practice with the applied arts, but the solution that it provided for the artisan did not conform to the Arts and Crafts ideal. The artisan, whilst provided with work, was constrained by the forms derived by the architect and the tradition that he was working under. The imaginative use of his skills was not developed in the way that those immersed in the ideas of romantic Arts and Crafts sensibilities would wish. This structural dilemma remained unresolved at the the Liverpool School of Architecture and Applied Art. The handful of student architects pursued their innovative studies, brushing up against arts practice of astonishing quality, but never fully connecting in the way that the scheme was originally conceived.[101]

In April 1902 the Art Sheds, as the Applied Art section's workshops had become affectionately known, began to be demolished[102] and by 1903 the future of the Applied Art section had been sealed. The City had the intention, and financial and administrative power, to ensure its integration into a new Municipal School of Art, and its Director was leaving for the University of London. Furthermore, its original partner in aesthetic study, Architecture, had secured its future in a degree from a University which had received its charter. The establishment of the University Grants Committee in 1904 would mean the University would no longer need the cooperation of the City in any future possible developments.

The University said goodbye to the Applied Art section with little public show of remorse, and no formality. A letter in *The Sphinx*[103] shows how far advanced the separation had become. The writer lamented the severing of the connections between the University and the Applied Art section, but made no mention at all of Architecture, or the way the Applied Art section had in the past related to it. The tone of the letter was languid and aesthetic; 'many of us have felt a sharp pang of sorrow and a chill to our enthusiasm'.[104] The anonymous writer apparently spoke for all who had 'artistic sympathies generally', and if this is so, indicated the distance between contemporary Liverpudlian design education and its principles of a decade earlier. In a report of the leaving party given for Simpson and his wife in the architecture studio (some time in December 1903) there is further evidence if we need it, of the erosion of the intended marriage between the two sections of the School: 'Old students were not merely represented by their work, for all generations were present, together with some representatives of the Applied Art School, who we were glad to see are interested in our doings'.[105] The polite pleasure from past and present architecture students at seeing representatives of the 'Applied Art School' at the farewell dinner for their director, must tell us something about the internal relations in the School.

When Charles Reilly took up his post in 1904 he was responsible solely for the School of Architecture, though the Applied Art section was not to unite formally with Mount Street and become the Municipal School of Art until 1905. Reilly represented the University on the management committee of the new School and was involved in the subsequent negotiations over the dispersal of Applied Art's staff. Charles Allen became Burridge's Vice-Principal at the new School of Art, whilst Herbert McNair and Gerard Chowne with disaffected students started a private art school, The Sandon Studios Society.

Traditionally, the demise of the integrated course has been seen as the result of the formal split between the Architecture and Applied Art sections in 1905. This view was first presented in the late 1960s by John Willet in his book *Art in a City*, when in examining the artistic personalities in late nineteenth century Liverpool he said, 'The Brief Art Nouveau movement seems to have fizzled out as soon as the Applied Art section parted company with the architects'.[106] Willet was referring to the physical closure of the Applied Art section and the instigation of the Municipal School of Art. Twenty years later this view was formalised in Quentin Hughes' *Before the Bauhaus*,[107] where Reilly is tacitly given the responsibility for the abandonment of the integrated course:

> With the appointment of Reilly, for better or for worse, the school became a school for architects, rather than a 'school for architecture' in Jackson's sense. It was to be tied firmly to the RIBA and, academically controlled by rigid examination, would soon receive exemption, first from the intermediate examination of the institute and later from its final examination.[108]

Two linked issues are immediately raised here. It is implied that Reilly's vision of architectural education was at odds with past practice at the School, and that he was responsible for the linking of the School with formal architectural structures. However, the Architectural degree scheme was initiated in 1901, and it was this restructuring of the course, this formalising of architectural education at the expense of the applied arts, that marks the end of the aesthetic and educational experiment every bit as much as the entry of the Applied Art section into the South Kensington System in 1902. By the time of Reilly's appointment, holders of the School's Certificate in Architecture had been exempt from the RIBA's Intermediate examination for two years.[109] It can be seen that Reilly's importance to the development of the 'old' course was minimal, the structures that enabled him to create a flourishing Beaux Arts school were already in place.

Hughes places great emphasis upon the role of Jackson in creating an educational methodology for the School, and as a pivotal point around which the programme of events at Liverpool unravelled. In doing so he neglects the possibilities of alternative contributions that also helped develop the School.[110] In ignoring the complexity of Liverpudlian artistic and political life he gives the impression that Jackson and his acolyte Simpson transcended their cultural environment, and were ultimately unable to implement their ideas because of hostile circumstances.[111] This emphasis upon personality rather than broader cultural issues has favoured an analysis based upon the separate achievements of dominant personalities. This is unsurprising given the lack of a formal educational structure in the Applied Arts section and the emphasis placed upon personality based teaching, but only compounds the felony, rather than explains it.

Reilly was a powerful, charismatic individual who invested much personal prestige in the development of the School as an international phenomenon. However, even Reilly was unable to alter the flow of historical circumstances, his skill lay in exploiting them to his advantage.

Notes

1 Quentin Hughes because he concentrated almost exclusively on the pronouncements of T. G. Jackson, and Mary Bennett because she examined the production of applied art objects. See Q. Hughes, 'Before the Bauhaus', *Architectural History*, vol. 25, 1982; and M. Bennett, *The Art Sheds*, Liverpool: Walker Art Gallery, 1981.

2 *Liverpool Daily Post*, 11 May 1895.

3 Perhaps disputable given the furore caused by Philip Rathbone's attempts to secure Stirling Lee's sculptural bas reliefs for St George's Hall.

4 'Now a public grant in aid of technical education would be available for the school, and he did not doubt that the status of the University would add greatly to its efficiency.' *Liverpool Daily Post*, 11 May 1895.

5 Ibid.

6 'The opening of the school was celebrated by a banquet, at which the Lord Mayor entertained at the Town hall a representative company of public men, architects and artists both of this city and of London. The rooms were handsomely decorated with plants from the botanical gardens. Several charming groups of exotic palms were arranged, interspersed among which were arum lilies, spireas and rhododendrons. The cut flowers included choice blooms of Chinese and South American orchids rich in colour and perfume.' Ibid.

7 *RIBA Journal*, vol. II, 1895 p. 626.

8 *The Builder*, 18 May 1895.

9 B. H. Jackson (ed.), *Recollections of T. G. Jackson*, Oxford, Oxford University Press, 1950, p. 88.

10 T. G. Jackson, *Modern Gothic Architecture*, H. S. King and Co., 1873.

11 Jackson, *Recollections of T. G. Jackson*, p. 218.

12 Ibid, p. 231: 'I said that in the triple election of a painter, a sculptor, and an architect one might hope to see the earliest of that reconciliation of the three arts so long sundered from one another, to which very many of us were hopefully looking forward.'

13 R. Norman Shaw, and T. G. Jackson (eds), *Architecture: A Profession or an Art?*, John Murray, 1892.

14 T. G. Jackson, 'On True and False Ideals in the Education of an Architect', p. 227 in ibid.

15 *The Builder*, 18 May 1895: 'Perhaps we may suggest that there is one side of the subject [of Jackson's opening speech], as regards the conditions under which architecture is practised, which has been a little overlooked. When Mr. Jackson implies that the architect should be a man working at the building itself than a man sitting in an office and making drawings for it … it may be replied that however well this system may have answered for a Mediaeval Cathedral the conditions are rather different in the case of a modern very complicated building, such as a Town Hall … Life moves faster than it did, and people want their large buildings produced quickly, and this will not be done without a great deal of division of labour.'

16 *Architectural Review*, November 1896, vol. 1, p. 132.

17 C. E. Mallows, 'Work of T. G. Jackson', p. 140 ibid.

18 Ibid., p. 154.

19 T. G. Jackson, *Some Thoughts on the Training of Architects*, Liverpool: D. Marples and Co., 1895.

20 'While the ordinary technical school stops short at the attainment of manual dexterity in the handicrafts, or such theoretical acquirements as can be had by studying text-books, and doing exercises on paper about building construction or simple engineering, you go further, and submit your training not only to the canons of utility but to those of beauty.' Ibid., pp. 3–4.

21 Ibid., p. 7.

22 Ibid., p. 22.

23 Ibid., p. 17.

24 '[There will always be work] left to the builder. But it does not follow that simple buildings should be ugly, or unarchitected buildings hideous, as is too frequently the case', ibid., p. 31.

25 '. . . it is certain that if every architectural student were to spend a year, or perhaps more, during his training, in the mason's yard and at the carpenter's bench himself, he would come to the task of original design furnished with a stock of ideas and capacity for invention not to be got in any other way', ibid., p. 25.

26 'A work of architecture without an architect is no more possible than a tale without an author', ibid., p. 17.

27 Ibid., p. 37.

28 'Imagine some school of architecture, to which anyone connected with building could have access, whether he intended to be an architect, a builder, or a craftsman in one of the arts connected with building. Let there be no conventional distinction of profession, no barriers of etiquette to divide the students. Furnish the school with competent teachers and appliances for study in every branch of the art. Let it be possible to learn all the mystery of good construction, but let construction never be taught except in connection with design, nor design except in connection with the proper and natural use of material. Let the school be regularly visited by those who are recognised as masters of the art, to whom the paid teachers should be subordinated, and to whom the students could look for direction, advice, and correction of their task. Let the students have every opportunity given them of seeing work actually done, and of themselves putting their hands to it. For those who have no workshop at home, which the young builder would naturally have, let there be attached to the school workshops, where the process of every handicraft could be demonstrated; where masonry, carpentry, joinery, could be practically taught, and a forge where iron could be wrought. Drawing of a practical kind

should, of course, be taught, so that every student might be able to set out and explain his ideas to the workmen or himself. Here those who mean to be ordinary builders might, if they please, stop. The school would, of course, be gradated, and it would not be necessary or desirable that everyone should go through the whole course of artistic training. We do not want our finer tools to do our rougher work, and we do not employ our most accomplished artists on ordinary occasions. The great thing would be that up to that point all should have been trained alike without distinction, and that the builders should have associated with those who aimed at higher flights, and should have shared in the same training under the best masters of the art. In this way we might hope to introduce into the building craft good taste, knowledge of design, restraint, and appreciation of simplicity … The further training of those students who aspire to be architects of a higher grade should run on the same lines … For acquainting themselves with practical design and the mode of carrying it out no better method exists than the old one of apprenticeship to an older architect … But never let them lose touch with actual handicraft; let them never make a design without understanding how it is to be carried out … Let them learn to handle the clay, so as to realise the difficulties and the possibilities of their own sculptured decoration; and if they go on to learn to carve, they will be but following the steps of their predecessors, who were the chief masons of the buildings they designed, and generally wrought on its sculptures with their own hands … Above all, let there be no folly of certificating or labelling the student as proficient at any period of his career. Let him remain a humble learner all his life; and let the school be open to him at any future part of his history whenever he wants instruction or advice, or desires to freshen his interest by contact with younger aspirants.' Ibid., pp. 35–37.

29 F. M. Simpson, *The Scheme of Architectural Education started at University College, Liverpool, in Connection with the City of Liverpool School of Architecture and Applied Art*, Liverpool: Marples and Co., 1905.

30 The first year timetable, of 27 hours study a week, encompassed; *Freehand Drawing*, 6 hours a week in the Autumn and Lent Terms, 3 hours a week in the summer; *Modelling*, 3 hours a week in the summer term; *History of Architecture*, 3 hours a week throughout the year; *Drawing Examples*, 5[?] hrs a week throughout the year; *Building Materials and Construction*, 7 hours a week in the Autumn and Summer Terms and 5 hours a week in the Lent Term; *Perspective*, 3 hours a week during the Lent Term; *Elementary Mechanics*, 3 hours a week throughout the year. In addition students were expected to attend some of the Applied Arts courses in the evening. It is clear from this how fundamental to the process of architectural design that drawing was seen to be; see ibid., p. 28.

31 'Any scheme must be on an utterly wrong basis which does not provide for a sound and systematic course of training from the very beginning.' Ibid., p. 3.

32 It has already been discussed at some length as to how pressure from the local architectural community was part and parcel of the formation of the School. Simpson asserted that; 'The aim of the school therefore is principally to provide a thorough course of training … for students before they enter an architects office. It is not intended to supercede pupilage but to be preparatory for it.' Ibid., p. 7. As such it is unsurprising to find Simpson quoting a resolution passed by the Liverpool Architectural Society on 20 June 1895 in support of the suggestion that 'Architects should shorten the the term of pupilage, and reduce the ordinary premium for students who, having attended a two year's course at University College, have been awarded the College certificate.' Ibid., p. 21. However this did not stop him summarising the benefits that the course would have for the local architectural community: see ibid., p. 22, where he lists eight reasons as to why the course should be supported.

33 'Those subjects which can be best taught by lectures will be taught in that way, but in all cases each lecture will be followed by two hours' class in the studio, during which the student will be set to work out studies illustrative of the lecture ... The lectures on the history of Architecture are intended to show how all architectural work is a matter of evolution, and how different factors, such as climate, religion, etc. and the altering requirements of everyday life influenced and necessitated the different forms of construction and design, and so produced the various styles.' Ibid., p. 17.

34 An extensive collection of contemporary photographs of Shelmedine's libraries can be found in *Liverpool Public Libraries*, Liverpool: Liverpool Public Library, 1912.

35 Simpson, *The Scheme of Architectural Education*, p. 8.

36 J. R. Clayton, *On the Isolation of 'Professional' Architecture from the other Arts*, p. 130, in Norman Shaw and Jackson (eds), *Architecture: A Profession or an Art?*

37 Ibid., p. 130.

38 Simpson, *The Scheme of Architectural Education*, 'The greater part of the work done today [in France] is on the same lines as that done in the last century. They still have a vernacular style in which their architects and workmen are trained, and although it may not be a perfect one, it is surely better than "the babel of tongues" which exists in England at the present time.' p. 14.

39 'France possesses a magnificent architecture, and its traditions have never been broken. It is curious that their great revolution, which more than anything else assisted in upsetting the traditions of art in other countries, hardly affected their own.' Ibid., p. 14.

40 'The University of Pennsylvania, at Philadelphia, which was started later, numbered last year sixty six students.' Ibid., p. 12.

41 Ibid., p. 33.

42 'That this course of study is generally approved of in America may be gathered from the following extract from a paper read by Professor Ware, of Columbia College – to whom I am indebted for much valuable information.' Ibid., p. 13.

43 W. Ware, 'Address before the Alumni Association of Columbia College on the Twelfth of June 1888', New York, 1888, p. 4.

44 This and subsequent information about Ware and his teaching has been taken from T. K. Rohdenburg, *A History of the School of Architecture, Columbia University*, New York: Columbia University Press, 1954.

45 'It is interesting that these two countries [USA and France], so widely different in many respects, should follow more or less the same course of instruction for architectural students. In America there are no old traditions, and practically no old architecture.' Simpson, *The Scheme of Architectural Education*, p. 14.

46 Ibid., p. 24.

47 *The Builder*, 23 March 1895.

48 C. H. Reilly, *Scaffolding in the Sky*, Routledge, 1938, p. 85. 'The Applied Art section of the old Department of Architecture, with which I had nothing to do officially, went on for a session after my arrival. Long before then its decease as a part of the University and its amalgamation with the City School of Art had been decided ... the Corporation, now having an art school of its own, did not see why it should subscribe a thousand a year to another which seemed to it to do practically the same work.'

49 Richard Anning Bell 1863–1933, was appointed to Liverpool in 1895 from a position as Lecturer at the Royal College of Art, at the beginning of a career that was

receiving a good deal of public notice. In the years that he taught at Liverpool it was unusual not to see some aspect of his work illustrated in *The Studio*, where he was given the equivalent sort of status as was afforded Ashbee and Crane (see *The Studio* vol. 9, pp. 122–24). His work ranged from bookplate design, poster design, frieze painting and bas relief plaster work. He left Liverpool in 1898 to take up the position of Chief of Design section at Glasgow School of Art, and was subsequently to become Professor of Design at the Royal College of Art. In 1916 he was elected an Hon. ARIBA, and in 1921 was Master of the Art Workers' Guild.

50 Charles Allen 1862–1956 was asked to apply for the post of Instructor in Modelling at Liverpool by Simpson, when he was working in the studio of Thorneycroft on architectural and monumental sculpture. He was trained at the Royal Academy where he was also a subsequent exhibitor. He was twice a Gold Medal winner at the Paris salon. His work in Liverpool was considerable, including panels for St George's Hall, sculpture for the the Victoria Monument and bas relief work for the Royal Insurance building. After the amalgamation of the Applied Art section and the Liverpool School of Art Allen became Vice-Principal of the new institution.

51 This quality of 'personality' teaching is mentioned with regard to both Anning Bell and McNair. In a review of Anning Bell's frieze exhibited at the New Gallery Arts and Crafts Show in 1896 the reviewer observed; 'Already a too-faithful group of disciples are imitating his manner', *The Studio*, vol. 9, 1896, p. 124. In talking of McNair's work, Gleeson White felt it necessary to legitimise McNair's personalised approach, suggesting that in some quarters it was questioned; 'It should not be necessary to disclaim on behalf of Mr. McNair and [MacIntosh] a charge of conscious affectation', 'Some Glasgow Designers', *The Studio*, vol. 11, 1897, p. 229.

52 See Bennett, *The Art Sheds*.

53 Architectural embellishment of contemporary buildings by the School was, with the exception of the Philharmonic Dining Rooms, to a very large extent at odds with the styling that emerges through a study of student work, and is in the main, interior decoration rather than the indissoluble meshing of the applied arts with architecture.

54 L. Budden (ed.), *The Book of the School of Architecture*, Liverpool: Liverpool University Press, 1932, p. 34.

55 The Birmingham School of Art's increasingly individualistic approach to design education was reported in a lengthy review of its students' applied art work in 'The Birmingham School of Art', *The Studio* vol. 2, pp. 90–98. Walter Crane's appointment as Head of the Municipal School of Art in Manchester in 1896 also meant extensive coverage in *The Studio* (see vol. 5, pp. 104–110), where it was seen as a further example of the break against the 'excessive domination of the central authority at South Kensington', p. 104. The initiative in Liverpool remained unremarked by *The Studio*.

56 A great number of the students in the Applied Arts section were middle-class women who wished to pass a leisurely hour in pursuit of the artistic. Their intentions were not to act as the shock troops of a new aesthetic, but were more in line with the Home Arts and Industries Association. This is not to say all women students were not serious in their studies, or that what was achieved by the majority of women students was not valuable (in social terms the Applied Art section was responsible for the cultural emancipation of many women) but rather that the original intention to train artisans alongside architects was largely unfulfilled. Bennett, *The Art Sheds*, p. 3, makes some interesting points about the women students and their subsequent successes.

57 Jackson, *Some Thoughts on the Training of Architects*, p. 37.

58 Published posthumously; B. H. Jackson (ed.), *Recollections of T. G. Jackson*, Spottiswoode and Co., 1950.

59 Calling it; 'An event of considerable importance', *The Builder*, 18 May 1895.

60 In *The Builder*, 11 May 1895, Hartley is reported as stating that Liverpool was the first centre to establish such an educational institution and that the school was; 'a great centre from which would spring new life and greater vigour in the development of art by the systematic training which [students] could now obtain'.

61 *The Builder*, 25 May 1895.

62 *The Builder* 7 September 1895, p. 166.

63 *RIBA Journal*, vol. V, 1897, Presidential Address, 1 November 1897, p. 8. In the same address Aitchison argued that the 'admiration' and 'gratitude' that architecture stimulated in enthusiasts was 'the very breath of its nostrils', and sufficient in terms of teaching its mysteries.

64 *RIBA Journal*, vol. II, 1894, pp. 601, 626, 635–42.

65 Ibid., p. 626.

66 *RIBA Journal*, vol. III, 1895, p. 509. The address was delivered to the Liverpool Architectural Society on 11 November 1895.

67 *The Builder*, 24 October 1896.

68 Ibid., Bradbury also said, 'It is useless for us to look to London for guidance'.

69 'The results … are highly gratifying, and by all accounts the department is in a flourishing and progressive condition.' *The Builder*, 4 July 1896.

70 The exhibition ran from 17–19 June 1899, and over 350 works were shown.

71 'Liverpool School of Architecture Exhibition', *The Builder*, 1 July 1899.

72 *The Builder*, 19 April 1905, reported on the Technical Instruction Committee's meeting in which it was recommended that the City Council be advised to establish a Municipal School of Art and that it be based at the School of Art at the Liverpool Institute. It was Alderman Ellis who laid charges that the Liverpool School had been unsuccessfully and extravagantly run.

73 Particularly Tyson Smith who worked extensively with Herbert Rowse and Lancelot Keay. Carter Preston worked mainly at the cathedral.

74 Bloomfield Bare reported regularly on artistic events in Liverpool in the 'Studio Talk' section, under the initials H.B.B. He was also a student at the School where he studied modelling and copperwork. See Bennett, *The Art Sheds*. He was responsible for the design of the gates to the Philharmonic Dining Rooms.

75 Fowler's studio was in Castle Street, in itself an indication of his financial success.

76 Anning Bell made it clear in his address to the Liverpool Architectural Society on 11 November 1895 (reported in the *RIBA Journal*, vol. III, p. 509) that artists must teach art, not 'schoolmasters'.

77 *The Studio*, vol. 3, p. 127.

78 See *The Studio*, vol. 9, pp. 122–24, report of the Arts and Crafts Exhibition at the New Gallery: '[The frieze was] … designed and executed by R. Anning Bell and Students of the Liverpool Municipal School of Art'.

79 Either formally or informally.

80 *The Studio*, vol. 8, 1896, p. 194: 'suggestions of secession of certain big towns from the South Kensington System, and the institution of locally maintained schools of art instead? That looks a very healthy sign'.

81 *The Studio*, vol. 13, 1898, pp. 189–93.

82 *The Studio*, vol. 17, 1899, pp. 187–90.

83 *The Builder*, 1 July 1899.

84 *The Studio*, vol. 20, 1900 p. 195.

85 *The Studio*, vol. 21, 1900, p. 195.

86 *The Studio*, vol. 30, 1903, pp. 45–51.

87 'Manufacturers desiring to make Mr. Lethaby's suggested experiment might do worse than seek assistance amongst craftsmen trained at the Mount Street School of Art.' Ibid., p. 51.

88 *The Studio*, vol. 34, 1905, p. 345. I think it reasonable to suggest that the absence of a review of the demise of the Applied Art section from Bloomfield Bare, must have at least some basis in a personal response to the direction that the School had taken towards the traditional Beaux Arts, Fine Arts approach, as exemplified in the Victoria Monument, as opposed to the Arts and Crafts approach favoured by Bloomfield Bare. In 1904 he was still writing enthusiastically of the Arts and Crafts remodelling of Thornton Hough by Douglas and Fordham, Grayson and Ould, and W. and S. Owen for W. H. Lever (see 'Thornton Hough Cheshire: A Rebuilt Village', *The Studio*, vol. 31, pp. 30–38).

89 'Needlework at Liverpool School of Art', *The Studio*, vol. 33, 1904 p. 149: Perhaps enough has been said to show that Mr. Burridge has succeeded in creating at Liverpool a school of needlework which claims real and serious recognition.'

90 'Work by the Students of the Liverpool School of Art', *The Studio*, vol. 25, 1902, pp. 170–80: '[The art Schools] ... are progressing along the right lines, and some among them are now doing for the arts and crafts what was done for them during the Renaissance by the famous guilds. In thinking of the Liverpool School of Art, and of others like it, we cannot but wish that they would carry out their usefulness a step nearer to that of the ancient guilds' (p. 172).

91 Hence Reilly's comment; 'The McNairs, husband and wife, both carrying out a queer art nouveau of their own and well known, we were told, in Berlin and Vienna if not in Liverpool.' Reilly, *Scaffolding in the Sky*.

92 'The National Competition of Schools of Art', *The Studio*, vol. 26, 1902; pp. 268–71, 'The National Competition of Schools of Art', *The Studio*, vol. 29, 1903, pp. 257–74.

93 Ibid., p. 257.

94 Technical Education Sub-Committee Minutes, 24 September 1900.

95 It is this that the following plaintive note in *The Sphinx* must refer to: 'We were rather taken aback in the studio one day last week by the announcement that work was to be continued during the Easter vacation. However, we have all calmly resigned ourselves to our fate.' 'Architectural Notes', *The Sphinx*, vol. 7, 1899–1900 p. 228.

96 Reilly, *Scaffolding in the Sky*, p. 85.

97 See W. H. G. Armytage, *Four Hundred Years of English Education*, Cambridge: Cambridge University Press, 1970.

98 I think it reasonable to assume that the changes in the administrative structure of the course, whilst formally altering the original notion of the course, were to a very large extent simply hastening the end, rather than strangling a successful enterprise. Apart from the vital matters of finance the following note from *The Sphinx* suggests that social relations between Architecture and Applied Arts students were not all sweetness and light: 'We have been asked to remind the Architecture students that there is serious work going on in the sheds, and that it is quite impossible for some people to work in the midst of noise. No one objects to talking in moderation, but it must be confessed that the continual dropping of easels and tumbling over stools is distracting. We feel sure that the Architecture students only have to have the matter brought to their consideration for them to see the reasonableness of this request.' *The Sphinx*, vol. 9, 1901–02, p. 172.

   99 K. Hewitt, 'Report on the Provision for Art Instruction in Liverpool', read to the Technical Instruction Committee, 28 April 1902.
  100 The City was financially responsible in varying degrees for the Mount Street School of Art, the Applied Art section at the Liverpool School of Architecture and Applied Art, art classes at the Walton and Kirkdale Technical Institute and the Wavertree Institute, and at the City's schools.
  101 The separation of the architecture studio situated at the top of the Victoria Building, from the 'art sheds' in what is now the quadrangle below, must have militated against the physical intimacy in which the exchange of ideas is made easier.
  102 Causing the pitiful remark: 'No one grudges that particular plot of ground to the science people, but we do wish that we were as lucky as they are.' *The Sphinx*, vol. 9, 1901–02, p. 201. A far cry from the imagined response of the emancipated radical artisan envisaged by Morris!
  103 *The Sphinx*, vol. 11, 1903–04 pp. 168–69.
  104 Ibid.
  105 *The Sphinx*, vol. 11, 1903–04 p. 67.
  106 Willet, *Art in a City*, p. 59.
  107 Q. Hughes, 'Before the Bauhaus', *Architectural History*, vol. 25, 1982.
  108 Ibid., p. 110.
  109 Budden, *The Book of The Liverpool School of Architecture*, p. 34.
  110 Whilst Hughes mentions the Liverpool Congress of 1888 he pays little attention to its role in focusing initiatives within the local artistic community.
  111 According to Hughes, Simpson had absorbed Jackson's 'advanced ideas on architectural education', ibid., p. 107. Hopefully I have previously demonstrated that these ideas were not really so advanced, belonging as they did to a body of thought evolved 50 years previously, and that Simpson's great contribution was the introduction of a systematised form of architectural instruction that was capable of absorbing the new building technologies. Hughes also demonstrates a misunderstanding of the evolution of the course in his analysis of its failure; 'Simpson's wish to have, side by side with the handycraft (sic) workshops, masons, plumbers, carpenters and joiners all taking part in practical work had not materialised. He had warned in 1896 [see F. Simpson, 'Architectural Education: A School of Architecture', *The Builders' Journal*, 3 March 1896, p. 51] that the jealousies of trades unions might come in its way and prevent the implementation of this interesting aspect of the course.' Ibid., p. 109. Despite initial enthusiasm from artisans, the course did not provide the basic craft education that was acquired more easily at the City Technical College. It was this as much as anything that determined the later targeting of the 'aesthetic' student, and the demise of the course's first intentions.

Chapter Five

Liverpool, the United States and the Beaux Arts Vision

Frederick Simpson's interest in the architectural education initiatives of the United States of America was not the only interest in the USA in Liverpool at the time of the inauguration of the Liverpool School. William Lever, who was such an important figure in both reflecting and moulding architectural attitudes in Merseyside, became interested in the new American architectural styles, and there is evidence of considerable traffic by the Liverpudlian architectural community between the city and the USA. Economic contacts between the port and the United States of America were of course fundamental to its survival, and along with trade connections there were also those of travel. It was possible to get to New York in a week, and to travel at a variety of levels of comfort and expense.[1] The passenger traffic to the USA was considerable and it would be surprising if there had not been any contact between the two cultures. There was a familiarity with American life in Liverpool at all social levels, from sailors to merchants. American news was regularly reported in the local papers, *The Courier* and *The Daily Post* – a necessity as there was a constant flow of visitors to and from the United States of America. Economically, New York was more important to Liverpool than London,[2] and lavish municipal entertainment for visiting American professionals was commonplace.[3]

General anecdotal awareness of the architectural wonders of the United States of America was high. On his world tour during 1892, Lever wrote a regular series of travel articles for the *Birkenhead News*.

A flavour of the local conception of the USA can be gleaned from his descriptions. From New York he wrote of 'the hustle and bustle of the place, the nervous energy, the vitality and force of the American people, and the high speed at which buildings there are being put up'.[4] He reported back to readers on the marvels of the architecture of the Chicago World's Fair a year before its formal opening,[5] and it can be assumed, as the Beaux Arts style was to so drastically modify the development of Port Sunlight village, discussed its merits with his architectural circle on his return.[6]

By 1895 Lever had opened offices in New York and Philadelphia, and thus opened a further channel by which cultural interchange could take place. His position as an architectural patron within the city was particularly important with the appointment of Charles Reilly as Roscoe Professor in 1904. It was Lever's patronage that enabled Reilly to visit the United States of America for the first time,[7] a visit that was to eventually to culminate in the use of American architectural firms for the Liverpool School's fourth year student office practice.[8]

The city and its intelligentsia were well aware of American cultural life. That the awareness of American architectural culture was stronger locally than nationally, can be seen in the British architectural press at the time of the inauguration of the Liverpool School. In 1894 a pamphlet was published in the UK called *Architectural Education in America*.[9] It was originally an American publication, containing four essays that examined aspects of American architectural education in general terms; The Ecole des Beaux Arts, the 'English' system, and the practicalities of American office training. The pamphlet was reviewed in both the *RIBA Journal*[10] and in *The Builder*.[11] Their respective commentaries throw an interesting light on the parochialism of English metropolitan thinking. In both publications the pamphlet was given a note length review, but more important than the length were the remarks. *The Builder* thought that the Beaux Arts style was inappropriate to the conditions in the United States, and the *RIBA Journal* made mention of the American Beaux Arts, referred to the incongruous nature of a French style in the United States of America, and made no attempt to interpret the style or its functions. The *Journal*'s main emphasis was upon the accuracy of the description of the Royal Institute of British Architects' examination system in Gibson's 'The English System', prosaically affirming that this article would be 'the essay most interesting to the British Student'.[12]

This indication of cultural introversion, and the lack of perception of the powerful role being played by the Beaux Arts in American architectural education, is further reinforced by the review of the Chicago World's Fair buildings published in the *Journal* earlier in the year.[13]

Its author, W. Emerson, was the UK's judge in architecture for the Fair. His article contained much that was generally favourable in response to the Fair's architecture, particularly to the 'classical' style, but he did not specifically mention the Beaux Arts and their contribution to the Fair and its styling. When describing the buildings of the 'Court of Honor' they were referred to by their specific classical order rather than the generic American term 'Beaux Arts'.

Information about American practice in architectural journals is scarce. It is limited in *The Builder* to brief technical notes, and when mentioned in the *RIBA Journal* it is almost exclusively through a Liverpool connection. The first indication of the Liverpudlian interest in American practice comes in a report of a paper read to the Liverpool Architectural Society, 'Three Years Architectural Experience in America' by James Cook.[14] Published several months before the article on American architectural education, it was an enthusiastic account of architectural practice in the United States of America that attributed the superiority of practice in New York and Philadelphia over that in the United Kingdom to college course training, emphasising this point by giving a brief account of that training.[15] He laid heavy emphasis upon the role of the Beaux Arts system, and the fact that American students travelled and studied abroad, particularly at the Ecole des Beaux Arts. He enthused; 'this must eventuate in the advancement of the country's architecture, and its influence is already strongly felt. Students, again, are being *taught*, instead of, as is so frequently the case in England, merely receiving opportunities to learn for themselves'.[16] The emphasis, as ever from the Liverpool Architectural Society, is upon education, and as can be seen, an emphasis upon a form of educational practice that was to have its parallels in Simpson's scheme of work for the new Liverpool School.

A year later the same Journal reported Bloomfield Bare's address, 'Philadelphia: An Architect's Notes in an American City',[17] given to the Manchester Society of Architects. Architectural training and the Beaux Arts were not mentioned by Bloomfield Bare, but the benefits of a planned city on a grid system were, and he noted approvingly how the cultural tastes of the city were those 'of Paris rather than London'. The issue of municipal control of communal facilities[18] was discussed in line with Rathbone's views of benevolent municipal paternalism, as was the keen sense of public responsibility in Philadelphia.[19] Bloomfield Bare built up a picture of a well-organised and planned city, and paid considerable attention to the development of 'semi-rural' residential areas built up around railway stations. (These concerns of course have close parallels with the development of Lever's village at Port Sunlight.) He had an interest in American frame built houses. Frame houses, he explained, grow 'very rapidly, and [the] system of construction permits a very great variety of plan and elevational designs'.[20] This insight, and his further examination of the construction of frame housing demonstrates the concern within the Liverpudlian architectural community for a marriage between the ideological and the practical.

American architectural education again loomed large in Liverpudlian eyes the following year in the Institute's journal, in a brief note entitled 'American Education'.[21] It is interesting to compare the response of Waterhouse (a member of the Liverpool Architectural Society) to that of the anonymous reviewer of *Architectural Education in America* eighteen months earlier. One is culturally introverted, the other culturally expansive. Two pamphlets by Professor William Ware were discussed; *The Instruction of Architecture at the School of Mines*, and *The Study of Architectural History at Columbia College*. Waterhouse discussed the worth of Ware's ideas in two areas, generally in reinforcing the importance of education as a valuable function in its own right, praising the American attitude; 'in America they have not given up thinking on the education question';[22] and by examining specific American educational proposals. He came to the conclusion that 'we may do worse than look to the Americans for an example of rational method of education'.

Waterhouse's piece was written a year after the scheme of work devised by Simpson for the Liverpool School was published. It is not possible to say for certain, but I think it reasonable to assume that Waterhouse's article sets out to do two things; firstly, to extend the debate about architectural education still further, and to combat the perceived complacency of the RIBA's Progressive Examinations. Secondly, given the architectural disinterest in American cultural affairs outside of Liverpool, the discussion of such a topic in an influential journal such as the Institute's would further legitimise the experiment in Liverpool. The City's intellectual community was so well known to one another, that it is impossible that one member of its architectural community, Waterhouse, would discuss an issue dear to the heart of another, Simpson, without some sort of collaboration existing.

A final, for the purposes of my narrative, Liverpudlian contribution to the dissemination of information concerning American architectural practice was a report in the *RIBA Journal* of another address to the Manchester Society. Gass was a member of the Liverpool Society of Architects and spoke on 'American Architecture and Architects, with Special Reference to the Work of the Late Richard Morris Hunt and Henry Hobson Richardson'.[23] In it, Gass gave a lucid account of the history of architecture in the United States of America, concentrating on the two great American architectural personalities, Richardson with his adaptation of the Romanesque, and the Beaux Arts practitioner

Hunt. Hunt was given more weight by Gass, who summed him up as an architect who was 'an enthusiastic disciple of the French School, and [who] exercised great influence therefrom'.

Once again it is American educational practice, in this case in the form of William Ware, that received the warmest praise. His educational principles and practice were treated by Gass as important as the buildings designed and constructed by Hunt and Richardson. Gass made his own position quite clear; 'In Professor William R. Ware, American Architecture has had an enthusiastic organising leader whose influence has been, and is far reaching for good.'

It is evident that there was a considerable interest in Professor Ware's educational practice in Liverpool. In the absence of documentation it is impossible to say whether the interest in Ware came entirely from Simpson, or whether it had been arrived at through general architectural channels in the city, with its great interest in architectural education. Simpson had not published anything on architectural education before his appointment at Liverpool, neither did he whilst Professor at University College, all his labours going into his study of the history of architecture.[24] It could be argued that just as he was prepared to initiate a system of design education in the Applied Arts section that had already been laid out by the city's architectural community seven years previously,[25] he was equally capable of implementing a set of ideas about architectural education that were already in the air locally. Charles Reilly's role as Simpson's successor would make him a less than objective commentator on Simpson, but he makes little mention of him in his autobiography, other than to say that architectural study at University College London, 'under Professor Simpson … did not seem to make much headway'.[26]

Lionel Budden suggests that the curriculum for the Certificate in Architecture had been decided in 1893 by a triumvirate of the University Council and Senate, the City Council and the Liverpool Architectural Society. If this was the case then Simpson's position as Director would have been one of administering and developing an already formed idea as to how architectural education would function within the new School.

Simpson's perception of cultural events was flexible and non dogmatic.[27] If it were the case that he simply put into operation a series of current educational principles, it would be to his credit that it ran efficiently. His own aesthetic taste was inclined towards the Beaux Arts, as the Victoria Monument in Derby Square indicates. A fuller indication of his tastes can be gathered from 'Old Architecture in Liverpool', a paper he read to the Warrington Literary and Philosophical Society in 1896.[28] In it Simpson discussed the qualities of design and detailing in the Georgian housing of Liverpool, quoting the Strozzi Palace and the Palace of the Antinori in Florence as further paradigms of elegant proportion. This rather suggests that Simpson's awareness of the design philosophy underlying the Beaux Arts was well developed if not before his residence in Liverpool, then certainly during the first couple of years of it, for his enthusiastic response to the architecture of Georgian Liverpool emphasises its uniqueness. His interest in town planning is demonstrated in his discussion of the Liverpool Town Hall–Custom House axis in the same paper. His observation that the removal of St George's Church would improve its aspects were later to be achieved with his design for the Victoria monument.

An example of the probable compatibility of Simpson's aims and those of the City's architectural community in implementing the influence of American design ideas is seen in the campaign to move the site of the proposed cathedral from St James' Mount (where it now stands) to Monument Place in London Road. The membership of the Petitioning Committee is not now known, but it would seem unlikely that Simpson in his role as President of the Liverpool Architectural Society was uninvolved, given the Society's and his own personal antagonism to the Cathedral Competition proposals. *The Builder*[29] extensively reported the Petitioning Committee's pamphlet and developed the debate. The implications of the placing of the proposed cathedral shows an interest in town planning unusual in an English context, with its emphasis on the development of the city centre, rather than with the planning of dwellings.[30] The municipal and symbolic aspect of city life had begun to have the same planning importance as the social aspect. In its small way, the Petitioning Committee's concern for the new cathedral to be placed centrally, prominently and with commanding vistas,[31] and its concerns for a symbolic building to be seen in terms of civic aggrandisement, relate more to the ideas of New York's *Municipal Affairs* journal with its talk of 'The City Beautiful', than it does to the developed architectural social conscience of Ebenezer Howard's *Tomorrow: A Peaceful Path to Real Reform.*[32]

Simpson's individual role in this issue is difficult to determine – his interest in Ware and his educational proposals are paralleled in general educational discussion in Liverpool, and certainly his interest in the Beaux Arts made him aware of American design. With this in mind, and with the obvious interest in American architecture emerging in Liverpool in the years after the 1888 congress, a mutual progress can be seen to be made by the city's architectural community and by Simpson. Most importantly there was a significant knowledge of American educational practice gained locally before it was gained nationally, and given expression at the Liverpool School of Architecture and Applied Art.

As we have seen, Simpson's *The Scheme of Architectural Education Started at University College Liverpool*,[33] mentioned two architectural college courses in the USA,[34] and cited them as paradigms. Both courses' educational practice was based on the Ecole des Beaux Arts in Paris. This Beaux Arts approach to architectural education in the developed American states was an important innovation in the 1890s. It provided a coherent structure to architectural practice in the USA at a time when a fragmented American profession was subject to the same demands as the British, that is, a need to set a standard for skills, the achievement of which guaranteed the architect public confidence.[35] General parallels can be made between the situation that American architects and Liverpudlian architects found themselves facing; an expansion of the building stock that needed to be regulated both technically and stylistically. The chosen educational scheme in Liverpool, whilst having obvious origins in the 'Gothic' debate, also looked to current practice in the USA. We have seen its relevance to educational practice in the Liverpool School, that was to grow under the Professorship of Charles Reilly. Its influence through the 'City Beautiful' movement in the USA was to be particularly important in the founding and subsequent teaching of the Department of Civic Design in Liverpool in 1909.

The 'World's Columbian Exposition' in Chicago in 1893 became a focal point for architectural debate in Liverpool, and stimulated an interest in Beaux Arts architecture in the USA. This interest became focused in the American architectural community with the formation of the *Society of Beaux Arts Architects* in 1894. The Chicago Fair's 'Court of Honor', known colloquially as 'The White City', was the USA's first glimpse of large-scale classical design integrating planning with architectural detail, combining the skills of painters and sculptors under the guidance of a coherent and consistent design principle. It was to exercise great influence upon 'mayors, industrialists, university presidents, and other potential patrons'.[36] It was this body of opinion that was to propel American Beaux Arts styling towards prestigious large-scale projects that were to ensure its status. So much so that Charles Reilly, in a monograph on McKim, Mead and White, felt able to refer to the style as one which summed up 'the finest aspirations of a great people at a great epoch'.[37]

Advocates of the architectural merits of the 'Court of Honor' at the Fair, saw the consistency of design principles espoused by Beaux Arts styling as being in opposition to the multiplicity of dynamic approaches to architecture in Chicago's commercial centre, where novelty of style and technology were substituted for a sense of architectural tradition.[38]

19 Liverpool Athenaeum, Harold Dod, completed 1928. This building shows the similarities and differences between the American Beaux arts and the work of Liverpool School practitioners (see plate 22).

20 The Midland Adelphi Hotel, Liverpool, Frank Atkinson, 1912. The façade is unusual in the shallowness of its surface decoration.

21 Boston Library, view of the stairway from the entrance hall. McKim, Mead and White, 1887–93. The Beaux Arts as signifier of civic virtue.

22 University Club, New York, McKim, Mead and White, 1900.

23 Pennsylvania Railway Station, New York, McKim, Mead and White, 1906–10.

Montgomery Schuyler, in an article in America's most prestigious architectural journal, the *Architectural Record*,[39] summarised the Court's success for the architectural community in the United States. The most important was its coherence as a design style in which individual architectural units could be seen as contributing to a wider conception of uniformity.[40] A major practical contributor to this was the virtually continuous skyline around the court with a uniform cornice line of 60 feet, so that uniformity of style and scale worked together. Because the classical style had become so well assimilated culturally, its forms had become disconnected from stone structure, and had become forms that were applicable to any material. This meant Beaux Arts styling could be used 'as a decorative envelope of any construction whatever without exciting in most observers any sense of incongruity, much less any sense of meanness'.[41] In addition to the unity of scale and formal principles, was the concept of 'magnitude'.[42] By this Schuyler did not simply mean bigness – as he pointed out, a pile of barrels the size of the great pyramid would astonish simply through its scale. What he meant by magnitude was the artistic manipulation of scale; 'an interminable repetition of the unit, the incessant application of the module'.

This manipulation of form was obviously aesthetic in approach, but independent of style. The fact that it was considered necessary to confront this issue casts a light on a particular perception of the commercial architecture of Chicago, where scale and height were prime architectural considerations, but in *economic* rather than in *aesthetic* terms.[43] What Beaux Arts styling was able to do in the eyes of its adherents, was to enable the construction of large buildings whose subsequent proportions were familiar enough culturally for them to be accessible, and so to become monumental in appearance, rather than incoherently large.

The point that can be drawn from Schuyler's article on the success of the World's Fair architecture, is purely ideological. Schuyler saw the architecture as that of illusion, of being 'holiday building', created purely for sensual delight. This should not be overly surprising as the architecture served a purely symbolic function, where to paraphrase Daniel Burnham, none of the buildings' facades expressed a plan, acting rather as full-sized models of buildings. In talking of the building's qualities of dignity, Schuyler referred to them as the 'Capital of No-Man's Land'. This could be interpreted as a disadvantage for an architectural style, that it represented not architectural principles but a festive event, but if one considers the Beaux Arts style as an amorphous representation of urbanity and sophistication its potency as a signifier of metropolitan values becomes clear. Its power is both that it can represent a capital, and one that is transnational, or international (No-Mans Land). It is culturally pervasive, and persuasive; and without being readily identifiable as the product of a specific culture, the style has transcended its material base and become a thing in itself.[44]

Charles Reilly's attitude to the style affirms this point. In referring to the issues of eclecticism and individualism in McKim, Mead and White's practice,[45] Reilly argued that the old notion of the architect as individual master must necessarily give way to an increasingly anonymous, less personal architecture. The issue of cultural universalism, so common in modern movement debate, was also present in the debate around the Beaux Arts style. In a highly prescriptive passage Reilly talked of McKim, Mead and White's 'noble' and 'reticent' buildings expressing 'a universal spirit such as our present-day civilisation should do, even if it does not'.[46]

In association with this idea comes the notion of internationalism, or perhaps more correctly in the context of Reilly's definition, *transnationalism*, where in its use of multicultural neo-classical imagery (Roman, Italian, English and American Colonial motifs), the architecture is applicable to a variety of contemporary urban environments. In what could be considered a curious use of metaphor for a neo-classical architecture, were the cultural origins of the debate that culminated in the Liverpool School not known, Reilly drew a comparison with McKim, Mead and White's architecture and that of the gothic cathedrals:

> At most we shall be able to say, as we do of our great gothic cathedrals, that a group of self-denying artists worked on this or that building and put so much knowledge, so much enthusiasm, so much of their spirit into it, that as long as it stands it will remain ... [great] ... all the greater, probably, because done in this semi-anonymous manner.[47]

The Beaux Arts style was valued by Reilly as a fitting symbol representing a universalised metropolitanism. This is something that can be reinforced in sociological terms[48] when talking of the evolution of the Beaux Arts style at the end of the nineteenth century in the United States. The style was successful because it fulfilled the demands of 'third generation nouveau wealth' that was prosperous, increasingly metropolitan and institutionalised.[49]

It would be wrong, however, to imagine that this process was an instantaneous one, and that the style was immediately and universally adopted. The Beaux Arts style had been used in the United States several years before the Chicago Fair with mixed success. It was the success of the Fair which ensured the success of the style. What is important to the general narrative of this book are the parallels of American Beaux

Arts practice and its adoption by the Liverpool School. Architecture in the USA was as deeply influenced by the ideas of John Ruskin as was that in Britain. McKim was particularly influenced by Ruskin early in his career;[50] the Gothic in all its forms was prevalent in most design areas. Reaction to McKim's Boston Library (1895), is a good indicator as to the form that opposition to the Beaux Arts took in its early stages. Built opposite Richardson's Romanesque influenced Trinity Church, the library's formal qualities were seen as quite inappropriate. *The Boston Herald* referred to the building as a 'Titanic cigar box',[51] and during its first years of construction wrote:

> As it grows the sense of disappointment in the architectural effect increases … [the partially completed building] stands like a great block of white granite, severe, unbroken, in the midst of warm colours, and richer forms … what opportunities for splendidly broken skylines that western background affords the architect, but this flat-backed, flat-chested structure promises to crash them to the earth.[52]

It took the 'Court of Honor' to give the Beaux Arts style a context in which to be read, and therefore made culturally acceptable. After the Chicago Fair had closed, *The Boston Herald* had changed its views on the library, calling it, 'severe and almost monastic in its simplicity, yet so genially beautiful; so palatial and dignified'.[53]

If the Beaux Arts style signified all that it did, how did it become a signifier? There can be no doubt that it emerged through the quest in the United States for a form of architectural training that could give the American architect the skills and status that he or she required in order to increase public confidence in his or her ability to build efficiently. Whereas in Britain a developed indigenous ideological debate and a rudimentary architectural educational structure channelled developments to some degree, in the United States architectural debate was historically tied to cultural links with France, and in crude terms, the Ecole des Beaux Arts principles were accepted or rejected,[54] but its educational processes were undertaken because there was no other alternative. A major difference between the British and American situations was that in Britain in the 1890s, architectural training was vocational and office-based, whilst on the eastern seaboard of the United States an architect was, ideally, 'schooled'. The reality was that in 1895, the year in which the City of Liverpool School of Architecture and Applied Art was inaugurated, the United States had nine schools of architecture; Massachusetts Institute of Technology (founded 1865), Cornell University (1871), University of Illinois (1873), Syracuse University (1873), Columbia University (1881), University of Pennsylvania

(1890), George Washington University (1893), Armour Institute of Technology (1895), and Harvard University (1895).[55] In 1898 there was a total enrolment of 384 students, and the 1900 census recorded 10,581 architects.[56] Questions could be raised as to the relationship between self-proclaimed and trained architects, but nevertheless a formal architectural educational structure was in place. Because there was no formal tradition of apprenticeship in the United States, there was no developed sense of architectural tradition [57] as exemplified by the Arts and Crafts approach in Britain. So, those ideas promulgated by Ecole des Beaux Arts trained architects who were administering formal courses were readily absorbed into the system as there was little coherent 'opposition' to them. The rise of the Beaux Arts style focused by the 'Court of Honor' was primarily the result of an evolved *educational* practice.

The objectives of the Ecole des Beaux Arts seemed particularly relevant to the purposes of American architecture at the time. In addition to the stylistic attractions, where the Beaux Arts style was ideally suited for large-scale architectural organisation, the educational system itself was also attractive. It was codified and regularised, and suited drawing office procedures where, because of the scale of contemporary American architecture, it was vital to integrate engineering systems into the structure as early as possible. These engineering systems in turn, were themselves regular and fixed.[58]

The first courses of architectural education run in the American universities, such as the Massachusetts Institute of Technology's School of Architecture,[59] concentrated upon construction and science to the exclusion of history and design. (This also must have contributed to a fragmented conception of the stylistic and formal role that architecture could play.) From the late 1880s in response to discussion in the architectural press,[60] architecture schools put an increasing emphasis upon design, and design that was Beaux Arts orientated, as it was only those trained at the Ecole des Beaux Arts who were able to put such schemes into operation. The Massachusetts Institute of Technology, the University of Pennsylvania and Harvard University all used French graduates of the Ecole to teach the new courses.

Until the 'World's Columbian Exposition' in Chicago in 1893 opened up the Beaux Arts style for consumption by continental America, the style had been almost exclusively a New York phenomenon. The Architectural League of New York (1881) took upon itself the role of disseminator of Beaux Arts ideas; it established a collection of photographs, drawings and plaster casts for educational purposes, and organised design competitions and drawing exhibitions. These activities were given a national focus by the Society of Beaux Arts Architects (1894) who sponsored competitions and independent ateliers for working architects, and in establishing the Paris Prize aimed to increase the number of Americans studying at the Ecole des Beaux Arts. It was instrumental in setting up the American Academy in Rome and the Rome Prize. Draper,[61] in summarising the Society's educational endeavours, identifies two basic objectives. Firstly, the establishment of a codified stylistic practice that 'would raise the general standard of taste' and produce 'a vital national style'. This would ensure the second objective, which was to develop 'artistic abilities' which would separate architects from builders and engineers. The parallels between the situation facing architects in the United States and England were close and the debate which was taking place in Liverpool, placed as it was between the two cultures, reflected both approaches, and drew heavily on American solutions.

Notes

1 R. Jones, *The American Connection*, Liverpool, 1986, pp. 55–68.

2 A special double issue of *The American European Newsletter*, June 1895, concentrated its entire contents on an examination of Liverpool's trading and social milieu with reference to the United States.

3 For example, 'Visit of American Engineers to the United Kingdom, Reception by the Mayor of Liverpool, programme', 6 June 1889, Liverpool City Library, Local History Archives.

4 W. H. Lever, *Following the Flag*, Liverpool: Simkin Marshall and Co., 1893, p. 4, first published as a series of articles for the *Birkenhead News*, 1893.

5 Ibid., p. 7: 'We spent a few days in Chicago [1892], visiting the World's fair and as far as one could judge in its present incomplete state, the Americans have every cause to feel proud of this monument of their energy … each building, from a purely architectural point of view, is well conceived, duly proportioned, and most admirably executed.'

6 Bloomfield Bare who had a studio in Port Sunlight village visited the United States in 1894.

7 C. H. Reilly, *Scaffolding in the Sky*, Routledge, 1938, p. 123. 'In 1909 I was sent by Lord Leverhulme [to America] and came back loaded with vast American prize drawings which I had been given or had managed to buy.'

8 Ibid., pp. 216–18.

9 B. Ferree (ed.), *Architectural Education in America*, publisher not known, 1894. The essays were: A. Rotch, 'The Ecole Des Beaux Arts'; R. D. Andrews, 'The Practical Side'; R. W. Gibson, 'The English System'; and B. Ferree, 'An Outsider's View'.

10 *RIBA Journal*, vol. I, 1893, p. 503.

11 *The Builder*, 4 August 1894.

12 *RIBA Journal*, vol. I, 1893, p. 503. 'The essay most interesting to the British Student is necessarily that of Mr. Gibson, who accurately describes the Progressive Examinations of the Institute.'

13 W. Emerson, 'The World's Fair Buildings, Chicago', *RIBA Journal*, vol. I, 1893, pp. 65–74.

14 J. H. Cook, 'Three Years Architectural Experience in America', paper read to the Liverpool Architectural Society, 5 March 1894, *RIBA Journal*, vol. I, 1893, pp. 362–63.

15 Ibid., p. 362: 'They had been instructed in the various branches of the arts, thoroughly grounded in the classical orders, and taught how to incorporate their knowledge in designs for modern buildings – how to plan, to detail, modelling in clay, perspective, together with the literary side of their art.'

16 Ibid., p. 363.

17 H. Bloomfield Bare, 'Philadelphia: An Architect's Notes in an American City', paper read before the Manchester Society of Architects, 5 March 1895. *RIBA Journal*, vol. II, 1894.

18 Ibid., p. 395. 'The lawns are beautifully trimmed and kept, no one tramples over corners or injures the grass edges, the flower-beds are liberally supplied with flowers and shrubs, no one plucks the flowers or injures the trees, and no one carves the wooden benches.'

19 Ibid., p. 397. 'One thoroughly appreciates the benefits derivable from the superior municipal government in English cities after a few years absence.'

20 Ibid., p. 397.

21 P. Waterhouse, 'American Education', *RIBA Journal*, vol. III, 1895.

22 Ibid., p. 440.

23 J. B. Gass, 'American Architecture and Architects, With Special Reference to the Works of the Late Richard Morris Hunt and Henry Hobson Richardson', paper read to the Manchester Society of Architects, 4 February 1896, *RIBA Journal*, vol. III, 1895.

24 F. M. Simpson, *A History of Architectural Development*, Longmans, 1905–11, 3 vols.

25 See in particular H. B. Bare, 'A School for Artistic Handicrafts' in 'Transactions of the National Association for the Advancement of Art and its Application to Industry: Liverpool Meeting 1888', conference proceedings, National Association for the Advancement of Art and its Application to Industry, London, 1888.

26 Reilly, *Scaffolding in the Sky*, p. 114.

27 His role as President of the Liverpool Architectural Society during the controversy over the Liverpool Cathedral Competition is a good indication of this.

28 F. M. Simpson, 'Old Architecture in Liverpool', paper read to the Warrington Literary and Philosophical Society, 16 March 1896.

29 'The Liverpool Cathedral Question', *The Builder*, 21 December 1901.'

30 Cf. 'The Environmental Debate and the Presentation of Two Rival Solutions' A. Sutcliffe, *Towards the Planned City*, Basil Blackwell, 1981, pp. 62–64.

31 'Objections to the Present Scheme for a Cathedral in Liverpool, 'The Builder*, 21 December 1901, pp. 548–49: 'That the site selected ... is not central; not readily accessible; not commandingly prominent; without vistas ... That there is a vista extending for nearly half a mile, which would be terminated by the west end of the Cathedral, were Monument-place site accepted; and the Cathedral would form the crowning feature of lines of streets, over a mile in length, commencing at the landing stage and riverside station, and passing the [city's civic buildings].'

32 This attitude was to find expression in the city through the Liverpool Garden Suburb, although there was considerable intellectual opposition to it.

33 F. M. Simpson, *The Scheme of Architectural Education Started at University College, Liverpool, in Connection with the City of Liverpool School of Architecture and Applied Art*, Liverpool: Marples and Co., 1895.

34 Columbia College, New York, and the University of Pennsylvania.

35 For a full account of this issue see J. Draper, 'The Ecole des Beaux Arts and the Architectural Profession in the United States' in S. Kostof (ed.), *The Architect*, New York: Oxford University Press, 1977.

36 Ibid., pp. 213–14.

37 C. H. Reilly, *McKim, Mead and White*, Ernest Benn, 1924, p. 24.

38 Cf. M. L. Peisch, *The Chicago School of Architecture*, Phaidon Press, 1964, pp. 17–38.

39 M. Schuyler, 'Last Words about the World's Fair', *Architectural Record*, Jan–March 1894.

40 Ibid., p. 293: 'In the first place the success is first of all a success of unity, a triumph of ensemble. The whole is better than any of its parts and greater than any of its parts, and its effect is one and indivisible.' Schuyler does not make the point, though it is one worth making, that five firms of architects worked together to produce a design that was consistent and unified through the use of a style, which in this particular instance can be considered as a neutral vehicle for expression.

41 Ibid., p. 294.

42 Ibid., p. 298: 'Next after unity, as a source and explanation of the unique impression made by the World's Fair buildings, comes magnitude. It may even be questioned whether it should not come first in an endeavour to account for that impression. If it be put second, it is only because unity, from an artistic point of view, is merely an advantage. The buildings are impressive by their size, and this impressiveness is enhanced by their number.'

43 Ibid., p. 398: 'To say of anything that it is the "greatest" thing of its kind in the world is a very favourite form of advertisement in Chicago. One cannot escape hearing it and seeing it there a dozen times a day.'

44 That the Beaux Arts style was seen as a style representing municipal virtues can be seen in C. Moore, *The Life and Times of Charles Follen McKim*, New York: Riverside Press, 1929, where the chapter on the Chicago Fair is headed, 'The Chicago World's Fair Marks the Beginnings of Civic Art in America' (p. 113), and includes 'Fully to appreciate the Chicago fair as the most significant event in the history of civic art in America …' (p. 116).

45 Reilly, *McKim, Mead and White*, p. 24.

46 Ibid., p. 10.

47 Ibid., p. 24.

48 *American Buildings and Their Architects, vol. 4*, W. H. Jordy, *Progressive and Academic Ideals at the turn of the Twentieth Century*, Oxford University Press, 1986.

49 Ibid., p. 344. Reilly makes much the same point with less objectivity but with far greater style when he refers in his book *McKim, Mead and White* to 'Mr. Morgan's spoil from Europe' (p. 17), and 'the vast stream of loot which was beginning to pour in from Europe' (p. 15). He talks also of American architecture 'sailing so safely in the mid-stream of European culture and not losing its way' (p. 22).

50 Ibid., p. 10. '[McKim] found it harder than most Americans did to reconcile himself to the Beaux Arts. Ruskin was then his prophet.'

51 *Boston Herald*, 13 October 1891, quoted in Jordy, *Progressive and Academic Ideals*, p. 330.

52 *Boston Herald* 3 November 1889, in ibid., p. 370.

53 *Boston Herald*, 15 May 1895, in ibid., p. 373.

54 Two American architects who can be considered the antithesis of all that the Ecole des Beaux Arts stood for, Henry Richardson and Louis Sullivan, were nonetheless graduates of it.

55 A. C. Weatherhead, *The History of Collegiate Education in Architecture in the United States*, Los Angeles: University of California Press, 1941.

56 Draper, 'The Ecole Des Beaux Arts' in Kostof, *The Architect*, p. 214.

57 See Simpson, *The Scheme of Architectural Education*, p. 14.

58 See Jordy, *Progressive and Academic Ideals*, pp. 344–46.

59 C. Shillaber, *Massachusetts Institute of Technology School of Architecture and Planning 1861–1961*, Cambridge, MA: MIT Press, 1963.

60 Draper, 'The Ecole Des Beaux Arts' in Kostof, *The Architect*, p. 214.

61 Ibid., p. 216.

Chapter Six

Charles Reilly, the Liverpool School of Architecture and the City Beautiful

IN 1915, after a national competition for a new Town Hall in Stepney, London, the architectural critic Randall Phillips wrote to Charles Reilly to say that 'eighty per cent of the designs were in the Liverpool manner'.[1] By this he meant an architectural style that had been consciously derived from the Ecole des Beaux Arts, a style that was a rationalised classical one, large in scale and restrained in detailing. This tale illustrates the considerable impact that the Liverpool School of Architecture made during the first decade of Reilly's Professorship. The influence of the School was exercised through two channels: the teaching of an architectural style that became synonymous with the School, and with the further dissemination of this style through the establishment of the first Civic Design course in the UK. Reilly was only in part responsible for the first aspect of the School's national reputation, drawing together as he did issues that were already current. In the latter though, he was an important instigator of events. Reilly's skill was in acting as a catalyst in the architectural education debate, and his ability in the manipulation of events.

When Reilly took over at Liverpool in 1904, the course of study no longer resembled that initially envisaged in 1894. Its formal organisation and the links that had already been established with the processes of architectural education in the United States, meant that Reilly's full adoption of Beaux Arts practices were not as radical as has often been been assumed, albeit primarily on the basis of his first-hand testimony.[2] Reilly was considerably aided in his task of making the

School one of national consequence by the deliberations of the RIBA's Board of Architectural Education.

The RIBA had initiated the Board in 1903 after informal approaches to interested professional associations and teaching establishments. Its brief was to establish a coherent architectural educational structure, and forestall the potential chaos that was latent in the disparate means by which architects could become professionally qualified. The Board's conclusions were read to the RIBA by Reginald Blomfield on 20 February 1905. The points made were pragmatic and devoid of the power broking that had characterised the attempts of the RIBA to rationalise architectural study a decade previously.[3] Essentially the report advised the gradual standardisation of existing educational practices in the varying schools examined, less emphasis upon 'abstract' examination practices and more on practical based study (a criticism of the RIBA's own examination procedures), and the erosion of pupillage.[4] In effect it was realised that the maintenance of a successful status quo was dependent upon the careful management of existing processes of change, rather than any attempt to manipulate events, which in the past had caused so many personality clashes. This broad based, non-confrontational atmosphere meant that Reilly could both cooperate with, and oppose, varying dominant ideas within the architectural system and its hierarchies without either losing face or becoming isolated, which had become the fate of the Liverpool School under the directorship of Simpson.

Reilly's autobiographical account of the first visit of the Board of Education to the Liverpool School[5] places the event 'a couple of years' after he had been at Liverpool. It has not been possible to ascertain the exact date of the visit, but as the report of the Board was submitted to the RIBA at the beginning of 1905, it must have been in 1904. As Reilly started in the Easter term of 1904, it can be assumed that the visit of the Board to the School was to examine the achievements of the previous administration, rather than as Reilly intimates, his own. In any case, it follows that the Board would have visited Liverpool in any circumstances, as its brief was to look at existing architectural education structures. This is not to decry Reilly's achievements. These were to be considerable, and he was later to be invited to serve on the Board. Initially however, he came to public attention in large part because of what he inherited at the school – despite his creative attitude to the chronicling of events.

Reilly's achievement in assuming responsibility for all aspects of the course at Liverpool can be partly explained by the lack of peer group acknowledgement of the achievements of the Liverpool School from 1895 to 1904. Subsequent to the Board of Architectural Education's reading of its report to the RIBA, Simpson, at this point Professor at the Bartlett School, had to remind the assembled panel that attempts to disestablish the pupillage system (the Board proposed its gradual integration into institutionalised course structures) had been underway for a decade in Liverpool in exactly the same way and with success.[6] This point was later reinforced by Maurice Adams who had worked for Lever at Port Sunlight, and Edmund Woodthorpe, a member of the Liverpool Architectural Society. That these Liverpudlian architects were still having to remind their peer group of activities a decade earlier is telling of the general level of awareness of the Liverpool experiment.

With these general points in mind it is interesting to look at Reilly's 'The Training of Architects'.[7] In this article Reilly set out a programme of study for the architectural student, and at the same time offered a (generally favourable) critique of the findings of the Board, which had just been made public. Reilly's review of the conditions in which the student architect would be studying differed little from that of his predecessors' analysis of architectural culture. The architect was still adrift in a society where there were no stylistic certainties, and where the new commercial patrons lacked a sense of the 'dignity of their own pursuits'. What was new in Reilly's analysis was the assertion that 'municipal bodies … are fast failing in England to understand their responsibilities'.

The municipal authorities in Liverpool had played a considerable part in helping to establish architectural education in the city. Its role in this area was now over, and whilst its role as patron was diminishing, in some ways this decline of the importance of regional autonomy was to facilitate the national reputation of the school. Within a national framework of educational structures, albeit a loosely-knit one,[8] Reilly and his ideas had a peer group arena in which to operate.

Just as a decade earlier a lack of cultural coherence was decried, so too Reilly commented upon the 'vast and preponderating' amount of architecture produced by 'persons styling themselves architects'. Reilly thought this contemporary work vulgar and absurd. The solution to non-signifying architecture in the heyday of the Arts and Crafts movement was the adoption of a vernacular form that was material based, making all architectural structures *original*, but in sympathy with one another. It must be remembered that the influence of the movement in its Art Nouveau form was still strong though waning (viz. the success of the Liverpool School of Art) which makes Reilly's proposals all the more unusual. Reilly's solution was to define the appearance of architecture through the conscious adoption of a predetermined style. This could ensure a consistently similar product, creating a coherent architectural culture, but through the mechanism of a process in which

24 Reilly's design for Liverpool School of Architecture, 1914, perspective by Harold Chalton Bradshaw. It is interesting to compare this industrial echo of the great Roman civic spaces with the modernist version of 15 years later (see plate 1).

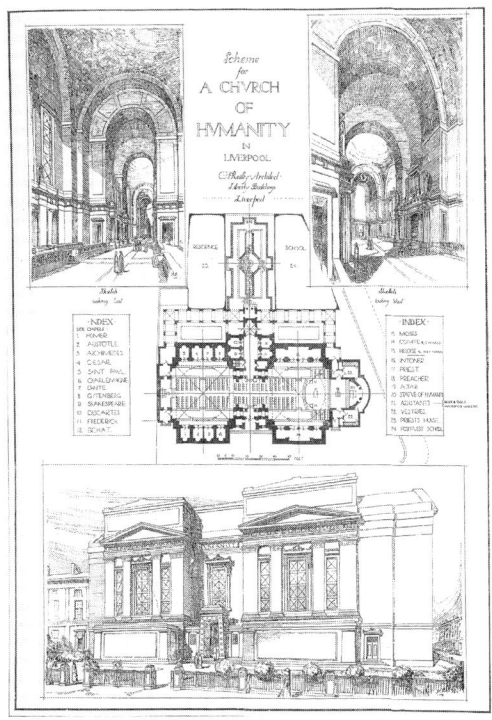

25 Reilly's proposal for Church of Humanity, commissioned by Edmund Rathbone, 1911, but never built.

originality in structure was sacrificed to *uniformity* of style. This did not mean that Reilly was antagonistic towards the 'truth to materials' argument of the Arts and Crafts movement. In a brief passage on architectural construction, he affirmed in a way which could have come from any adherent of Ruskin 50 years previously, that an understanding of the suitability of construction to the purpose of the building was fundamental to preventing revivalism.[9]

The 'absurdities' of Art Nouveau in Reilly's eyes were partly due to the excessive emphasis upon originality in design, and in a passage reminiscent of Simpson's *Scheme of Education* he talks of the success of architectural education in France and the United States, but made his personal admiration for the Beaux Arts more explicit than Simpson did. At its most rudimentary, Reilly's idea was not to encourage genius, but to make 'mediocrity as respectable and sober in its architecture as it generally manages to be elsewhere'.[10]

Beaux Arts educational practice, derived substantially I think from the sources I have already outlined, provided him with a methodology of design that produced students skilled in executing large-scale projects, at the expense of individuality of approach. This was not a disadvantage in Reilly's opinion, as the level of technical expertise acquired by students taught in this way[11] was far greater than that achieved through office based training. This was accepted by Reilly as sufficient compensation for any perceived loss of originality.

Reilly praised the Board's proposals for a four year course: two years in a recognised school of architecture, and two as an articled pupil, as a 'very excellent compromise',[12] and used the opportunity to lay out a set of general principles for the development of schools of architecture in universities, using the American system as a model. He considered the universities the most suitable setting for schools of architecture because of the ready accessibility of the technical and scientific information necessary for contemporary architectural practice. There are a number of possible reasons why he should adopt this technologically orientated stance.

In suggesting the universities as the base for architectural education Reilly would have strengthened his own personal position, and because of the decade of development at Liverpool within the university system, he would have a secure base from which to develop further. Secondly, by identifying 'technology' as a leading factor for contemporary architectural practice he was reaffirming his own skills as a graduate engineer, and giving them wider validation. He would also, now that the new building technologies were firmly ensconced in practice, be perceived as being in the vanguard of commercial, as opposed to domestic architecture, and thus Arts and Crafts practice. This would have enabled him to distance himself immediately from any legacy of discredited craft practices that might still be lingering in the air from the previous Liverpudlian initiative.[13]

However, Reilly's conceptual links with the school that Simpson created are stronger than might be imagined. The awareness of new technology and American architectural practice in the city preceded Reilly, and Reilly's advocacy of a Liberal Arts content for an architectural degree[14] was not so very far from the structure of the then existing Liverpool University degree. For this qualification students pursued a three year course, the first year of which was that of a normal arts degree before they specialised. It is interesting that as a model, Reilly offered not the school where he was Professor, but the school at Harvard University.[15]

Another idea that was close to Reilly's heart,[16] but not his exclusive preserve as we have already seen, was the Beaux Arts conception of architecture as the focus for the union of the fine arts. In his article, developing the idea of the necessity of a liberal arts content for the student architect, Reilly argued for the study of the 'sister arts' sculpture and painting alongside that of architecture. This he explained 'must be if the sympathetic relationship between them and architecture is to be maintained and strengthened'.[17]

It is clear from an examination of Reilly's text that his proposals for architectural education were closely linked with the practice of the Liverpool School in the decade previously. Architecture was to be a subject biased towards the arts rather than the sciences. To talk of 'strengthening and maintaining' links between the fine arts and architecture rather than *developing* them, is a tacit acknowledgement by Reilly that architectural practice was developing successfully in that direction already. This is echoed in his own architectural tastes of that time – he was for example, an admirer of Lancaster and Rickards' work.

Reilly's final remarks about the constructive nature of the atelier system can similarly be seen as close to those espoused by the School in earlier years. The system was to be prized because the teacher would also be a practising architect, which, according to Reilly's argument, would obviate pedantry and doctrinaire views. The value of working with a practitioner was the same as it had always been, students would be able to study, 'under his guidance, the building he is erecting, these will become for them, in every stage of their construction, a series of practical experiments carried out under the most advantageous circumstances and the best laboratory in which an architectural student can work.'[18] Apart from the language, which uses the terminology of technology rather than of art, this passage has close links with the pronouncements in Simpson's *Scheme of Education*. This of course does not mean that Reilly plagiarised Simpson's scheme, but rather that both owed a substantial debt to the practices of the Ecole des Beaux Arts. Reilly's skill at the Liverpool School lay in his amplification and elaboration of these practices, rather than their instigation. By 1908, when *The Builder* devoted an enthusiastic article to the School,[19] these practices had been refined and put into operation with some success. *The Builder* talked of 'various changes' in the curriculum. Because of the lack of information as to what constituted the courses in the days of the School of Architecture and Applied Art it is impossible to say how substantial the curriculum changes in the courses were. However it is possible to examine the wide-ranging effects of the organisational changes made in 1906.

The Certificate course had its daytime hours increased, and a new Diploma that built on the Certificate course was introduced. Budden remarks in *The Book of the Liverpool School of Architecture* that the 'basis of this course was that adopted in 1894'.[20] The ordinances for the School's Bachelor of Arts with Honours in Architecture, and the Master of Arts had been approved in 1903. Reilly instigated a Bachelor of Architecture, which involved a further two years' office practice in addition to the existing BA Honours degree (in line with the Board of Architectural Education's proposals). The article in *The Builder* was written in October 1908, so information about the numbers of students affected by Reilly's innovations at the date of the article's publication finishes with those completing their studies at the end of the academic year 1907.[21] All those graduating in 1905 and 1906 had enrolled in the days of Simpson, as had those who gained the Certificate. In 1907 there were no Bachelor degrees awarded, but the department's first Master's degree was, as were seven Certificates. The first Diploma was awarded in 1908,[22] the next was not awarded until 1911. The first Degree of Bachelor of Architecture was not awarded until 1915.

What all this indicates is that Reilly's great success at the School was not due to any substantial structural innovations in the architectural education system, nor was it due to any radical remodelling of existing course content. This point can be further reinforced by the following point from *The Builder*'s 'Architectural Education at the University of Liverpool'; 'Professor Reilly, regarding design as the primary essential of architecture, teaches history and building construction merely as a means to that end'.[23] This of course was the way that Simpson envisaged making the teaching of history and construction relevant to architectural study,[24] and it is hard to imagine anyone emerging from an Arts and Crafts tradition approaching this area of study in any other way. This methodology, with its origins in past practice, was not the means by which Reilly transformed architectural education in the UK. Reilly's

success was achieved through an understanding of the cultural importance of stylistic coherence and its power as a unifying cultural principle.

The Builder was close to making this point when it referred to Reilly
teaching his students the Classic orders as a 'vocabulary of architecture'.
In order to fully understand the potency of this simple act, it is necessary
to put it into its historical perspective. The immediate tradition that
Simpson was working in, was a tradition of the vernacular. To design in
the vernacular, because of its regional vagaries and its range of building
materials, the process had to be a fluid, non-dogmatic one. The contradiction that was becoming increasingly obvious in the School under
Simpson's directorship – the tensions between a new trans-cultural
design principle in architecture, ill at ease with an applied arts tradition
rooted in the past – was essentially resolved when the two sections
were parted in 1904. Whilst this can be interpreted as a collapse of the
Arts and Crafts experiment, it can also be read as a timely move away
from design concepts that had ceased to signal their ideological concerns
in a lucid and eloquent way. Reilly's skill was to imbue the Beaux Arts
style with the sort of ideological values that the vernacular had previously held, those of the anonymous, collaborative, collective and
cooperative.[25] This is substantially demonstrated in the following extract
from *The Builder*'s article:

> In these [design] exercises [26] students are not allowed to in-
> dulge too far their undisciplined fancies but must adhere
> closely to specified conditions, and so in the one case the Order
> to be used is always stated, and in the other the style, which
> is usually Georgian, early or late, and the materials. Thus when
> all try to solve the same problem in the same manner, the
> students learn more from each other and attain a higher
> standard of design than they would if their efforts were
> diffused through a large variety of channels of expression.[27]

Reilly gave what could have been a purely prescriptive exercise a
relevance, by relating it directly to the environment in which the students found themselves, that of the city. The study of the orders was
not new. Reilly pointed out in his autobiography that the study of the
orders was insisted on by the RIBA for its examinations, but what *was*
new was his ability to give this lifeless form a meaning. By taking the
study of the orders away from the realm of abstract knowledge, and
by having students make measured drawings of those buildings in the
city, Reilly was able to bring these forms back into currency with a
newly acquired symbolic meaning. It is ironic that *The Builder* concluded
its article with the assertion that the criticisms of the School, that it was
overly influenced by the Ecole des Beaux Arts were 'more apparent

than real'.[28] As part of his process of 'propaganda' for the school, Reilly, in his role as consulting editor of *The Builder's Journal*, was publishing illustrations of 'developed classical architecture',[29] and also a selection of the measured drawings made by students at Liverpool, which were published as a separate annual known as the *Liverpool Sketch Book*.[30] As early as February 1907,[31] Reilly had written to the secretary of the Ecole des Beaux Arts in Paris, sending a volume of measured drawings from the Liverpool School and requesting an exchange of publications. There are no records of any further attempts at communication, and Reilly makes no mention of the incident in his autobiography, so it can be assumed the attempt to establish links was stillborn. What this letter shows is Reilly's recognition of the importance of the Ecole and the benefits that it would bring, and his ceaseless activity in spreading the word as to the studies at Liverpool, and their success.

It is clear that the transition from an Arts and Crafts to a Beaux Arts design sensibility was not as clear-cut as has been previously thought, but issues of methodology, and how and what designed objects should signify, link the two approaches. Other areas reveal these links; the City Beautiful movement, which in its earliest manifestations contained elements of both the Arts and Crafts, and also the new planning ideas of the Beaux Arts. The involvement of William Lever in the mainstream of Liverpudlian architectural life and his move from an 'Arts and Crafts' style for Port Sunlight village to one that exploited the possibilities inherent in the new Beaux Arts styling illustrates this.

Because it was Lever who *funded* the UK's first Department of Civic Design at Liverpool University in 1909, and because of his use of its principles in the development of Port Sunlight village from 1910, Lever has been credited with a considerable influence in the *founding* of the Department of Civic Design.[32] Important though he was in facilitating its inception, the department's origins within the city's culture were wider. Reilly's view of the creation of the Department of Civic Design concentrates upon his own central role, of course. According to his autobiography, Reilly went to the University Club and wrote a letter to Lever after pondering that during John Burn's presentation of the 1909 Town Planning Act in the House of Commons, there had been no mention of architecture at all. In his letter he suggested 'an endowment for a Chair, for a Lectureship and for a Journal in the subject. By return of post I had an encouraging letter asking me to come and see him ... The deed was done in a few days.'[33] The reality of course was similar to events surrounding the Liverpool School of Architecture and Applied Art where contemporary concerns found a focus. The Department of Civic Design can be seen as the first formalisation of ideas that had been current nationally for a number of years, and which had become increasingly important within the city.

Municipal concerns for the planning and development of urban areas had developed into responsibilities as the infrastructure necessary for the successful running of towns and cities became increasingly complex.[34] This process in Liverpool was well advanced. John Foster, the City Surveyor, had formally planned the development of Abercromby and Faulkner Square at the beginning of the nineteenth century and the first municipal attempts at solving the city's housing problems had begun in 1869.

Professional Associations and their respective conferences were also important in summarising and directing cultural agendas. Concurrent with the City Beautiful conference in Liverpool in 1907, was the less glamorous Association of Municipal and County Engineers Annual Meeting in Liverpool, in which the Liverpool City's policy of road widening and planned development of the suburbs was enthusiastically approved.[35]

In 1898 Ebenezer Howard's *Tomorrow: A Peaceful Path to Real Reform* was published, emerging from the Utopian Socialist milieu of the Arts and Crafts movement.[36] Within the year the planning ideas contained in the book began to gain a wider currency with the establishment of the Garden City Association. By the time of the first national conference of the Garden City Association in Bourneville in 1901, the idea of Garden Cities had been popularised by its national chairman, Ralph Neville, a Liberal Party luminary who had introduced Howard to Lever.[37] The year 1902 saw the republication of Howard's book under the new title *Garden Cities of Tomorrow*.[38] By 1904 work on the development of Letchworth had commenced. Whilst the Garden City movement was developing, the Co-operative movement had taken its first steps towards its entry into the provision of housing with the setting up of Tenant Co-operators Ltd in 1888. This initiative came to fruition with the drawing of this, and other similar societies, under the umbrella organisation of the Co-Partnership Tenants Housing Council in 1905.[39]

Both the organisations were represented at the City Beautiful Conference in Liverpool in 1907, the origin of which lay in the formation of the Liverpudlian 'City Beautiful Society'. In 1906 the Liverpool Architectural Society initiated a city-wide debate on planning. An article in The *Liverpool Daily Post* reported the call for the rational organisation of the city's architectural and social future.[40] A week later these issues were picked up nationally by the *Tribune*, which in the course of its report quoted from The *Liverpool Daily Post*; 'In a modern City like Liverpool practically no historic associations exist, and we have therefore to depend wholly on our aesthetic resources.'[41]

In identifying this issue amongst many in the debate about planning, it is evident that to a large extent, though obviously not exclusively, the debate in Liverpool was about *appearance* – the appearance of architecture, and the way that it affected the appearance of the city as a whole. The way that the city looked determined the way that it would be understood by both its inhabitants and visitors. The way that the city looked was significant, because it was seen as a recent expression of collective and communal experience. With a limited and stylistically focused architectural heritage to build on, with a building programme of formidable size, and with a reputation as 'a dull, ugly and commercial city',[42] there was a perceived need for an expression of the city in newly created, self-determined form.

In March 1906 there was a response to the Liverpool Architectural Society's initiative from the Liverpool Academy of Arts in a lecture, 'The City Beautiful'. There is no record of what was said although it is known that members of the ubiquitous Liverpool Architectural Society were present. It is safe to assume that the role of architecture as a form of civic aesthetic instruction was probably mentioned. It is probably also safe to assume that the use of the American phrase 'The City Beautiful' would not be without its particular resonances for a Liverpudlian audience. The phrase had become formalised in American debate with its repeated use in the New York journal *Municipal Affairs* in December 1899,[43] although its usage had been current for a number of years before that. Its first recorded use in Liverpool was in 1895 in the University journal *Sphinx*.[44]

The man who had popularised the idea of the City Beautiful in the English speaking world was an American, Charles Mulford Robinson. Whilst there is no specific reference to Robinson in contemporary literature in Liverpool, his books were part of the Department of Civic Design's early library. Perhaps his most influential book was *The Improvement of Towns and Cities*,[45] published in 1901. It is a rambling, enumerative text that examines the processes Robinson thought necessary for the practical and aesthetic enrichment of urban life, drawing from examples of tree planting to statue placing in the United States and Europe. There was no coherent ideological position to the book, and no defined stance as to architectural or planning style. His position has in the past been described as confused.[46] It is perhaps fairer to say that what is now seen as a clear-cut division between Arts and Crafts domesticity and other more urbane design approaches, was not at the time understood as such, but seen as part of the same concern. The City Beautiful movement was seen as a continuation of the ideas of the Arts and Crafts movement. In this way, the demands for the rationalisation of a city's organisation were enough to enable Robinson to unify the new chain system of American parks, the Boston Public Library, William Morris and Walter Crane into a programme for future change.

In November 1906, the *Liverpool Daily Post*[47] reported the proposed formation of a society for the promulgation of the aims of the 'City Beautiful' movement. Reilly was voted on to the executive, as was Willink. By the time that this initiative had been reported nationally,[48] the society was formally known as the 'City Beautiful Society'. Whilst the genesis of the City Beautiful Conference in Liverpool is not known, it makes sense that it was the direct consequence of the efforts of the City Beautiful Society in alliance with interested partners in the municipal authorities, who offered the Town Hall for the purpose. Within two years the City Beautiful Society had amalgamated with the Trees Preservation and Open Spaces Association and the local Kyrle Society,[49] into an organisation called the Liverpool City Guild.[50] By this time, it had done its job in sufficiently motivating the local intelligentsia to back what was substantially Reilly's personal City Beautiful Conference.

The City Beautiful Conference took place on 27 June 1907. (Reilly had written to the editors of *The Architectural Review*, *The Building News* and *The Builder*, promising them *all* exclusive use of pre-conference material, at the beginning of May).[51] At this time the agenda was proposed in three parts; 'The Planning of Cities', 'The Beautifying of Cities' and 'Garden Cities'. In the event the agenda had only two parts, 'Town and Suburban Planning' and 'Garden Cities'. In the event only Reilly's paper 'Urban and Suburban Planning' was reported in full.[52] Other contributions have been lost, but the fact that such prominent members of the organisations agitating for planning change were present, indicates that the debating position of the organisations were presented at the highest level. Nationally, the only mention of the conference was the footnote to Reilly's paper published in *The Builder*, however the conference was referred to significantly by H. V. Lanchester in his article 'Park Systems for Great Cities', a year later.[53] This article was important in establishing the innovative role of the Liverpool conference in bringing together those interested in issues of urban planning. Lanchester made several references to the conference in the introduction to his article where he used both Horsfall's contribution on German town planning, and most particularly that of Sybella Gurney's, in establishing a paradigmatic model of radial parkways for urban development.[54]

Reilly's contribution is interesting in that he combined the wider national and international issues of city planning and made it pertinent to Liverpool (at the same time increasing the city's – and his own – importance through the nature of his comparisons). Essentially, Reilly demanded the rational planning of cities modelled on the paradigm of Wren, the Woods (again creating an historical importance for Liverpool) and nineteenth century Paris. He decried the breaking up of the uniformity of Georgian urban architecture in London and Liverpool,[55] particularly for the purposes of commercial development. His underlying assumption was that civic significance was of greater importance than commercial. Reilly demanded uniformity in the way that a city should present itself. For example, in acknowledging that the width and position of Castle Street gave it certain planning advantages, he thought that it would be greatly improved if 'the buildings on either side [were] of one height and one material, not to mention the more debatable point of one style'.[56] The lessons from the Chicago World's Fair had been well learned.

Reilly argued that city planning was 'asleep' in the UK, but active in French and American towns giving them a 'consciously regulated life'. This civic self-awareness led to both aesthetic and material prosperity, and Reilly saw Paris as the supreme example of this. We may well baulk at this shorthand interpretation of the wealth of an imperial centre, but just as the Middles Ages were a conceptual starting point for Ruskin's ideas, so too was Reilly's symbolic use of Paris. Reilly's main argument revolved around an idea of planning as an aesthetic activity, so it would be in partnership with planning as a solution to 'those problems of traffic and sewerage which have till now completely held the field'.[57]

Reilly used the Beaux Arts design principle of the ground plan as a device for planning the city. The site provided for urban development should contribute towards the development of 'balanced, symmetrical, dignified buildings'. This of course rejects the process of piecemeal, speculative commercial development. With his rejection of 'individualism' and the promotion of a coherent, consistent architectural practice, Reilly envisaged the planned city as a place where 'whole districts ... could be made parts of a harmonious composition'.[58]

If one thinks of the broad approach of Robinson to the issues of town planning, an openminded potpourri of drives, drains and dahlias, and compare it to the singleminded and localised demands of Reilly, one becomes aware of the genuinely innovative position of Reilly in transferring the aesthetic stance of the Liverpool School from architecture to town planning. Equally, the stylistic and visual emphasis of Reilly's position is profoundly evident compared to the dry dissection of German planning principles offered by Horsfall.[59] It is illuminating to compare Reilly's vision of the city with the programme proposed by the advocates of the Garden City. Although the views expressed by Rose and Neville at the conference in Liverpool have been lost, they

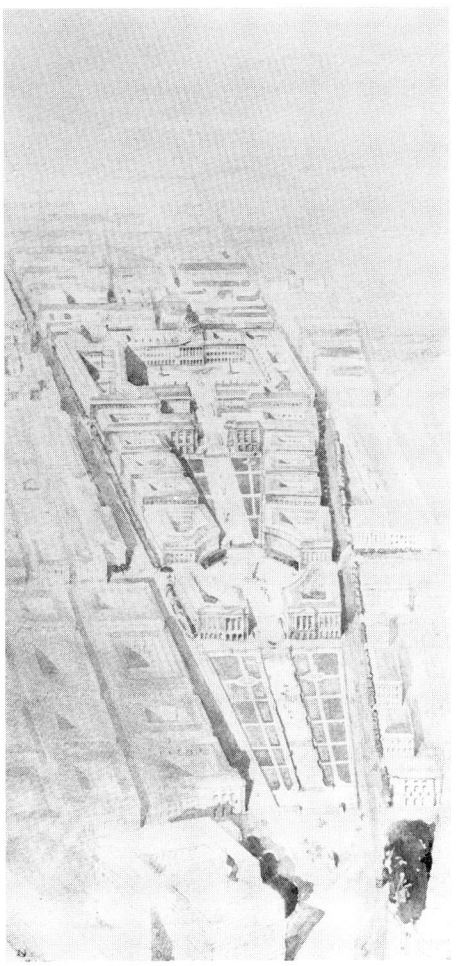

26 Beaux Arts visions of Brownlow Hill: Liverpool Reconstruction Scheme, perspective drawing of Newbold's design, entry for the Lever Prize 1912.

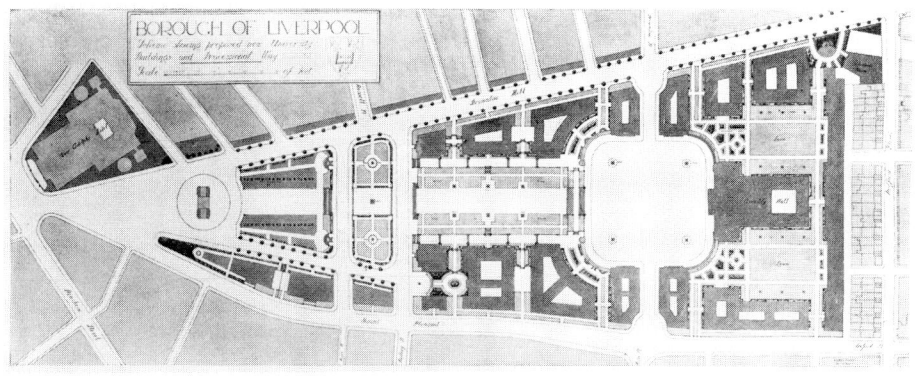

27 Redesign of Brownlow Hill, Liverpool: drawings by R. H. Mattocks.

cannot have differed greatly from those usually expressed by the Garden City Association at the time. In opposition Reilly expressed a vision of the city that was urbane and cosmopolitan. The advocates of the Garden City had argued for a number of years for the development of cities in which the urban and country environment intermixed, so that the city took on a pastoral quality akin to that achieved by Lever at Port Sunlight village.[60] In a proselytising paper given at Port Sunlight in 1904,[61] Ralph Neville acknowledged (though in retrospect it appears self evident) that the 'central idea of the the Garden City scheme is taken from Mr. Ebeneezer Howard's book *Garden Cities of Tomorrow*.'

It is clear that apart from the desire for rational planning which united the two approaches,[62] what separated them was the conception of the city as a domestic environment, in opposition to the city as an expression of a collective civic culture. This allows us to make a stylistic connection between the Garden City and the Arts and Crafts, and the City Beautiful with the Beaux Arts derived style of the new Liverpool School. Initially it might appear incongruous that two such seemingly different approaches to architectural style and planning principles should be sharing the same platform provided at the Liverpool City Beautiful Conference. However that division between the two – put crudely, between the Gothic romantics and the rational neo-classicists – was not as closely defined as it has become in retrospect, and was to become within the next few years. Stanley Adshead's article, 'An Introduction to Town Planning',[63] in which the new design paradigms were spelled out with such prescriptive rigour was still three years away. As it was, it was remarkably easy for leading figures in the Arts and Crafts to find themselves working alongside Reilly, and later Adshead, because of the shared ideology of the collective and the collaborative. Charles Ashbee for example, who had adopted a resolutely bucolic stance in transporting the Guild of Handicrafts to the Gloucestershire countryside, was able, after his tour of the USA in 1908–09, and his introductions to the City Beautiful Movement, to approach the design issues of the Liverpool School with equanimity, seeing in its planning terms a vision of a corporate future.[64]

The Liverpool City Beautiful Conference was an important transitional point on the way to the formation of the Department of Civic Design and had further importance in creating a precedent for many such conferences on Town Planning. It was part of the process that set the cultural agenda for the 1909 Housing and Town Planning Act.

Notes

1 Quoted in C. Reilly, *Scaffolding in the Sky*, Routledge, 1938, p. 121. In a review of Reilly's autobiography in the *Architect's Journal* 17 November 1938, in the course

of a brief biographical introduction it was said, 'by 1914 the work of the School had profoundly influenced the course of English Architecture'.

2 The School grew substantially under the guidance of Reilly and his assiduous promulgation of its practices. There can be no doubt that without his strength of personality there would have been no Liverpool School as we know it. However, when he refers to the School in his autobiography (*Scaffolding in the Sky*, p. 69) as; 'That ... little Department of Architecture, not yet called a School and certainly not worthy of such a name' he is belittling the considerable progress made at the Liverpool School of Architecture and Applied Art towards a formalised progressive architectural education. Reilly's ability to be creative with fact was well known amongst both his friends and those who were not. Reilly received considerable mail on the publication of his autobiography, one letter was from Maurice Webb, the son of Aston Webb, who wrote: 'You're indeed an honest crook', Liverpool University Archive, no. D207/7/1. Maud Budden, the wife of Lionel, wrote a skit for the Sandon Society, which reviewed the Liverpudlian life of Reilly. She sent him the script which contained the following line: 'TRUTH [played by a beautiful girl] coming forward. "Professor Reilly. I am TRUTH. And we have never met".' Liverpool University Archive, no. D207/7/1. Others were less tolerant. The *RIBA Journal*'s review of *Scaffolding in the Sky* said, 'One only wishes that his information was as reliable as are his descriptions interesting.' *RIBA Journal*, 5 December 1938.

3 This is unsurprising when one considers that amongst the members of the Board of Enquiry, besides Blomfield, were Mervyn McCartney and Ernest Newton, who along with Frederick Simpson had resigned from the RIBA in 1891 in the course of the 'Profession or an Art' debate.

4 A key passage in Blomfield's presentation is the following which gives a clear indication as to the rationale behind the exercise in the eyes of one of its principal protagonists: 'The object of the Board throughout has been to avail itself of all that is sound in existing methods, and to develop and co-ordinate existing systems on such lines as will get the best out of them for the practical training of architectural students.' *RIBA Journal*, vol. XII, 1905, p. 245.

5 Reilly, *Scaffolding in the Sky*, Routledge, 1938, pp. 115–16.

6 *RIBA Journal*, vol. XII, 1905, p. 248.

7 C. Reilly, 'The Training of Architects' in *University Review*, July 1905 (published in the USA), and also published in pamphlet form by Sherratt and Hughes, London, 1905.

8 Reilly was well aware of the problems that a too tight a system of national structures might have caused: 'The danger I saw was the establishment of a sort of South Kensington System, with the great architects in London dictating what the schools everywhere should do and what they should not do, but without that experience as actual teachers which the similar leading architects in France, with their ateliers allied to the Ecole des Beaux Arts, always possessed.' Reilly, *Scaffolding in the Sky*, p. 116.

9 'To construct with the beauty born of directness, simplicity, and suitability, is the first step to fine architecture. It is the strict observance of this vital relation of construction to actual needs and conditions which can alone prevent copyism and the revival of forms, which have long lost their meaning.' Reilly, *The Training of Architects*, pp. 244–45.

10 Ibid., p. 243.

11 And presumably correctly so, as later successful practice was to demonstrate.

12 Reilly, *The Training of Architects*, p. 247.

13 It cannot have escaped Reilly's notice that the year of his arrival saw the finish of

construction of the Royal Insurance Building in Liverpool, using steel-frame technology to create a vast open ground floor office space, with further buildings in the city in the process of construction using this method. This was not his first introduction to steel-frame construction, whilst working for Belcher in the late 1890s, he was aware of Belcher's partner Joass's 'queer marble casings hung on their tall steel frames' (*Scaffolding in the Sky*, p. 49.) Belcher's office had been responsible for the Royal Insurance building in Piccadilly. This was before the 'official' first use of steel-frame technology in the UK by Mewes and Davies for the Ritz Hotel in 1903–05. I have already discussed the awareness within the city of this new technology from the USA.

14 Reilly, *The Training of Architects*, p. 254.

15 Where students architects were required to graduate with a BA first.

16 His account of how he tried to found a Faculty of Fine Arts can be found in *Scaffolding in the Sky*, pp. 124–25.

17 Reilly, *The Training of Architects*, p. 253.

18 Ibid., p. 248.

19 'Architectural Education at the University of Liverpool', *The Builder*, 3 October 1908, pp. 341–43.

20 Budden (ed.), *The Book of The Liverpool School of Architecture*, Liverpool: Liverpool University Press, 1932, p. 35.

21 The following figures are abstracted from Budden, *The Book of the Liverpool School of Architecture*, p. 59:

	B.A. Hons	B.A.	M.A.	Cert.
1905	1	2	0	6
1906	2	0	0	4
1907	0	0	1	7

22 By a previous holder of the Certificate who enrolled at the start of the academic year 1904.

23 'Architectural Education at the University of Liverpool', *The Builder*, 3 October 1908, p. 341.

24 F. Simpson, *The Scheme of Architectural Education Started at University College, Liverpool*, Liverpool: Marples and Co., 1895. See p. 17.

25 I am not suggesting here that Reilly was solely responsible for the new readings of neo-classical form. The civic function of the neo-classical had become increasingly evident since the late nineteenth century, and many commercial buildings had been constructed in a florid baroque style during the same period. However I think that it is reasonable to argue that Reilly was among the first in reclaiming the neo-classical as a *modern* style, and articulating the idea that it had an ideological value of contemporary relevance. Writing in 1924, and aware of the stylistic implications of the emerging modern style, Reilly had developed his arguments for significant style more clearly. In disparaging the newly completed Selfridges building his main criticism was the inappropriateness of the elaborate neo-classical facade for the merchandising of 'soft goods'; 'You would think from looking at its vast ornate colonnade that shop keeping was really the height of our ideals.' C. Reilly, *Some Architectural Problems of Today*, Liverpool: Liverpool University Press, 1924, p. 3.

  Further to Reilly's argument was the relative nature of urban architecture – what made the Selfridges building so inappropriate in his eyes was its comparison to the British Museum. The more important the cultural significance of a building the more architectural emphasis needed placing upon it. According to this argument, the architectural paradigm of the British Museum should not be infringed upon. This argument was directly related to that of the suitability of individual architectural expression in housing. 'In the eighteenth century most people lived in terraces of houses, in which externally each individual house did not differ materially from its neighbours. This was a fine sign of urbanity, a tribute to the community ... Any excessive expression of individuality or of personal importance in a building was considered bad manners.' Ibid., p. 6.

Whilst the above was expressed in its most coherent form in the 1920s, the ideas were the same ones that Reilly was formalising in 1907. His views were sufficiently unusual to be reported soon after his appointment to the post in Liverpool. In a public lecture given in Liverpool he was reported by *Building News*, 12 May 1905 (Charles Reilly's cutting books, Liverpool University Archive no. S3214/15/16), as having argued for; 'The value of the Classic style, modified by English taste, in domestic as well as public architecture.'

Some indication of the innovative nature of Reilly's adoption of this stylistic stance, and its cultural significance can be gleaned from a brief examination of Geoffrey Scott's *Architecture of Humanism*. In his foreword to the edition published in 1980 by The Architectural Press, David Watkin quotes Clough William Ellis in support of his view that Scott provided an intellectual justification for classicism not otherwise provided in English architectural theory. He says; '*The Architecture of Humanism* was, of course published at a singularly unpropitious moment in the summer of 1914, and but for the war would undoubtedly have been even more of a bible to architects anxious to bring about a classical renaissance in English architecture similar to that which had swept America after the World's Fair at Chicago in 1893.' (p. xxiii.)

It is outside of the scope of this particular chapter to argue the first part of Watkin's assertion, but it should be clear from points already made about the relationship between Liverpool and the American experiments with the Beaux Arts style that it is possible to assert that any evidence of a 'classical renaissance' in the UK – possible, probable or real – could in considerable part have its roots traced back to the 1890s in Liverpool, where such ideas had been well rehearsed before they were popularised by Reilly.

For the purposes of my argument the relevance of Scott's work lies in his reinforcement of the new set of cultural values that were attached to the new neo-classical building style. In examining the history of architectural styles and in an attempt to quantify their symbolic significance, Scott came to the conclusion that: 'For the material of architecture, no system of accepted meaning has been organised' (Ibid., p. 61). This point, that the general architectural values of mass and space were dependent as much upon learned responses as a material reality, meant that the Renaissance remodelling of the classical styles was to be valued because, 'It realised that for certain purposes in architecture, fact counted for everything, and that in certain others, appearance counted for everything.' It is this acknowledgement of the ideological nature of the new classical designs that legitimises the assumption that Reilly was able to impose a set of cultural values upon this style.

One final point about the innovative nature of Reilly's position with regard to a neo-classical style and its value as a progressive secular and collective one. Scott's book, which is considered as creating a stylistic paradigm, can also be seen as reflecting a commonly held attitude amongst certain architectural circles. In its title

The Architecture of Humanism, the ideological programme of Scott's book is laid bare; it was first published in 1914, and later in 1924. When the School of Architecture was based in what is now the Bluecoat Chambers, Reilly published a proposed scheme for a 'Church for Humanity' in Liverpool, a proposed institute for Humanist scholarship. The drawing was illustrated in the March 1911 issue of *Architectural Review*. All this is meant to demonstrate is that ideas which Scott is supposed to have initiated can in fact be seen reflected in the arena of architectural production in Liverpool concurrent with his analysis, if not before.

26 Students were expected to produce five substantial design schemes in two years. These were part of a system of continual assessment that went hand-in-hand with a loose examination system. In a letter to Reginald Blomfield (23 January 1906, Charles Reilly's letterbooks, Liverpool University Archive, no. D207/2/1), Reilly wrote; 'It must not be considered because the courses are divided by examinations, so called, that this (the School's course structure) is a purely examination system'.

27 'Architectural Education at the University of Liverpool', *The Builder*, 3 October 1908, p. 342.

28 On the grounds that 'the whole spirit of the designing is restrained and shows none of that desire to over decorate, which is the fault of so much French work', Ibid., p. 343.

29 Work by students from the Liverpool School was also extensively illustrated, for example; *The Builder's Journal*, 24 March 1909, 2 March 1910, 20 April 1910.

30 For a full account of this see Reilly, *Scaffolding in the Sky*, pp. 119–21.

31 Letter dated 27 February 1907, Charles Reilly's letterbooks, Liverpool University Archives, no. D207/2/2.

32 See particularly; M. Wright, *Lord Leverhulme's Unknown Venture: The Lever Chair and the Beginning of Town and Regional Planning, 1908–48*, Hutchinson Benham Ltd, 1982.

33 Reilly, *Scaffolding in the Sky*, pp. 125–26.

34 See A. Sutcliffe, *Towards the Planned City*, Basil Blackwell, 1981, pp. 48–87.

35 'Association of Municipal and County Engineers – Meeting in Liverpool', *The Builder*, 6 July 1907.

36 E. Howard, *To-Morrow: A Peaceful Path to Real Reform*, published by the author, 1898. (Charles Reilly's cutting books, Liverpool University Archive no. S3214/15/16).

37 Like Lever, Neville was an advocate of profit sharing as the main means for an evolutionary move towards social egalitarianism.

38 E. Howard, *Garden Cities of To-Morrow*, 1902 (reprinted, Faber & Faber, 1946).

39 See *Town Planning Review*, vol. 1:1, 1910, pp. 119–24.

40 *Liverpool Daily Post and Mercury*, 23 January 1906.

41 *Tribune*, 2 February 1906.

42 A. John, *Chiaroscuro*, Jonathan Cape, 1954. 'Liverpool, commonly considered a dull, ugly and commercial city, for me abounded in interest and surprise' (p. 39).

43 See Sutcliffe, *Towards the Planned City*, p. 103.

44 *The Sphinx*, vol. 2, 1894–95 p. 124 'beholding … the City Beautiful – the New Liverpool'.

45 C. H. Robinson, *The Improvement of Towns and Cities, or the Practical Basis of Civic Aesthetics*, Putnam, 1901. See also C. H. Robinson, *Modern Civic Art, or the City made Beautiful*, Putnam, 1903. The latter title does not appear to have been acquired by the Department of Civic Design's library.

46 See Sutcliffe, *Towards the Planned City*, 'Consistency of thought and clarity of expression were not his strongest points' (p. 104).

47 *Liverpool Daily Post and Mercury*, 16 November 1906. (Charles Reilly's cutting books, Liverpool University Archive no. S3214/15/16).

48 *Building News*, 30 November 1906. (Charles Reilly's cutting books).

49 The Kyrle Societies were philanthropic, encouraged people to keep window boxes, and fostered 'a knowledge and love of art by such means as may be available', Robinson, *The Improvement of Towns and Cities*, p. 196.

50 The Chairman of the Liverpool City Guild was the Marquis of Salisbury. It was on his land that Liverpool Co-partnership Tenants Ltd built Liverpool Garden Suburb.

51 18 May 1907, Charles Reilly's letterbooks, Liverpool University Archives, no. D207/2/2.

52 *The Builder*, 6 July 1907.

53 H. V. Lanchester, 'Park Systems for Great Cities', *The Builder*, 3 October 1908.

54 Ibid., Lanchester used Sybella Gurney's illustration for the development of Liverpool as a radially planned city using a parkway system, as the proposed model for a number of cities.

55 C. Reilly, Urban and Suburban Planning, *The Builder*, 6 July 1907, p. 11. 'It was possible less than ten years ago for Nash's fine architectural scheme in Regent Street to be broken up by two odd and ugly domes erected to advertise certain shops. It is still possible in Liverpool to introduce a yellow terra-cotta dressed building into the quiet dignity and repose of Rodney Street.' p. 11.

56 Reilly, 'Urban and Suburban Planning', p. 11.

57 Ibid., p. 12.

58 Ibid., p. 13.

59 See T. C. Horsfall, *The Improvement of the Dwellings and Surroundings of the People: The example of Germany*, Manchester: Manchester University Press, 1904.

60 See Sutcliffe, *Towards the Planned City*, p. 6.

61 R. Neville, 'The Economic Aspect of the Garden City Movement,' a paper read at Port Sunlight, 6 November 1905, in R. Neville, *Some Papers and Addresses on Social Questions*, Spottiswood, Ballantyne and Company, n.d.

62 Ibid., p. 57: 'Laissez-faire has proved a conspicuous and disastrous failure.' This bears obvious comparison with Reilly's remarks.

63 S. Adshead, 'An Introduction to Town Planning', *Town Planning Review*, vol. 1:1.

64 '[Ashbee] admired the monumental, axial approach of the Liverpool School, seeing in it the expression of a corporate spirit', A. Crawford, *C. R. Ashbee: Architect, Designer and Romantic Socialist*, New Haven, CT: Yale University Press, 1985, p. 157.

Chapter Seven

Town Planning Review: Design Ideology and Practice

Without their local cultural environment, William Lever and Charles Reilly would not have been able to contribute to the development of town planning as they did. Equally however, they were themselves an important component part of that culture, and without their energies the channelling of contemporary ideas about planning in the city into the Department of Civic Design would not have taken place. Reilly first met Lever in 1904 after his appointment as Head of the School of Architecture. Reilly wrote to Lever in April of that year,[1] and in his letter invited himself and his students to look at the church and one of the dwellings in Port Sunlight village. After some misunderstandings the meeting between the two men went ahead. 'It did not,' Reilly was to say some 30 years later, 'seem a propitious beginning'.[2] When Conway, formally Roscoe Professor, now Sir Martin, came to Port Sunlight to formally open Hulme Hall later that year, Reilly was invited to dinner by Lever and from this point on their mutually advantageous relationship began. Reilly provided Lever with proposals of a suitable dignity on which to spend his money, and thus enhance his reputation as an architectural patron,[3] and Lever provided the finance by which Reilly was able to extend his power base, both within the University and nationally.

In July 1907 Lever was the victor in a libel case he had instigated against the *Daily Mail*.[4] Encouraged by Reilly, Lever developed a 'patronly interest'[5] in the School of Architecture and proceeded to spend the awarded damages on the School of Architecture and the Department of Civic Design. His first act of benevolence in June 1908 was the purchase of the Blue Coat Hospital. Within a week of Reilly's suggestion to Lever that it would be a good site for the School, Lever purchased an option on the building and then offered it to Reilly (or more correctly the University) rent free. Obviously emboldened by this success Reilly then suggested the formation of a Department of Civic Design within the School of Architecture. The wider cultural background to this event has already been discussed, but it does not diminish the sense of astonishment at the alacrity at which Reilly's initiative was taken up by Lever.

In February 1909, the Faculty of Arts had been guaranteed the funding to be able to recommend that a Department of Civic Design, offering both day and evening classes, should be established. The role of the Professor was to conduct and direct research into the problems of the design and development of towns.[6] Thus, the UK had its first institution devoted to the discipline. As well as funding the Chair, Lever also paid for a research fellowship, and the publication of a quarterly journal, which was to be *Town Planning Review.* Stanley Adshead was appointed Associate Professor in May 1909,[7] and in June, Patrick Abercrombie was given editorship of *Town Planning Review* as Research Fellow in Civic Design.

It is not within the scope of this chapter to look at the career of Adshead, but certain aspects of it are pertinent. The creation of the Department of Civic Design was a further tool for Reilly to use to advance his ideas for the new architecture. Adshead had been an acquaintance of Reilly's for a number of years; he had first met him in 1899 whilst working in practice in London.[8] It was Adshead who drew the perspectives for Reilly's submission to the Liverpool Cathedral competition, and it is his drawing that makes him particularly important in this narrative. His early career was as a perspectivist for other architects, and from 1904 till his appointment to Liverpool he taught at King's College as a studio instructor. In 1907 he published an article[9] in which he argued for the adoption of an 'academic French' style of drawing, as opposed to the usual purely linear competition style that was current at the time. Good drawing, he argued, produced good architecture, and whilst he was Professor of Civic Design he spent a good deal of time in the studio of the School of Architecture teaching it.

Adshead's approach to architecture was a visual one; his articles in *Town Planning Review*, 'Furnishing the City', would demonstrate this even if his work on drawing did not. His approach to town planning was similar to Reilly's, where the emphasis was upon the aesthetic qualities of buildings and their arrangements, and the way that these had, and have, a cultural significance. Adshead shared Reilly's orientation towards the Beaux Arts at the expense of the Arts and Crafts legacy. Considering that he was Reilly's appointment it would be surprising if he had not.

Before looking more closely at the content of *Town Planning Review* and determining how the new ideas at the Liverpool School fitted in with the national debate, it is interesting to examine Adshead's statement of intent for the new department, 'An Introduction to Town Planning'.[10] It was the first article in the newly published *Town Planning Review*, and was a wonderful opportunity for the Liverpool School to address a national public in prestigious circumstances. For despite Abercrombie's first editorial where he said, 'it is hoped that the journal will, from its independent position, be able to deal fairly but critically with the various town planning schemes that arise in this country and abroad',[11] the emphasis upon those ideas that adhered to the principles of the Liverpool School became increasingly evident after a number of issues.

Adshead's 'Introduction to Town Planning' introduced the reader to a programmatic review of the principles of town planning, in a way that must have seemed quite startling to those who had been introduced to the discipline through Charles Robinson. The article[12] has a tone that is noticeably dismissive of the received values of the Arts and Crafts, and proposes a clearly defined model for the future development of urban sites. In making so clear a stand,[13] Adshead was echoing the polemic of the previous five years from Reilly as he attempted to mould the architectural profession's perception of architectural style. To anyone who had been following the stylistic debate that had emerged from Liverpool,[14] there could have been no confusion as to the stylistic position that the new Department of Civic Design would take. It is indicative of the final break with the transitional phase between the Arts and Crafts and the Beaux Arts.

Adshead's first premise was the fundamental and immutable success, in both practical and aesthetic terms, of the Roman town plan. This was because the format was flexible, unlike the 'monotony of America's chequered plan',[15] and therefore inexhaustible in its application.[16] The prearranged plan encompassed symmetrical sub-units arranged asymmetrically and axially connected, thus creating a comprehensible unity to the city, whilst ensuring within that whole unit a multiplicity of visual experiences. The Gothic was given little attention by Adshead, the origin of the tree-lined boulevard and its implications[17] were afforded as much attention as was the whole of the previously much loved Middle Ages. The paragraph devoted to the medieval says as much in its omissions as it does in its content: 'The mediaeval age with its feudalism and hereditary craftsmanship, gave us cities striking in the interest of their individual conception, and by reason of their narrow environment, harmonious in the style of their general expression, but usually lacking in systematic arrangement, the essential of a later classicism.' [18]

Explicit here is the idea of the necessity of order, of harmony, and the idea that before this can be achieved formally there must be a unified conceptual structure upon which to build. Implicit, is the notion that individualism leads to a destabilising and anarchic approach to form where both formal, and social, consensus in interpreting that form, is subsidiary to the process of creating and making. This means that form created in this way becomes more difficult to read. Its connoted meanings, if any, are no longer shared by groups, or are increasingly difficult to decipher. This was one of Reilly's concerns in his imposition of a single stylistic approach in his teaching. This is of course not an absolute truth, but an ideological judgement which appears in varying forms throughout Adshead's article. In talking of the late eighteenth century architecture in Liverpool, and in putting the city's regional development into a national context, Adshead wrote that; 'the interest of the movement lies, not only in the administration which brought it about, but also in the education of the architects responsible for its effects'.[19]

Here it is possible to see an endorsement of a system within which formal rules (in this case consisting of interchangeable but essentially unchanging components) are administered to create a universally applicable and understandable style. This view is further reinforced by Adshead's reference to the 'disturbing influence of the great Gothic revival'. The elements of the picturesque, of revivalism and historicism, all of them seen as negative aspects by Adshead (and Reilly), can also be seen as transitory and correctable aberrations. What is problematic about them is the Gothic's perceived underlying ideology of 'individual conception' and its lack of 'systematic arrangement'.

Adshead dealt briefly with contemporary influences, those of German and American municipal construction. Given the cultural agenda established, the United States is particularly seen as a cultural force to emulate. In mentioning the plans for civic development for Washington, Chicago and St Louis, Adshead's approach was an endorsement for an architectural style that sets out deliberately to convey a grandiloquent view of urban life; 'Approaching their civic centres around which are to be ranged their judicial and official groups [of buildings], are avenues, tree lined and flanked with public and other important buildings on well arranged sites. Their railway approaches and waterfronts are on a scale of breadth and magnificence previously unknown.' [20] This view concentrates upon the city as a municipal creation, where public

buildings constitute the body of the city. It is from this point on, where
assumptions about the stylistic appearance of cities start to include
assumptions about the role of the city, that the limits of the Liverpool
School's ideological stance start to emerge. This can be clearly understood if we look at the last two sections of Adshead's article, 'The
Sociological Aspect' and 'The Influence of the City on City Life'. In
these sections the assumptions of the previous two, in which a Beaux
Arts style had been defined historically, were placed in an ideological
framework. Thus, the 'moral force and intellectual vigour'[21] of the
citizen is ensured by the rational organisation of the city into zones;
business, residential and recreational. In 'progressive' cities like Washington, Düsseldorf and Vienna, Adshead remarks, 'an architectural
grouping of buildings with reference to their relative uses is very
conspicuous'. No mention is made of industrialised zones, and the
nature of an industrialised, capitalist society is largely ignored. The
large industrial cities, according to the new concerns, were in need of
demolition, 'Haussmanising', and re-erecting. This was to be the task
of municipal authorities in partnership with town planners. Compared
to this view of the future development of cities, the proposals of the
Garden City movement look rigorously pragmatic.

It cannot be argued that Adshead was a visionary of a post-industrial
society, rather that the limits of his design ideology could only take
him so far. Adshead's views were conditioned by the circumstances
that he found himself in, where industry was apparently incidental to
the production of wealth. He had lived in London and was now living
in Liverpool, duplicating Reilly's experience. Both cities' wealth was
the result of trading goods rather than their manufacture. Outside of
London, Liverpool had the largest number of banks and merchant house
concerns in the UK, and its working population was engaged primarily
in casual labour and the service industries. To them the city was to be
an intellectual and commercial centre, a shop rather than a factory, a
museum rather than a workshop. This attitude becomes increasingly
clear as Adshead talks about the city's role. He quotes Wilde's aphorism,
'Art holds a mirror to nature', and develops it to suggest that 'the city
is the model to which the country needs to conform ... Convincing is
its merit when the persistent formality of its streets is conducive to a
sense of respect, and arouses in the heart of the citizen that pride of
citizenship alone engendered by civic art.'[22]

The city had another symbolic role and that was to express modernity
(after all, the conception of modernity was not the exclusive property
of the European avant-garde). Adshead talked admiringly of the 'wonderful machinery' that enabled the rapid construction, erection and
completion of buildings. He enthused about the 'splendid trains, smooth

running trams and rapid cars'. His vision of the city was one that was forward-looking and dynamic, but was a little vague as to the precise social and economic means by which progress was to be made. The inherent contradiction in the idea of a dynamic and growing city constrained by a centralised prearranged plan was never fully dealt with. The nearest Adshead came to dealing with this was his suggestion that a modern and progressive society needed the controlling influence of the 'Greek style', (presumably because of the city's dynamism and thus potential instability). The city was in effect separated from the domestic life of its inhabitants who were allowed to 'partake' of suburbs with the character of old towns with their 'mullioned windows and rough hewn beams'. Unlike the non-hierarchal city of the Arts and Crafts movement, with Adshead the city takes on a powerful role as an abstract device where the expressive power of style takes precedence: 'In the city proper where throbs the pulse of life, new conditions must prevail … We must have a character about the buildings of our streets which suggest strength held in reserve, and abundance of force subtly controlled.'[23] The buildings of the planned city were to act as a background to events, to complement the activities of city life. To this end Adshead proposed that buildings should be simple and strongly composed, with hard surfaces and delicate decoration. The architecture of Paris was used once again as an aspirational model. The colour of cities also became a significant ideological pointer in Adshead's article. All great cities, he argued, were white or grey, such as Athens or New York. For obvious reasons he emphasised the grey city, which he saw as suggestive of endurance, romance and grandeur. 'Grey cities', he felt 'are very fitting for these humid and northern climes'. Adshead went further and compared Morris's vision of the city,[24] and that of the Garden City movement's, with the new vision of the city: 'That [city] which is a golden red harmonising with the rich green verdure of the surrounding land, will ever suggest ease of existence, simplicity, and primitive life. Such a harmony can never suggest solidity of existence as does grey, nor vivacity as does white or cream.'[25]

In developing the ideas of the Liverpool School, in giving the stylistic demands of Reilly their full expression and in taking the Beaux Arts classicism out from the localised context of individual buildings in Liverpool and putting them into an international, metropolitan context, Adshead exposed the limit of the efficacy of the Liverpool School approach. The designer (of buildings, furniture or cities), was seen as operating from a closely defined stylistic base, in which the use of forms and their significance was clearly articulated within its own terms. This meant that every artefact had an immediately understood cultural context. It is the complete opposite of the Arts and Crafts approach of organising design in an organic and piecemeal way. The consequence of the legacy of the Arts and Crafts approach, seen by Reilly and Adshead as offering only incoherent individualism, was that it was unable to offer a consistent form of cultural signification. Whilst this point can be accepted within the logic of Adshead's and Reilly's arguments, it also helps to erode the potency of their own argument. If the modern world of 1909 was one of dynamism, of everchanging technology, then the imposition of a fixed style upon its products points to the inability of that style to encompass the notion of change. As already discussed, part of Adshead's reasoning was that of controlling, or modifying the nature of technology in symbolic terms. There is a profound contradiction in encouraging and encompassing change only to demand that it then becomes static. In this way long-term architectural development is sacrificed in order to achieve short-term architectural legibility. Alternatively, it could be argued, (and may well have, had Reilly and Adshead been confronted with these questions), that once a formal design language has been established, nurtured within the context of instructional mechanisms and institutions, its evolution as a widely acceptable language would mean that it could invent new forms from within itself to encompass technological innovation.[26] It is in this sense where a design language is so ubiquitous as to be invisible, and in the concern for rationalised, collective design action, that there are still links between the Liverpool School and the Arts and Crafts. It is this seemingly strange pairing, and its subsequent divorce that I wish to examine next.

It is possible to read the early editions of *Town Planning Review* as an ideological text. By this I mean that it is possible to look at the issues discussed within its pages as a reflection of a set of values pertinent to those who ran the journal. If it is acknowledged that *Town Planning Review* was as much a mouthpiece for the Liverpool School as it was an objective journal examining the nature of town planning, then through an analysis of its pages it should be possible to determine the relationship between the Liverpool School and the rest of the architectural and planning community.

   During the first five years of *Town Planning Review* it was edited by Patrick Abercrombie. When Adshead accepted Frederick Simpson's invitation to set up a department of Civic Design in the University of London in 1914, Abercrombie was made the Professor at Liverpool. During his editorship of the journal in its first five years, a distinct pattern of articles and material emerges, which in effect becomes a dialogue between the Garden City movement and the more formal proposals of the Liverpool School.

The city of Liverpool took up a good deal of space in the first four editions of the journal where the fabric of the city was subjected to a number of analyses and hypothetical schemes.[27] This can in part be explained by a lack of material on the subject in the early days of the discipline,[28] and also that the city provided ready raw material needed for the working out of plans and schemes. From the beginning of his headship of the Liverpool School, Reilly had established that architecture, like charity, began at home. This concern with local issues gives the journal a sense of place, and acts as an illustration of the possibilities inherent in the new town planning, but is not in itself the clearest indication of the direction of the debate.

The similarities of the ideological base of the Liverpool School and of the Garden City movement have already been discussed; how they shared a demand for the rational organisation of the city in order to facilitate the health and convenience of its inhabitants. They shared also the ideological premise of the importance of collective and collaborative action that was their common heritage from the Arts and Crafts movement. It was because of this, that it was possible for Reilly and Adshead to be on the same advisory panel as Walter Crane and Charles Ashbee when *Architectural Review* began to publish its *Town Planning and Housing Supplement* in 1910,[29] although it must not be thought that there was no opposition to the institutionalisation of the ideas of the Liverpool School. There was some, though it was neither consistent nor organised. In an article, 'The Recovery of Art and Craft'[30] in *New Age*, Huntly Carter viewed a substantial part of *Town Planning Review*'s content with suspicion. In his eyes it exemplified 'Town planning not hobnobbing with the citizen and calling upon his soul for guidance, encouragement and inspiration. On the contrary, it may be seen entering parliament on the arm of a distinguished Cabinet Minister'. Carter went on to condemn the revival of the classical style as the revival of a style of oppression. From the other side of the ideological spectrum, criticism centred around the cosmopolitanism of the Liverpool School style. In an extensive article in the national newspaper the *Morning Post*[31] the Liverpool School was described in terms of a cosmopolitan intrusion into the stable traditions of British design:

> Modern Architecture (of which the Liverpool School is held to be important) has in reality no more foundation, no more stability, than so much stage scenery. That it seems to me is an encouraging thought. Passively acquiesced in, allowed to be the fashion, apparently secure, it is nevertheless not in a position to resist for a single moment the challenge of a style sanctioned by the national instinct.[32]

For a month this debate entered into the fringes of the architectural press before it fizzled out. *The Builder* [33] took up the side of the Liverpool School, whilst *The British Architect* took up a stance for moderation, fudging the issue: 'we must be cosmopolitan in many ways, no doubt, but the cosmopolitan art which effaces nationality and individuality, which loses the unpersonal (sic) in the general, will bring about a culture at the cost of much that makes architecture worth the while'.[34] Such culturally undeveloped criticism of the stylistic stance of the Liverpool School is a good indication of the way that Reilly and Adshead were able to impose their views through the pages of *Town Planning Review*. The ideas of the Liverpool School were coherent and unified against an intellectual opposition which lacked those qualities.

Initially extensive coverage was given in *Town Planning Review* to Garden Suburb schemes. In his article 'A Comparative Review of Examples of Modern Town Planning and Garden City Schemes in England',[35] Abercrombie established the planning paradigm for such schemes in identifying their sources as 'The twin garden villages of Port Sunlight and Bourneville, Mr. Howard's book, and the Tenant Co-operators Ltd. These four form the foundation of the movement'. From this cultural point on, a number of articles dealt with the development of such schemes.[36] Within the year the journal had felt it had largely done its duty towards the Garden City movement when in an editorial it made clear that the journal had 'put before our readers a retrospective view of the Garden City and Suburban schemes in England'.[37]

Other articles and forays into the world of applied planning in England were to continue during the next couple of years but with less emphasis upon full articles and more upon endnotes. This initial examination of the Garden City movement was balanced out by numerous reviews of planning schemes in the USA. These in effect amounted to theoretical proposals from the Liverpool School for cities in the UK. Reilly's article 'Town Planning Schemes in America' [38] is a good example of this (by this time Reilly had visited the Eastern seaboard of the USA at Lever's expense),[39] for alongside his review of planning issues in the USA, Reilly conducted a parallel commentary of the discipline in the UK. Planning in the United States, in Reilly's eyes, was distinct from the 'hygienic and humanitarian' practice in the UK and Germany, because of the provision of a civic centre, where public building expressed the importance and dignity of the town. This differed considerably, he argued, to town planning in England which started 'with the idea of the garden suburb – the little imitation village on the edge of a big town, – and as yet [has] hardly got beyond it'.[40] The Americans on the other hand had gone to France for their architectural inspiration and thought of town planning in terms of 'encircling boulevards, wide diagonal streets leading from one open space to another, monumental bridges and quays, grandiose vistas are everywhere projected, and in some places in the course of construction'.

Thus a dialogue between two different sets of planning paradigms was established by Reilly, and whilst he identified them as working in separate areas there was no overt antagonism as yet displayed towards the Garden Suburb. That antagonism first emerged in his paper 'The City of the Future', given at the Royal Institute of British Architects' *Town Planning* conference held in London in 1910. The conference itself (rapidly organised by the RIBA in an attempt to exert as much pressure over town planning as it could)[41] was reported in *Town Planning Review* in précis form, with Reilly's, Adshead's and Dowdall's (Lecturer in Civic Law in the Department and past Lord Mayor of Liverpool) papers reproduced in full. Charles Robinson's paper, in comparison, was summarised as having 'dealt with the standardisation of streets'.

Reilly's paper started with a criticism of British suburbs and their stylistic incoherence, and I doubt whether his views would have taken his audience by surprise. (In July a flattering article[42] in *The Builder* had identified the promotion of a single architectural style as being one of the distinguishing qualities of the Liverpool School.) Reilly went on to argue that the cultural force behind the new Garden Suburbs was one of organisation, and the suppression of 'rampant individualism' for the provision of general amenities. With this in mind he asked whether the buildings of the Garden Suburbs adequately expressed 'the best contemporary culture. And if they do not do this, how can they serve for any length of time the culture that is to come?'[43] In answer to his own rhetoric Reilly rehearsed, once again, the Liverpool School's argument in favour of the axially planned, cosmopolitan city, using modern French and American architecture as the source for the necessary new signification. This was picked up by Adshead in his paper 'City Improvement'[44] in a far more combative way. He argued that in an age of emerging internationalism the first cultural edifice to be eroded was that of national distinctions and directions in the arts. Once more, the solution to this problem was the provision of an architectural style best exemplified by the work of McKim. The forms of the city, symmetrically expressed, were to be given coherence under this unified, and unifying, design principle. Adshead's tone in parts was distinctly, and deliberately provocative; 'I have an impression that to drag the word style into a discussion on modern architecture is considered bad form'.

It is from this point on that a new element can be seen emerging in the relationship between the accepted, and now dominant, town planning practices of the Garden Suburbs, and those proposed by the Liverpool School. The sense of duality that existed initially between the two, though it was never clearly articulated, was deliberately disrupted by Adshead in his promotion of the 'new' town planning. In effect Adshead was responsible for the opening up of the planning dialogue and turning it into an oppositional debate. This was first clearly expressed in 1913, when he wrote in a signed editorial in *Town Planning Review*, 'modern Town Planning seems tacitly to have admitted that the garden suburb is the only solution of town development ... we believe that there are two sides to the question, which has not yet been thoroughly discussed'.[45]

To this end a number of articles were published which brought into question the correctness of the Garden Suburb as the form by which the city should rationalise itself. The Garden City movement was condemned for both its romantic ideology and its design in 'A Criticism of the Garden City Movement' by Trystan-Edwards.[46] The architecture of the Garden Suburb was criticised by Trystan-Edwards for its 'perfect hatred of design', by which he meant its variety of style and its lack of formality, echoing Reilly's attitude to the Garden Suburbs. This architectural design was further condemned for its rural quality, its cultural common denominator; 'but if the buildings show no restraint in their form, if they are inclined to be a little frisky, at any rate in their character they are uniformity itself. One note pervades them all, the note of country domesticity'.

A reply to this article[47] concentrated on the issues of health and hygiene and ignored the issue of style as an irrelevance compared to the importance of these. Trystan-Edwards was to further respond[48] on stylistic grounds referring to the 'monotonous diffuseness of the Garden Cities'. This debate, briefly aired in the pages of *Town Planning Review* was considered all but closed by an editorial which acknowledged the important role that the Garden City movement had played in the past, but argued that its contribution had been made, and that in contemporary design 'it has been absorbed in others of wider significance'.[49] During the course of this examination and debate, the journal's pages were substantially filled with material that can be seen as an attempt to provide an alternative design ideology to the domestic, drawing on the best examples of European and American classically derived architecture and townscape. This stance was given a sustained and continuous importance with Adshead's series of articles, 'Furnishing the City', in which those forms considered appropriate for the city were examined methodically and in detail.[50]

28 Garden suburb ruralism: Liverpool Garden Suburb, Childwall, Wavertree Nook Road.

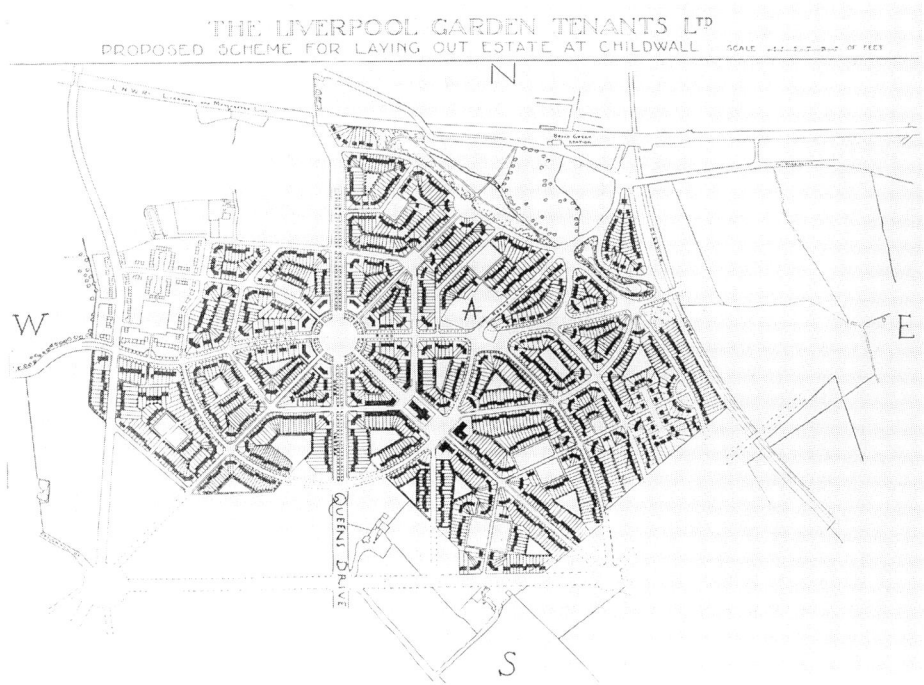

29 It is possible to see in these three designs (Plates 29, 30, 31) the beginnings of the more formal geometry used in the layout of later Liverpool corporation modernist housing estates. Liverpool Garden Suburb: plan by Dixon.

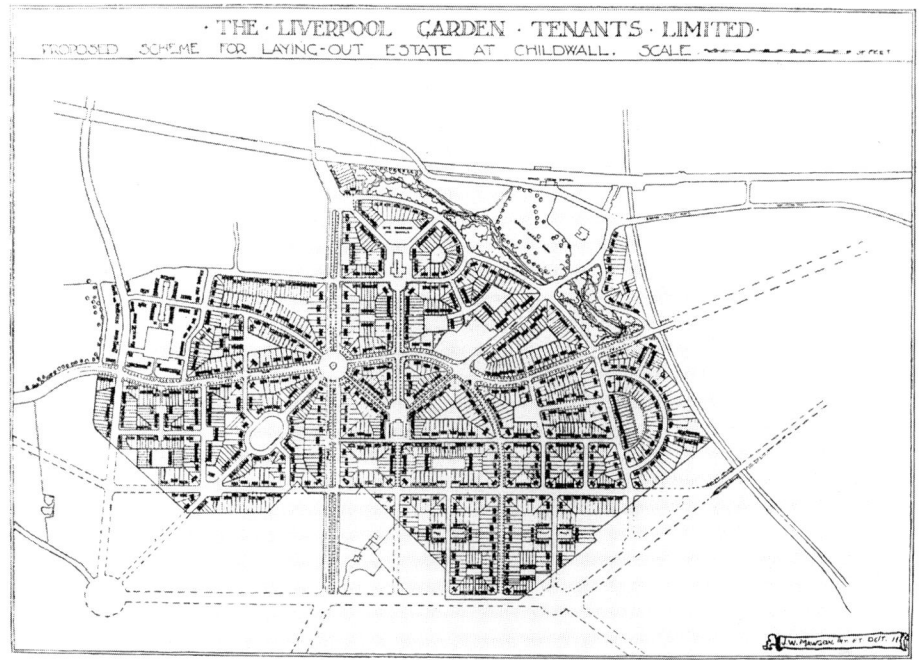

30 Liverpool Garden Suburb: plan by Mawson.

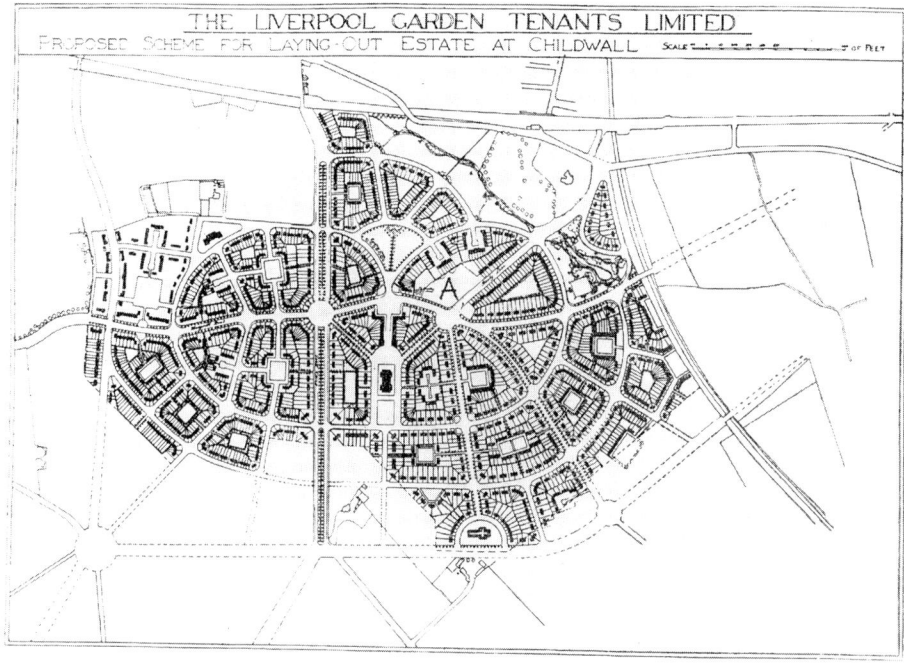

31 Liverpool Garden Suburb: plan by Mattocks.

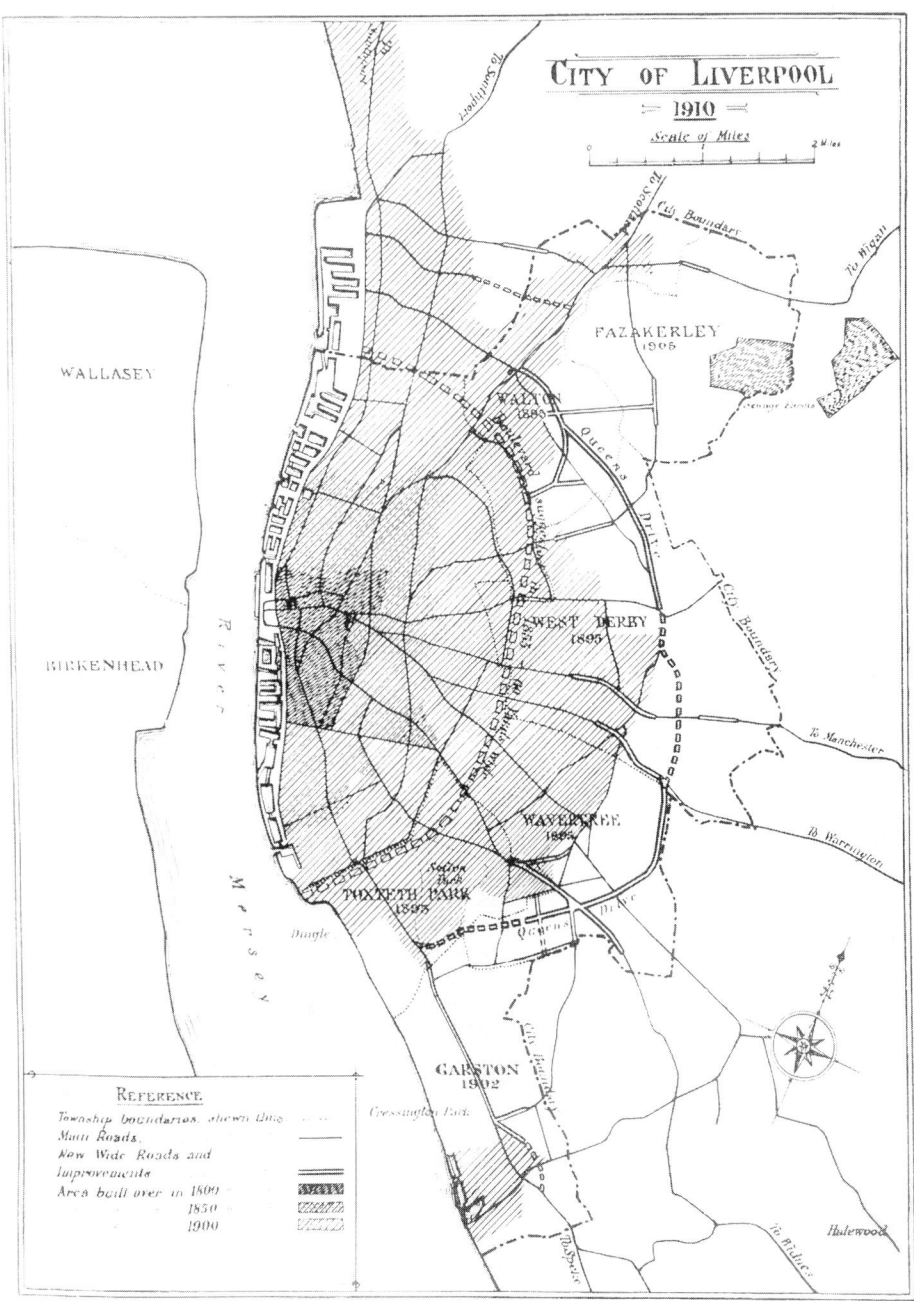

32 This plan shows the scope of Brodie's planning vision: Plan of Liverpool
showing Queens Drive, 1910.

At the outbreak of the First World War the debate in Town Planning was no longer whether it was a discipline that demanded attention. Directed through the pages of *Town Planning Review*, it had become a debate over the nature of the design style that the discipline should adopt. This is not to say that the Liverpool School was in a position to supplant the dominant forms of the Garden Suburb, but it was important enough as a cultural force to demand the reassessment of the direction that the discipline should take. The last remnants of the ideas of the Arts and Crafts movement were at this point severed from importance within the city.

In the years immediately before the First World War two planning ventures were undertaken in Liverpool which illustrate well the duality of approach that was debated in the pages of *Town Planning Review*. They were the Liverpool Garden Suburb, and Liverpool's circumferential boulevard, Queen's Drive. The first was a co-operative housing venture; the second part of a larger scale municipal vision of town planning, planned and instigated by the City Engineer John Brodie. Brodie was an important figure in municipal planning, open to new ideas and innovative in his thinking.[51] His cooperation had been sought by the University's Faculty of Arts during the process of the formation of the Department of Civic Design[52] and a special Lectureship in Civic Engineering was created for him within the School[53] where he held the post of Associate Professor. As such, he was fully aware of the practical issues and theoretical debates in town planning. His standing with Reilly was high, as is evident in the following description by Reilly of Queen's Drive: 'both in its conception and in the detail of its creation, especially in the way in which it connects with Sefton Park, [Queen's Drive] is one of the finest gifts the imagination of Mr. Brodie – a city engineer with that rare endowment – has given to the town.'[54]

Queen's Drive was begun in 1904. Six and a half miles long, with a minimum width of 120 feet, it was the result of the need for better cross-town traffic, and it acted as a connecting link for the radial arterial routes that emanated from the city centre, which had arisen naturally but which were developed by Brodie. It was a national innovation needing a series of Parliamentary Acts culminating in that of 1908, to permit the building of a road system of such considerable size. It was designed by Brodie on a heroic scale in anticipation of increased motorised traffic, earned him the nickname 'More Roads Brodie' and caused considerable disquiet during its construction as it cut its modern mechanised way through farmland on the outer perimeter of town.[55]

It was one of the first pieces of large-scale municipal planning in the UK that was to become more commonplace after the First World

War. Whilst it cannot be argued that Brodie was directly influenced by specific instances in the development of urban centres in America, it has to be assumed, because of the circles in which he moved, and his interest in the automobile, that American urban planning was not a mystery to him. The links for example between Brodie's plan for Liverpool, and Burnham and Bennett's for Chicago, where radial routes from the city centre waterfront are connected by a broad circulatory boulevard, are not those of direct influence (Queen's Drive was already under construction when Burnham and Bennett's plan was published) but of mutual cultural influences, that of the city of Paris and the work of McKim.[56]

Brodie's own view of the road [57] stressed its importance as a mechanism to increase the speed by which traffic travelled, and as a way of increasing green open space into the city. Brodie's plan was that radial routes would be widened 'so that the present day idea of parks as areas through which it is not proper to provide main thoroughfares and modern methods of travel, might be modified, and that wide belts of planted open spaces leading out into the country would be better essentially and from every point of view'. These green 'radial lungs' have more to do with what Charles Robinson called the 'fast roads' [58] of urban America than they do with the Champs-Elysées or the Unter der Linden, but still have a distinct quality of their own. Robinson still saw the urban parkways as 'glorified drives' catering to wealth, but Brodie saw them as essential practical components for the working of the modern city, where motorised transport was not the sole prerogative of the wealthy individual but the rational solution to getting workers rapidly from the edge of town to their work in the centre. Such road systems also have a connection with the 'wide streets and boulevards' [59] of Raymond Unwin, the difference being that Unwin wished to constrain their development if the width of the road encroached on building land. If this was to happen, in order to reap any financial benefits from the development of a site, buildings would have to be built higher. Large-scale development would have been an absolute necessity if boulevards were to be constructed within an existing urban environment as in Liverpool. It was this sense of scale that appalled Unwin, which was so attractive to the Liverpool School.

Brodie saw the planned city in terms of municipal development in preference to the piecemeal approach of the Garden Suburb. He remained unconvinced that legislation on its own would transform the areas surrounding towns into Garden Cities [60] and thought that only municipal authorities had the wealth and organising capability to develop and maintain housing and open spaces. In this he held views similar to those of Adshead.[61]

This position, where public authority was both the generator of ideas and the mechanism by which they were implemented, is obviously at odds with the philosophy of the Garden Suburb. They can probably be best distinguished from one another as the difference between the corporate and the collective. Ironically, Brodie's development of the perimeter of the city was to enable the construction of the Liverpool Garden Suburb. Indeed *Town Planning Review* was to remark, 'Queen's Drive ... passes through the suburb, and it is fortunate for the estate that this fine boulevard has already been planted and laid out'.[62]

There was really little option for the development of the Liverpool Garden Suburb anywhere but on the outermost edge of the city. As Brodie pointed out in *Some Guiding Principles in City Planning*,[63] the intensity of smoke pollution made the upkeep of 'green' areas very difficult. The new estate was to be developed several miles away from the main body of by-law terrace housing that lay on the slopes of the Liverpool upland,[64] and a little way from the village of Wavertree. It was to be the first substantial development along Queen's Drive. The drive was to be instrumental in the doubling of the population in the outer suburbs between 1911 and 1931.

In the summer of 1910 Co-Partnership Tenants Ltd formally announced their plans for a Garden Suburb in Liverpool, now known as Wavertree Garden Suburb, then called The Liverpool Garden Suburb Tenants Ltd.[65] Negotiations with the Marquis of Salisbury (owner of the land and Chairman of the Liverpool Guild) had taken three years, and the original intention was for the development of 185 acres providing 1,900 homes. The site had been carefully chosen with consideration for ease of access to rail and tram termini, a necessity considering the scale of the initial plans.[66] Two competitions were announced,[67] one for the layout of the site for Civic Design students in the Liverpool School, and the other for the design of cottages for the architectural students. Raymond Unwin was to assess the competition for the site plan.

By the beginning of 1911 substantial developments had taken place at Wavertree; 16 semi-detatched houses had been built, some of them occupied, and 38 further houses were close to completion. Roads had been widened aesthetically: 'In order to keep the rural character of the neighbourhood, the hedge on the west side of Wavertree North Road is being retained and the boundaries of the gardens of these houses have been planted with young privets about two feet high.'[68]

Town Planning Review reported Brodie, in his capacity as City Engineer, cooperating fully with the developers in trying to fit the original conception of the scheme into the planning demands of the time as closely as possible. In doing so Brodie was obviously fulfilling the task for which he was paid, but he did it in a way that demonstrated both his professionalism and his flexibility, bearing in mind his personal attitudes towards the Garden Suburb movement.[69]

In April 1911 the competition instigated by the Liverpool Garden Suburb Tenants Ltd for students at the Department of Civic Design was judged by Raymond Unwin and prizes awarded at the Liverpool Town Planning Conference held at Liberty Buildings.[70] Whilst none of the plans were taken up by the company, surviving illustrations give an indication both of the proposed scope of the original site, and a clear idea of the design principles of the Department of Civic Design. There is no record of the fate of the architectural competition.

The design solutions to the problem have a certain similarity with one another. A major junction (between Queen's Drive and Thingwall Road) became a major nodal point in the plan, and there is an emphasis upon an underlying geometry and vistas within the estate. The scope of the site compared to the scale of existing developments documented and illustrated in *Town Planning Review*, and in Unwin's *Town Planning in Practice* [71] was large. This is because that whilst the size of the Letchworth and Hampstead sites were themselves large, they were developed in a piecemeal way. The unreality of the competition meant that the Wavertree site could be thought of as a piece of unified design, although in reality it was developed pragmatically in a varied fashion.

Nook Rise, completed by the time of the judging of the competition, can be seen as a design piece closely modelled on planning at Letchworth and Hampstead. The winning competition entries obviously paid less attention to the individual component parts of the site and more to the general distribution of them. The overall winner (J. N. Dixon) of the three finalists chosen by Unwin is differentiated from the others predominately by the broken building line of the houses, conforming to one of the design principles of Unwin.[72] Whilst the plans for the Wavertree site were student work, in addition to the planning principles promulgated by Unwin, it is still possible to see in them the beginnings of the more formal geometry used in the layout of the Liverpool Corporation housing estates, Norris Green and Dovecote, in the early 1920s which is so strongly representative of Liverpool School design. This link is stronger than that with the plan for Letchworth which was still being used as a paradigmical example by Ashbee in 1917.[73]

The close involvement of the School (Brodie's involvement was obviously on a different level) with the early development of the site can be interpreted in a number of ways, which in the absence of tangible evidence, can all be given equal credence. It could indicate that duality of approach between the Liverpool School and the Garden

Suburb movement already discussed. Alternatively it could be that Reilly saw advantages in collaborating with the scheme in the hope of influencing its direction and moulding it to a form that could act as a physical paradigm of the Liverpool School's theories, in the same way that Port Sunlight acted as an example of Lever's ideas as to the social function of architecture. As it was, after 1911, and the failure of the School to influence the nature of the development's layout, and presumably architecture, *Town Planning Review* no longer reported on the development. This must also be seen in the light of the development of the Liverpool School's public stance towards the Garden City movement.

In returning to the architecture of the Wavertree estate, it is clear from its domestic appearance that its roots ran deep in the Arts and Crafts vernacular tradition (but without the decorative flamboyance of Port Sunlight). It is almost identical in its appearance to the architecture of Letchworth and Hampstead, and conforms to the principles laid out in the following passage by Unwin:

> To the picturesque style of architecture, [what Unwin calls *Gothic* in a previous paragraph], irregularity of site and lack of symmetry in arrangement offer no difficulty. English domestic architecture very largely belongs to this class. Though many classical buildings have been successfully designed for irregular sites ... it does not lend itself to the production of picturesque irregularities, nor do clusters of such buildings ... produce successful groupings, as often happens with similar groupings of the more picturesque types of buildings.[74]

This conception of domestic architecture can be contrasted with housing designed by Brodie that was completed seven years earlier. Eldon Grove Flats shows how Brodie's vision of architecture was antithetical to the Garden City movement and can been seen as parallelling certain of the design principles of the Liverpool School. The flats were a block of dwellings constructed entirely of reinforced concrete.[75] In 1901 Brodie was experimenting with pre-cast concrete construction methods, perhaps with the purpose of planning its mass use for corporation housing. In 1903 Brodie presented his plans to the Council to construct a block of 12 flats, with a communal playground on the roof, made from pre-cast concrete panels which were to be transported to the site and erected. Internal fittings, such as the sink, were also to be included in the pre-casting, and doors were to hang directly onto the concrete structure. By November 1904 the flats were substantially completed and Brodie's report back to the Council was published in April 1905.[76] The building of the flats had exceeded its

33 Reinforced concrete using neo-classical styling: Eldon Grove Flats, Liverpool, 1905. (Architect John Brodie.)

initial budget by 400 per cent, and Brodie concluded that the only way to bring down costs was to mass produce them in large numbers. This was not to be. The structure was still sound when the flats were demolished in 1966.

I am not attempting directly to compare Eldon Grove with the development at Wavertree. After all, one was a suburban development, large in scale, co-operatively built, the other an experimental, municipal, small-scale inner city development. It is possible, however to make to make some observations about the stylistic forms that were used in the two instances, and what they might signify. It has already been observed that the architecture of the Garden Suburb was domestic, and almost rural in quality. This can be contrasted dramatically with the uncompromisingly urbane block of Brodie's flats, with its clearly articulated conception of communal living. Perhaps this is most obviously demonstrated by the external central stairwell, that, in its climb to the communal roof space gives the building its open, elevated aspect. The detailing, restrained in ornament but somewhat heavy in appearance, nevertheless strongly signifies the rational ordering of the neo-classical. It has the solidity and weight of a gentleman's club, though at no time does the design attempt to obscure what the building is – a block of flats. If one compares what must have been a grey concrete building, with the brown brick and decorative timberwork of the Wavertree development one finds two opposing poles of the conception of group living.

This mixture of the formally planned and the informally domestic, rooted in a similar ideological base is best examined in terms of the development of Port Sunlight immediately before the First World War, intimately connected as it was with the Liverpool School.

The narrative threads that have stretched from Port Sunlight village and its place in the Arts and Crafts pantheon, from the mutation of Arts and Crafts ideas to those of the Beaux Arts as represented by the Liverpool School of Architecture finally come together in events immediately before the First World War. As part of the funding programme for the Department of Civic Design within the School of Architecture, Lever instigated a series of competition prizes within the School. By 1912 these had been dignified with the appellation 'Lever Prize'. They are important because they indicate the direction that the Liverpool School was taking in theoretical design, and one competition result had a direct bearing upon the development of Port Sunlight village. In addition the publicity that was generated by the prizes had a contemporary importance as a national showcase for the display of talent associated with the School's students. Lever's initial conception of Port Sunlight village as a quasi-rural environment, where the first housing development took place around the informality of the Dell, was to change substantially in 1910 when he instigated a competition at the School of Architecture for a plan suitable for the completion of the village. The village development had spread out from the first section by the factory and had extended to the perimeter of the site. The winning entry by a third year student at the School, Ernest Prestwick, proposed a wholesale remodelling of the interior on Beaux Arts lines. Prestwick's scheme shows the imposition of a rigorous formality. The most fundamental change from the village as originally conceived, was Prestwick's introduction of intersecting boulevards creating dramatic vistas within the undeveloped internal space. By 1914, with the exception of the proposed group of civic buildings, Prestwick's plan had been largely implemented, with the addition of provision for an Art Gallery and the end of the main axial boulevard (the Diamond). The Art Gallery was designed in 1913 by William and Segar Owen,[77] and at Lever's suggestion was in Beaux Arts style. This is in marked contrast to other civic buildings on the estate, built in rustic and vernacular styles. Hubbard and Shippobottom suggest in *A Guide to Port Sunlight*

Village,[78] that the 'work of Professor Reilly and the Liverpool School of Architecture must have played a part in influencing him'. I think it must be clear that this comment is a massive understatement, and that the whole design ethos of the Liverpool School had been substantially absorbed by Lever, who was in part responsible for its promulgation. This is further proved by even a cursory examination of the Lever Prize Competitions where winning entries reflect the teachings of Reilly and Adshead.

The Lever Prizes for 1912, 1913 and 1914, unlike the competition for Port Sunlight remained paper exercises. They all have a coherence that stems from the teaching programme at the School. In 1912 the competition involved a redesigning of Brownlow Hill, Liverpool, where the area from Lime Street to the University was to 'be reconstructed as an example of monumental Town Planning'.[79] Illustrations of designs show the scale and scope of the redesign as envisaged by the student competitors and give a good indication of the ambitions of the School's teaching programme. Vistas of heroic size are framed by architecture that *The Builder* had struggled to describe two years earlier:

> It is difficult to say which school this one [Liverpool] more nearly approximates to – it is certainly very different from the present day Beaux Arts work ... nor is it a heavy correct Palladian school. Perhaps the influence of Cockerell ... is as strong as that of any one. We also felt that the severer works of McKim, Mead and White must have been studied, and were wondering if the [work] were like that of an American School of Architecture; but a copy of the Columbian University Year Book ... betrays a much closer connection with the Beaux Arts'[80]

In 1913 this monumental design philosophy was applied to the design of 'A New Liverpool River Front'.[81] The designs and illustrations submitted for these schemes show a conception of the city form rooted in architectural display rather than in questions of function, and if compared to drawings by Adshead show how closely student work followed the ideas and premises of that of their staff. Even given that the competition was fixed in that curious limbo that exists between the tangible world and that of architectural fantasy, the designs submitted bear little relationship to any logical extrapolation of the city form and become pieces of purely ideological design. Large buildings of loosely defined function (offices, hotels) line the riverfront creating an architectural fantasy illustrating a conception of an ideal city form. Designed to be viewed from the river, the development takes on the air of a stage set for the future, tellingly closer to exposition architecture than to that of real commercial development. This of course was a large part of its conceptual origin and substantially its purpose, an attempt to force the pace of design to match its rapidly developing ideological base.

Although there was a Lever Prize competition held and judged in 1914 before the outbreak of war (involving the redesign of St John's Gardens behind St George's Hall) [82] it is the 1913 competition that is the best evocation of the grandiose nature of Liverpool School design, and one that bears ideological comparison with the Ecole des Beaux Arts conceptual plan for the ideal city, 'A World Centre of Communication', a symmetrical and harmonious fantasy 'supposed to be The City Beautiful, the complete and perfect metropolis'.[83]

In both cases, on different scales, the conception of design for the city has become abstracted in a way, and on a scale, that would have been inconceivable to the Arts and Crafts practitioners. The legacy of the Arts and Crafts in the form of the piecemeal development of the cities using the Garden Suburb, available technology, and a conception of design rooted in traditional technology, contrasts strongly with the Liverpool School's Beaux Arts derived conception of wholesale redevelopment, using new technologies and transcending historical stylistic precedent. What the Lever Prize design submissions show is a design vision of the world almost purely ideologically motivated, and which because of the impossible scope of the vision, was inevitably doomed to exist only in fragments.

It was this trans-national gigantism, this overwhelming obsession with the unification of design parts under a coherent design ideology, that made it easy for Reilly, and later Lionel Budden and others at the Liverpool School, to absorb and promote the new ideas of modernism in the post-war world,[84] ideas that at first glance might appear to be at odds with the Liverpool School stylistically, but which shared similar ideological expectations. A key text of modernist practice in Britain, *Circle*, was published in 1937. In it we read of the potential of anonymous design, of 'the irrelevances of architectural "self-expression" and the confusion of idea that accompanies it',[85] reflecting the aspirations of design culture in Liverpool at the turn of the nineteenth century. When Marcel Breuer writes, 'the basis of modern architecture, however, is not the new materials, nor even the new form, but the new mentality; that is to say, the view we take and the manner in which we judge our needs'[86] he is articulating an idea that has been central to this book's narrative.

34 The Pier Head: a scheme for reconstruction by students of the School of Civic Design, Liverpool University.

35 A Beaux Arts vision of the Liverpool waterfront: Lever Prize winning design by H. C. Bradshaw.

Notes

1 Letter, Reilly to Lever, 23 April 1904, Charles Reilly's letterbooks, Liverpool University Archives no. D207/2/1,.

2 C. Reilly, *Scaffolding in the Sky*, Routledge, 1938, p. 93.

3 '[Lever] kindly said I was at liberty to suggest any such way of using up his surplus money provided he was equally free to refuse', ibid., p. 123. See also pp. 124–28.

4 *Liverpool Daily Post and Mercury*, 11 July 1906.

5 E. Hubbard and M. Shippobottom, *A Guide to Port Sunlight Village*, Liverpool: Liverpool University Press, 1988, p. 3.

6 22 February 1909, Liverpool University Senate Papers, vol. 3 no. 23, Liverpool University Archives.

7 To be made full Professor in 1912.

8 Details of Adshead's early career can be found in an unpublished autobiographical manuscript in the Liverpool University Archives, *Architects I have Known*, no. D 247/1. The following paragraph creates a less than heroic vision of the Department's inception; 'I did fourteen competitions without success. I seemed to fail in everything and was reduced to running my office with one boy, and busying myself with reading papers on architecture before societies. When one day through the instrumentality of my friend Professor Reilly, I received an invitation to occupy the newly funded Chair of Civic Design at the Liverpool University.'

9 A. Adshead, 'Style in Architectural Draughtsmanship', *RIBA Journal*, vol. XIV, 1907, p. 485.

10 P. Abercrombie, 'Editorial', *Town Planning Review*, vol. 1:1, 1909, p. 1.

11 S. Adshead, 'An Introduction to Civic Design', *Town Planning Review*, vol. 1:1, 1909.

12 The article was broken down into four parts; 'The Prearranged Plan', 'Historical Retrospect', 'Sociological Aspect', 'The Influence of the City on City Life'. This compares to such headings in Robinson's *The Improvement of Towns and Cities* as 'Beauty in the Street', 'Aesthetic Phase of Social and Philanthropic Effort', 'Aesthetic Phase of Education Effort', 'Means to secure Civic Aesthetics'.

13 See also 'Under Professor Reilly's guidance the Liverpool School has to come to be recognised as the first, if not the only school in England which stands for monumental architecture and Classic tradition' (p. 2). 'Like the Liverpool School of Architecture of which it is a department, our school of Town Planning has a distinct point of view. It believes and teaches that a well organised society expresses its existence only in a well directed and well planned way.' (p. 6). S. Adshead, 'The School of Civic Design at the Liverpool University', unpublished manuscript, no. D 247/2, Liverpool University Archives.

14 'The teaching of Design at this school [The Liverpool School] is based on the methods of the Ecole Des Beaux Arts in Paris and on those of the great American Schools of Architecture adapted to meet our somewhat different requirements.' *Architectural Review*, August 1910, p. 41.

15 Adshead, 'An Introduction to Civic Design', p. 10.

16 'Rome in the laying out of her forums, her palaces, her pleasure places, and her public ways, was unity itself; and the adjustment of her symmetrical units, unsymmetrically arranged, offers solutions of problems so varied and of so great an interest as to remain to this day a precedent for axial connection unrivalled in the world,' ibid., p. 5.

17 'Still it is the genius of Louis XIV, assisted by his architects Bullet and Blondel, and by his landscape architect Andre le Notre, that we are indebted for the great Champs Elysee and the Place de l'Etoile, and it is they who first originated the

tree lined boulevard, with its clearly defined roadway, its trottoirs, and its prome-
nades.' Ibid., p. 6.

18 Ibid., p. 6.
19 Ibid., p. 8.
20 Ibid., p. 10.
21 Adshead thought that with efficient distribution and communication mechanisms the city simplifies itself into varying zones; residential, parks, business, recreational. It is the proper provision of these mechanisms that ensures the citizen's 'moral force etc.'.
22 Ibid., p. 14.
23 Ibid., p. 16.
24 For example, see; W. Morris, *News from Nowhere*, Longmans, 1910, pp. 24–25.
25 Adshead, 'An Introduction to Civic Design', p. 16.
26 I am inclined to think that this was the case if one looks not only at the work of Herbert Rowse pre-war, but also some of the immediate post-war building by Shennon, particularly Spinney House. As it was Reilly was sufficiently flexible in his approach to architectural matters to be able to embrace Modernism in the late 1920s, partly due to the stance of the classicising nature of a great part of it.
27 Major articles on Liverpool in *Town Planning Review*: S. Adshead, 'A Suggestion for the Reconstruction of St Johns Gardens, St George's Hall Liverpool', vol. 1:1; S. Adshead, 'Liverpool: A Preliminary Survey, with Some Suggestions for Remod-elling its Central Area', vol. 1:2; J. Brodie, 'The Development of Liverpool and its Circumferential Boulevard', vol. 1:2; R. Muir, 'Liverpool: An Analysis of the Geo-graphical Distribution of Civic Functions: Part One', vol. 1:3; S. Adshead, 'King Edward Schemes', vol. 1:4; R. Muir, 'Liverpool: An Analysis of the Geographical Distribution of Civic Functions: Part Two', S. Adshead, 'Liverpool: A Preliminary Survey, Being a Reply to Professor Muir's Articles', vol. 1:4. Subsequent volumes of *TPR* to 1914 contained no further substantial writing on Liverpool although there continued to be a steady stream of material about planning and planning education in the city.
28 It is a measure of the newness and innovation of the journal that there were few people equipped to write on the discipline. John Burns wrote on the consequences of the 1909 Act in the 'Town Planning Supplement' in *Architectural Review*, and it was not until 1912 that Patrick Geddes contributed to *Town Planning Review* ('The two fold aspect of the Industrial Age'.) A year later Lanchester and Unwin began their contributions.
29 'Special Town Planning Supplement', *Architectural Review*, 1910.
30 H. Carter, 'The Recovery of Art and Craft', *New Age*, 9 January 1911.
31 L. March Phillips 'Liverpool and its Architecture', *Morning Post*, 9 June 1913. The following brief extract gives a good indication of the cultural position of the *Morning Post*; '[H. H. Munroe] was endowed with just the right touch of "educated scorn" which has always distinguished that superior paper. Like his paper, "Saki" was suspicious of all enthusiasm, and stood ready to mock at the zeal and aspirations of all "faddists" and "cranks"'. H. W. Nevison, Introduction to H. H. Munroe, *Beasts and Superbeasts*, Bodley Head, 1914, p. vii.
32 March Philips, 'Liverpool and its Architecture'.
33 Editorial, *The Builder*, 13 June 1913.
34 Editorial, 'Cosmopolitan Art', *The British Architect*, 20 June 1913.
35 P. Abercrombie, 'A Comparative Review of Examples of Modern Town Planning and Garden City Schemes in England,' *Town Planning Review*, vol. 1:1.
36 Substantially achieved in the two parts of the article ibid., but also in endnotes and

articles such as W. Tuckett, 'Corporate life in a Garden Suburb', *Town and Planning Review*, vol. 2:2, pp. 128–30; and C. Hobson, 'Walkley – A working man's suburb', *Town Planning Review*, vol. 3:1, pp. 39–46.

37 Editorial, *Town Planning Review*, vol. 1:4, p. 269.

38 C. Reilly, 'Town Planning Schemes in America', *Town Planning Review*, vol. 1:1 pp. 54–55.

39 'It was decided that that he [Adshead] and I should divide the world between us at [Lever's] expense. Adshead was to travel through Europe collecting information as to what was being done in town planning in Germany, Austria and elsewhere and I was to go to the Eastern States of America and do the same.' Reilly, *Scaffolding in the Sky*, p. 127. Whilst in Chicago, Reilly met Burnham.

40 Reilly, 'Town Planning Schemes in America,' p. 54.

41 'Few of the numerous foreign delegates were fully aware of the RIBA's ulterior motive of cornering the practice of town planning … and most were genuinely impressed and even moved by a magnificently set international occasion.' A. Sutcliffe, *Towards the Planned City*, Blackwell, 1981, p. 171.

42 'the Liverpool School seems to be quite considerable enough to take a stand of itself, and perhaps even to suggest a style to others. We feel acutely the value of a strong common speech among a body of men … is preferable to a babel of polyglot talk.' 'The Liverpool School of Architecture', *The Builder*, 16 July 1910, p. 64.

43 C. Reilly, 'The City of the Future', *Town Planning Review*, vol. 1:3, p. 195.

44 S. Adshead, 'City Improvement', *Town Planning Review* vol. 1:3, pp. 198–204.

45 S. Adshead, 'Editorial', *Town Planning Review*, vol. 4:2.

46 A. T. Edwards, 'A criticism of the Garden City Movement', *Town Planning Review*, vol. 4:2, pp. 150–57.

47 C. Reade, 'A Defence of the Garden City Movement', *Town Planning Review*, vol. 4:3, pp. 245–51.

48 E. T. Edwards, 'A Further Criticism of the Garden City Movement', *Town Planning Review*, vol. 4:4, pp. 313–18.

49 Editorial, 'A Controversy', *Town Planning Review*, vol. 4:4, p. 275.

50 S. Adshead, 'The Decoration and Furnishing of the City', a series of articles beginning in *Town Planning Review* vol. 2:1 and continuing until Adshead's departure for London. Reilly saw these as one of Adshead's major contributions; 'His series of articles on the furnishing of towns have made those early numbers of the *Town Planning Review* much sought after and of a considerably enhanced value today.' Reilly, *Scaffolding in the Sky*, p. 129.

51 As some indication of Brodie's attitudes, he read a paper, 'Application of the Electric Light' at the Free Public Library, Liverpool, (Engineering Society Transactions vol. 2, 1880–81, pp. 32–39) to the Engineering Society in 1880 whilst still working for the Mersey Dock Estate. He was also an early advocate of the motor car, becoming Vice-President of the Self-Propelled Traffic Association. He was appointed City Engineer in 1898 after six years in private practice. He was a national expert on Motor Vehicle regulations and Street Traffic (see *University of Liverpool Engineering Society Journal*, vol. 3, 1915, pp. 10–11) and it was this expertise that led to his involvement with the siting and planning of New Delhi.

52 See Liverpool University Senate Papers, vol. 3 no. 23, 22 February 1909, Liverpool University Archives.

53 He held this post from 1910–28.

54 C. Reilly, 'A Note on the Architecture of Liverpool' in A. Holt (ed.), *Merseyside*, Liverpool: University Press of Liverpool, 1923, p. 51.

55 See F. Hyde, *Liverpool and the Mersey: An Economic History*, David and Charles, 1971, p. 174.

56 See M. Peisch, *The Chicago School of Architecture*, Phaidon, 1964, pp. 91–94.

57 J. Brodie, 'The development of Liverpool and its circumferential boulevard', *Town Planning Review*, vol. 1:2, pp. 100–10.

58 See C. Robinson, *The Improvement of Towns and Cities*, Putnam's, 1901, pp. 152–72.

59 R. Unwin, *Town Planning in Practice*, Fisher Unwin, 1911 p. 242: 'These wide streets or boulevards are further decorated with avenues of trees, and are favourite promenading grounds in the evening, when the amount of traffic is reduced. Such roads, however, are costly, both in the amount of land required for them and in the construction and maintenance of the numerous tracks, and, while roads of this form are desirable and their expense justified for main thoroughfares in large towns, they must not be recklessly adopted. Continental cities are undoubtedly, in many cases, suffering severely from needless extravagance in the laying out of roads of much greater width than the requirements justified. This has had the effect of increasing greatly the return necessary to be obtained from the land, and has consequently intensified a tendency already strong, to crowd too many buildings upon the lane, and to carry these buildings too high.' It is interesting to compare this pragmatic capitalist approach to land values with the romantic corporatism of Brodie.

60 J. Brodie, 'Some Guiding Principles in City Planning', *Town Planning Review*, vol. 1:2, pp. 109–10.

61 S. Adshead, 'A Symposium on the Municipal Ownership of Land,' *Town Planning Review*, vol. 3:4, pp. 232–39.

62 *Town Planning Review*, vol. 1:2, p. 174.

63 J. Brodie, 'Some Guiding Principles in City Planning'. It is difficult to overestimate the practical difficulties in establishing 'garden cultures' in the cities before the First World War. The following extract gives some indication: 'The villa-dweller will tell you, "I am so fond of flowers, but nothing will grow in my garden." Ask why, and you will nearly always receive the reply, "I suppose it's the smoke." Now it is quite true that many beautiful things will not grow in smoky towns. There are people so innocent as to dig up bracken and parsley fern and plant them in tremulous hope beneath the sooty rhododendron in the front garden.' H. Swanwick, *The Small Town Garden*, Sherratt and Hughes, 1907, p. 23.

64 See W. Smith, 'The Urban Structure of Liverpool', pp. 196–99 in W. Smith (ed.), *A Scientific Survey of Merseyside*, Liverpool: Liverpool University Press, 1953.

65 For fuller details concerning the development of the Liverpool Garden Suburb see K. Sloane, 'Copartnership housing in Liverpool: The emergence of the Liverpool Garden Suburb,' unpublished MA Thesis, University of Liverpool, 1988.

66 The development was severely curtailed by the outbreak of the First World War.

67 *Town Planning Review*, vol. 1:3, p. 263.

68 *Town Planning Review*, vol. 1:4, p. 334.

69 See note 10.

70 See S. Adshead and P. Abercrombie (eds), *Liverpool Town Planning and Housing Exhibition 1914*, Liverpool: Liverpool University Press, 1914.

71 R. Unwin, *Town Planning in Practice*, Fisher Unwin, 1909.

72 Ibid., second edition, 1911, pp. 330–59.

73 C. Ashbee, *Where the Great City Stands*, Batsford, 1917, p. 44.

74 Unwin, *Town Planning in Practice*, 1911, second edition, p. 368.

75 A material developed to a large extent in Liverpool by L. G. Mouchel. Brodie's experiments in the material were studied by a New York architect, Grosvenor

Atterbury, who developed the system for multi-storey development between 1906 and 1927. See R. Moore, 'An Early System of Large-panel Building', *RIBA Journal*, vol. 76, 1969, pp. 383–86.

76 J. Brodie, 'Concrete Dwellings, Eldon Street. Report of the City Engineer 22.4.05', proceeding of the City Council, Liverpool, 1904–05.

77 It was William Owen who had designed the first sets of housing for Lever in 1890. Segar was his son.

78 Hubbard and Shippobottom, *A Guide to Port Sunlight Village*, p. 40.

79 *Town Planning Review*, vol. 3:1, pp. 80–81.

80 *The Builder*, 16 July 1910, p. 64. The article carries on to say; 'Perhaps after all it is idle to compare the "Liverpool School" with others to find traces of its origin, as it seems considerable enough to take a stand of itself, and perhaps even to suggest a style to others. We feel acutely the value of a strong common speech among a body of men … is preferable to a babel of polyglot talk.'

81 *Town Planning Review*, vol. 4:1, p. 66.

82 *Town Planning Review*, vol. 5:1, p. 82.

83 A. T. Edwards, 'A World Centre of Communication', *Town Planning Review* vol. 5:1, p. 14.

84 Whilst Blomfield was never able to accept modernism, referring to it disparagingly as 'Modernismus', emphasising what he saw as its un-Englishness.

85 J. M. Richards, 'The Condition of Architecture and the Principle of Anonymity' in J. L. Martin, et al. (eds), *Circle*, Faber and Faber, 1939, p. 189.

86 M. Breuer, 'Architecture and material' in ibid., p. 194.

Select Bibliography

Adams, M. *Modern Cottage Architecture*, Batsford 1904.

Adshead, S. 'An Introduction to Civic Design', *Town Planning Review*, vol. 1:1.

Ashbee, C. *Where the Great City Stands*, Batsford, 1917.

Bare, H. B. 'A School for Artistic Handicrafts' in *Transactions of the National Association for the Advancement of Art and its Application to Industry. Liverpool Meeting 1888*.

Bibby, C. *T. H. Huxley: Scientist, Humanist and Educator*, Watts, 1959.

Bisson, R. *The Sandon Studios Society and the Arts*, Liverpool: Parry Books, 1965.

Budden, L. *The Book of the Liverpool School of Architecture*, Liverpool: Liverpool University Press, 1932.

Chandler, G. *William Roscoe of Liverpool 1753–1831*, Batsford, 1953.

Collingwood, W. G. *The Life of John Ruskin*, Methuen, 1900.

Conway, W. M. *Episodes in a Varied Life*, Country Life, 1932.

Conway, W. M. *Liverpool Royal Institute Gallery of Art*, Seeley, Jackson and Halliday, 1884.

Conway, W. M. *The Succession of Ideals: An address delivered in St. Georges Hall at the opening of the College Session October 2nd 1886*, Liverpool: Thompson, 1886.

Cotgrove, S. F. *Technical Education and Social Change*, Allen and Unwin, 1958.

Creese, W. L. *The Search for Environment*, New Haven, CT: Yale University Press, 1966.

Darley, G. *Villages of Vision*, The Architectural Press, 1975.

Dixon Scott, W. *Liverpool 1907*, A. & C. Black, 1907.

Evans, J. *The Conways: A History of Three Generations*, Museum Press, 1966.

Forwood, W. B. *Liverpool Cathedral – The Story of its Foundation*, Liverpool: Lee and Nightingale, 1925.

George, W. L. *Labour and Housing in Port Sunlight*, Alston Rivers, 1909.

Hewitt, W. *The Technical Instruction Committee and its Work 1890–1903*, Liverpool: Liverpool University Press, 1927.

Hikins, H. *The Liverpool General Transport Strike 1911*, Liverpool: Toulouse Press, 1980.

Horsfall, T. C. *The Improvement of the Dwellings and Surroundings of the People: The Example of Germany*, Manchester: Manchester University Press, 1904.

Holt, A. (ed.) *Merseyside*, Liverpool: University Press of Liverpool, 1923.

Hubbard, E. and Shippobottom, M. *A Guide to Port Sunlight Village*, Liverpool: Liverpool University Press, 1988.

Hughes, Q. 'Before the Bauhaus', *Architectural History*, vol. 25, 1982.

Hyde, F. E. *Liverpool and the Mersey: The development of A Port 1700–1970*, David and Charles, 1971.

Jackson, B. H. (ed.) *Recollections of T. G. Jackson*, Oxford: Oxford University Press, 1950.

Jackson, T. G. *Some Thoughts on the Training of Architects*, Liverpool: D. Marples and Co., 1895.

Jackson, T. and Shaw, R. (eds) *Architecture: A Profession or an Art?* John Murray, 1892.

John, A. *Chiaroscuro*, Jonathan Cape, 1954.

Jolly, W. P. *Lord Leverhulme: A Biography*, Constable, 1976.

Jordy, W. H. *Progressive and Academic Ideals at the Turn of the Twentieth Century*, Oxford: Oxford University Press, 1986.

Kelly, T. *For Advancement of Learning*, Liverpool: Liverpool University Press, 1981.

Kornwolf, J. D. *Baillie Scott and the Arts and Crafts Movement*, Baltimore, MD: Baltimore University Press, 1972.

Lever, W. H. *Following the Flag*, Liverpool and London: Simpkin Marshall and Co., 1893.

Lund, T. W. M. *The Ideal Citizen*, Liverpool, 1896.

Marillier, H. C. *The Liverpool School of Painters*, John Murray, 1904.

Mather, M. *John Ruskin, His Life and Teaching*, Warne, 1898.

Midwinter, E. *Old Liverpool*, David & Charles, 1971.

Moore, C. *The Life and Times of Charles Follen McKim*, New York: Riverside Press, 1929.

Morris, W. *News from Nowhere*, Longmans, 1910.

Neville, R. *Some Papers and Addresses on Social Questions*, Spottiswoode, Ballantyne and Company, n.d.

Orchard, B. G. *Liverpool's Legion of Honours*, Birkenhead: published by the author, 1893.

Ould, E. *Old Cottages, Farm Houses and other Half Timbered Buildings in Shropshire, Herefordshire and Cheshire*, Batsford, 1904.

Peisch, M. L. *The Chicago School of Architecture*, Phaidon Press, 1964.

Rathbone, P. *Architecture as a Necessary Element in National Economy*, Paper read to the Liverpool Architectural Society, 3 December 1894.

Rathbone, P. *Impressionism in Art*, Liverpool, 1890.

Rathbone, P. *Lessons from France as to Imperial and Municipal Encouragement of National Art*, Liverpool, 1888.

Rathbone, P. *The Mission of the Undraped Figure in Art*, Liverpool, 1878.

Rathbone, P. *The Object and Scope of an Art Professorship*, sole extant copy without its cover, Liverpool(?) Early 1880s(?)

Rathbone, P. *The Place of Art in The Future Industrial Progress of the Nation*, paper read to the Social Science Congress, Birmingham, 1884.

Rathbone, P. *The Political Value of Art to the Municipal Life of a Nation*, Liverpool, 1875.

Rathbone, P. *Realism, Idealism, and the Grotesque in Art: Their Limits and Functions*, Liverpool, 1877.

Rathbone, P. *The School of English Impressionists*, Liverpool, 1883.

Reilly, C. H. *McKim, Mead and White*, Ernest Benn, 1924.

Reilly, C. H. *Scaffolding in the Sky*, Routledge, 1938.

Reilly, C. H. *Some Architectural Problems of Today*, Liverpool: Liverpool University Press, 1924.

Reilly, C. H. *The Training of Architects*, Sherratt and Hughes, 1905. Also in: *University Review*, July 1905 (USA).

Reilly, C. H. 'Town Planning Schemes in America', *Town Planning Review*, vol. 1:1.

Rendall, G. *Education in Liverpool Past and Present*, Liverpool: Marples, 1894.

Rendall, G. 'Inaugural Address', Cambridge 1882.

Rendall, G. and Conway W. M. 'Liverpool Cathedral: A Letter to the Lord Bishop of Liverpool', Liverpool, 1886

Robinson, C. H. *The Improvement of Towns and Cities, or the Practical Basis of Civic Aesthetics*, Putnams, 1901.

Robinson, C. H. *Modern Civic Art, or the City made Beautiful*, Putnams, 1903.

Rohdenburg, T. K. *A History of the School of Architecture, Columbia University*, New York: Columbia University Press, 1954.

Roscoe, H. E. *The Life and Experiences of Sir Henry Enfield Roscoe*, Macmillan, 1906.

Ruskin, J. *Notes by Mr Ruskin on Samuel Prout and William Hunt*, Fine Art Society, 1879.

Ruskin, J. *Sesame and Lilies*, George Allan, 1906.

Ruskin, J. *The Stones of Venice*, George Allan, 1874.

Ruskin, J. *The Two Paths*, George Allan, 1901.

Ruskin, J. *Unto This Last*, Everyman, 1907.

Scott, G. *The Architecture of Humanism*, The Architectural Press, 1980.

Sharpe, C. W. *The Sport of Civic Life, or Art and the Municipality*, Liverpool: published by the author, 1909.

Shillaber, C. *Massachusetts Institute of Technology School of Architecture and Planning 1861–1961*, Cambridge, MA: MIT Press, 1963.

Simpson, F. M. *Old Architecture in Liverpool*, Paper read to the Warrington Literary and Philosophical Society, 16 March 1896.

Simpson, F. M. *The Scheme of Architectural Education Started at University College, Liverpool, in Connection with the City of Liverpool School of Architecture and Applied Art*, Liverpool: Marples and Co., 1905.

Simpson, F. M. *Two Presidential Addresses* Liverpool: Liverpool University Press, 1901.

Smith, W. (ed.) *A Scientific Survey of Merseyside*, Liverpool: Liverpool University Press, 1953.

Stansky, P. *Redesigning the World*, Princeton, NJ: Princeton University Press, 1983.

Swenarton, M. *Artisans and Architects: The Ruskinian Tradition in Architectural Thought*, Macmillan Press, 1989.

Tooley, B. H. *Liverpool and the American Cotton Trade*, Longman, 1978.

Tyndale Harries, W. *Landmarks in Liverpool History*, Philip, Son and Nephew, 1946.

Unwin, R. *Town Planning in Practice*, Fisher Unwin, 1911.

Ware, W. *Address before the Alumini Association of Columbia College on the Twelfth of June 1888*, New York, 1888.

Weatherhead, A. C. *The History of Collegiate Education in Architecture in the United States*, Los Angeles: University of California Press, 1941.

Willet, J. *Art in a City*, Methuen, 1967.

Wilson, C. *The History of Unilever*, Cassel, 1954.

Wright, M. *Lord Leverhulme's Unknown Venture*, Hutchinson Benham Ltd, 1981.

A Miscellany Presented to J. M. Mackay, Liverpool: Liverpool University Press, 1914.

Index